DIED 13 JUNE 1983.

Good Friday

The Films
of
NORMA SHEARER

Norma Shearer.

The Films
of
NORMA SHEARER

Jack Jacobs and Myron Braum

SOUTH BRUNSWICK AND NEW YORK: A. S. BARNES AND COMPANY
LONDON: THOMAS YOSELOFF LTD

© 1976 by A. S. Barnes and Co., Inc.

A. S. Barnes and Co., Inc.
Cranbury, New Jersey 08512

Thomas Yoseloff Ltd
108 New Bond Street
London W1Y OQX, England

Library of Congress Cataloging in Publication Data

Jacobs, Jack, 1919-
    The films of Norma Shearer.

    Filmography: p.
    1. Shearer, Norma, 1900-   I. Braum, Myron, joint
author.   II. Title.
PN2287.S37J3   791.43'028'0924 [B]   74-9286
ISBN 0-498-01552-1

Contents

Foreword

Norma Shearer reminds me of a very precious jewel in a glamorous setting of fame.

Her tapestry of life has been brilliantly shaded with exciting experiences, dramatic episodes, and outstanding successes, both here and abroad.

She was and still is the personification of femininity and charm—she possesses a certain spiritual quality and a sweet sincerity in manner that have entranced all who have been privileged to know her.

Our paths crossed often, professionally and socially, during the luxurious star-studded era of Hollywood, when stars were presented like royalty. In all the years I knew Norma, I never heard her speak one word of criticism of anyone.

Norma was one of the few motion-picture stars who dressed with excellent taste off screen as well as in her productions. She possessed a unique chic and a certain scintillating quality that, coupled with her talent and beauty, captivated her audiences throughout the world. Her exquisite gowns and costumes for her glamorous roles were designed by Adrian, the world-renowned MGM fashion designer and artist, whose creations were works of art, and Norma Shearer knew how to wear them with dignity and grace.

After her marriage to Irving Thalberg, the genius, director-producer of MGM Studios, Norma seemed to increase her fame and, through his direction and inspiration, she further developed her many talents. As Angelo Patri expressed it, "Behind each great achievement there is usually a friend...who stirs the ashes of our spent dreams...to him all honor, all love is due."

Norma Shearer will always shine as a brilliant star in the Hall of Fame.

Peggy Hamilton

One of Peggy Hamilton's famous star-studded luncheons at the Biltmore Hotel in the mid 1920's. Back row, left to right: Helen Delaine, Ruth Clifford, Peggy Hamilton, Ruth Roland, Mrs. Edith B. Thompson, Patsy Ruth Miller, Lilyan Tashman, Mabel Smith and Beverly Bayne. Front row, left to right: Mrs. W. M. Hamilton Cline, Dorothy Phillips, Olive Larkin, Helen Ferguson, Kathleen Clifford, Norma Shearer and Wanda Hawley.

I truly feel someone of more importance than I should write the foreword to a book about Norma Shearer. It should be one of her peers, one of the movie greats, not someone she discovered.

Not that I am not honored. My feelings about Miss Shearer are very deep, and I am always proud to share them. As a child she gave me great enjoyment through all of her motion pictures. She is an idol, with her talent, her beauty, her glamour, and more important, her warmth and love as a person.

She was responsible for my discovery, she made it possible for me to have a chance: she opened a whole new world for me. I love her. I love her because she is a beautiful person. I don't know how to express my appreciation for a human being any better than that.

Janet Leigh Brandt

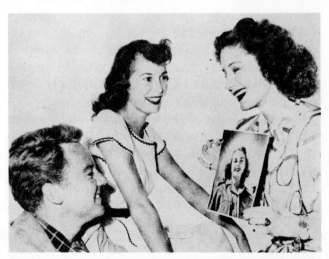

Norma Shearer, who went to the lodge and saw the photo of receptionist's daughter, Jeanett Morrison, who won opposite Van Johnson, who tabbed her Janet Leigh.

8

Acknowledgments

We wish to express our sincere thanks to the following people who have contributed additional photographic material and other important data to this book:

The staff of the Academy of Motion Picture Arts and Sciences Research Library
Michael Bach
Paul Ballard
Bill Bass
Eddie Brandt's Saturday Matinee
Loraine Burdick
Bill Chapman
Bob Cushman
Oliver Dernberger and the Cherokee Book Store
John Graham
Peggy Hamilton
Janet Leigh Brandt
Ken Hollywood, Jr. and Sr.
Richard Hudson
Talbert Kanigher
Raymond Lee

Albert Lord
The Memory Shop (Mark Ricci)
Peter Morris, Curator of the Canadian Film Institute
Paul Myers and the staff of the Theatre Collection of the New York Public Library, Lincoln Center
Charles Silver and the staff of the Museum of Modern Art
David Noh
Virginia Reidy
Lou Valentino
Mark Vieira
Allan Smith
Fred Santon

In England:
The British Film Institute
John Kobal
Arthur Nicholson
John Phillips

The Films
of
NORMA SHEARER

I
BIOGRAPHY

EDITH NORMA SHEARER was born on August 10, 1900, in a suburb of Montreal, known as Westmount, in a two-story brick house at 507 Grosvenor Street. On the roof of the building was a spiral, the kind usually associated with European castles that dominated part of the area and further enhanced it. There, Norma was reared with her sister, Athole, and her brother, Douglas, both of whom were a few years older than she. Their father, Andrew Shearer, a Scotsman, was an executive with a construction company, and their mother, Edith Fisher Shearer, was English and a descendent of a lineage of clergymen. The family was not wealthy, but quite comfortably off.

As a child, Norma suffered from various ailments, most of which were diagnosed as bad colds that were probably attributed to the harsh Canadian winters. Because of this she was confined to her bed for long periods of the time, which kept her out of school until the age of ten. But being indisposed as she was did not interfere with her education, for she was taught the necessary fundamentals by her parents. Eventually, Norma's resistance grew stronger and she was able to attend primary classes and later Westmount High, which she attended for two years.

Most Canadians loved the outdoors, and the Shearer family was no exception. Mr. Shearer was an enthusiastic sportsman, a fine horseman and hockey player. Mrs. Shearer was also athletically inclined, and the children were encouraged to participate in sports as much as possible. It was indeed a happy, carefree, and pleasant home. The seasons were ideal for outdoor activities. In the winter there was skiing, tobogganing, and ice skating, in the summer, swimming, canoeing, games, and parties. "Life," said Miss Shearer years later, "was a pleasant dream, between the ages of thirteen and sixteen."

Although she was never a tomboy in the sense of the word, Norma preferred the comradeship of boys and always claimed that she was their equal. She would participate with them in snowball fights, and on more than one occasion had risked her life with her playmates when they were foolhardy enough to skate on a lake on which the ice had not quite hardened. But despite what seemed like male behavior she was completely feminine.

She also had a great love for animals and hated to see them mistreated. One day, she encountered a group of boys torturing a squirrel that they had cornered in a maple tree on the Humber River bank where Norma would spend much time relaxing.

The first thing she knew, they had tied a rope around the helpless creature and began to drag it down the road. Tearfully, Norma pleaded with the young tormentors to free the animal, but they merely laughed at her. Norma could not contain herself any longer and before she realized what she was doing she lunged at the little rascals and pounded them with her fists. The boys were stunned at this sudden attack from a girl and they quickly released the squirrel and fled. This, apparently, was an early sampling of the grit she was to display in her quest for theatrical jobs some years later.

As to Norma's future, her mother had first planned a career for her as a concert pianist and soon made preparations for her daughter's enrollment at the Royal Academy of Music, where she would be placed under the tutelage of Blossom Connelly, a prominent music teacher. Miss Connelly's death, however, brought these plans to a sudden halt.

When she was fifteen, people were beginning to notice Norma and regarded her as a special type of beauty. As a result, shortly after, she won a local beauty contest, receiving first prize. This im-

Norma Shearer at the age of three years.

mediately inspired Mrs. Shearer to consider a stage career for her daughter, whose thoughts soon turned in the same direction. Norma soon joined an amateur theatrical group and for practice she would recite "Dangerous Dan M'Grew" and "The Face on the Bar Room Floor," both by her favorite author, Robert W. Service, who was also a Canadian.

Another celebrity Norma idolized was Pearl White, the serial queen of the movies, whose pictures she sat through for hours, thrilled and fascinated by Miss White's daring exploits. When the star made a special personal appearance at the Strand Theatre in Montreal, Norma waited outside with other admirers to catch an eager glimpse of her. Then, when Miss White got into her automobile, Norma mounted her bicycle and followed her down the street. She was certainly a high-spirited, fun-loving girl in those days and not without a certain tenacity. Impudence was said to be another one of her traits in which she would mimic everybody she met. At the time, she was a blonde, with a piquant prettiness.

Early in 1920, a depression hit the country, as well as other parts of the world, with Mr. Shearer suffering heavy losses from his business. Forced to economize, he put up his home for sale, among other prized possessions, and moved his family to more modest quarters in a less imposing neighborhood.

At the age of sixteen Norma decided to quit school in order to help bolster the family's dwindling resources by going to work. She soon found a job in a music store plugging sheet music and demonstrating such popular ditties of the day as "They're Wearing Them Higher in Hawaii" and "On the Beach at Waikiki." Mrs. Shearer offered her services as a saleswoman in a department store, while Athole became an office clerk and Douglas obtained employment as an assistant technician with an engineering firm specializing in electrical apparatus.

Amid this breadwinning, however, Mrs. Shearer saw no future in Montreal for her daughters, especially Norma, whose beauty she felt could lend itself to a possible stage career in New York. The idea not only appealed to Norma, but to Athole as well, and it was proposed that the piano on which Norma had been practicing for so long be sold, which would enable them to make the trip. It finally was for four hundred and fifty dollars, but

not without Norma shedding a few tears, since she had attached much sentiment to the instrument.

The winter of 1920 was just beginning when Norma, her mother, and Athole arrived in New York armed with several letters of introduction that Mrs. Shearer had obtained from Montreal theatre managers whom she knew. One of them happened to be Florenz Ziegfeld, the legendary producer of the Follies.

The three soon found cheap lodgings in a dilapidated apartment building at 57th Street and 8th Avenue for which they paid $7.50 for one room that was utilized for both sleeping and cooking. The furnishings were practically bare and the Shearer's trunk used for a table and other necessities. The building was near the el and the noise was deafening when the trains roared by, affording the three women little sleep, plus the fact that an all-night electric sign added to their discomfort. It was a far cry from Westmount, but a new experience nevertheless and a challenging one. Mrs. Shearer again found work in a department store and Norma and Athole proceeded to make the rounds of agents and producers.

The first impresario Norma went to see was Mr. Ziegfeld, who was then lining up one of his usual super productions, but the great glorifier was not impressed with the young Canadian aspirant who appeared somewhat ill at ease in his presence. He told her that her legs were not quite up to the requirements of a show girl, that her teeth needed straightening, and that her eye, in which she had a cast, would mar her appearance. This struck Norma as ironic, considering that she had been the winner of a beauty contest back home. Not too many years after her meeting with him, she recollected: "I saw him six months later. He then told me he didn't know what he could fit me into. I wasn't a dancer. I couldn't be a pony. I wasn't tall enough to be a show girl. But that he would try to fit me into something." Ziegfeld never did. The other introductory letters didn't do any good either.

Months of trudging the streets in search of work only developed holes in Norma's shoes and she had to conceal them with pasteboard. Regardless of her unstable footwear, she always appeared neat and comely in her attire and no one was the wiser as to her plight.

One day, a motion-picture registration bureau, where the Shearer girls had left their names, sent them over to Universal, where eight girls were needed for a two-reel comedy. Norma and Athole arrived to find fifty girls ahead of them. Norma tried to attract the casting director's attention by coughing and shuffling her feet. It worked and she was promptly hired, persuading the director to give Athole a job, too. It was extra work, but a beginning. They were paid five dollars a day when it was sunny, as a lot of scenes were filmed outdoors. If it rained, they weren't used, or paid. More extra work followed for Norma and she was practically obliterated in a romantic comedy about a boarding school for girls called *The Flapper* in which Olive Thomas, a one-time Follies girl, was the star and which was made at the original Selznick studio in Manhattan. The other film, a drama about an unfortunate marriage that leads to tragedy, titled *The Restless Sex* starred Marion Davies, with whom Miss Shearer was to vie for certain roles in the not-too-distant future. This, too, was produced locally, at Famous Players.

Norma next approached D. W. Griffith, who, like Ziegfeld, gave her very little encouragement. He did, however use her as an extra in *Way Down East*, with which she went up to Mamaroneck, New York, for location filming. Norma's appearance in this classic about the old homestead was indeed fleeting and one had to look very closely in order to spot her. She was supposed to have been among those riding in a sleigh.

Despite Griffith dissuading her from a screen career, she was tremendously impressed with him and his devotion and passionate interest in his work. "I always remember his amazing habit of disregarding time," she once recalled. "We knocked off for meals at any time, and at the end of the day, work was just as likely to be twelve or one o'clock that night. But we didn't mind it because of the tremendous thrill of working for the great D. W."

With film work now becoming scarce, Norma managed to obtain some modeling jobs with an advertising illustrator at five dollars a sitting. She subsequently posed for such well-known artists as James Montgomery Flagg, Charles Dana Gibson, Rolf Armstrong, and others of note. Soon, her face began to adorn automobile tires, particularly the Kelly-Springfield ones in which she went under the pseudonym of "Miss Lottie Miles." Toothpaste ads, house coats, magazine covers, and twenty-four-sheet billboards also became part of her displays. It was valuable experience and she

claimed that her facial expressions in these advertisements helped her to express different facial characteristics when she was before the cameras. But most important of all, it did much to overcome her physical deficiencies, such as her mishaped teeth, under which she had been wearing a brace, her lack of poise, and her homely legs that Ziegfeld had thought so uninteresting. These barriers never broke Norma Shearer's spirit to reach her goal. Athole, though, despaired of ever becoming an actress and decided against a career on the stage or in films. Some years later she married film director Howard Hawks.

When Norma was no longer required for modeling engagements she applied for a job as a movie-theatre pianist, but the manager wasn't too pleased with her renditions, explaining that he catered to a more discriminating patronage who preferred their music in a classical vein. She also needed a union card.

Finally, Norma met a talent agent whose name was Edward Small and who got her a small part in a Johnny Hines short feature comedy called *Torchy's Millions*. Small later became one of Hollywood's leading independent producers during the thirties and established a production unit known as Reliance Pictures, which he released through United Artists. Among his credits under this aegis was *The Count of Monte Cristo*, starring Robert Donat, *The Last of the Mohicans, Let Em' Have It*, a crime melodrama dealing with the FBI, and other well-produced films that never approached the excellence and distinction of *The Count of Monte Cristo*. Small is semiretired, but still maintains an office in the Taft Building at Hollywood and Vine having left the Samuel Goldwyn lot where he was based for many years. Small is in the process of writing his autobiography. Although *Torchy's Millions* did nothing at all for Norma, except to make her look appealing, *The Stealers*, her first full-length feature, did, which Small was further instrumental in getting for her. In it, she had a solid supporting role, being billed fourth, and played the wholesome daughter of a minister who, because of domestic problems, resorted to leading a criminal organization that embezzled law abiding residents of a rural community. *The Stealers* was widely exploited as a super-special and hailed as a powerful human document along the lines of *The Miracle Man*. It was written and directed by Christy Cabbane and had a gala opening at the Broadway Theatre in New York in 1920. To catch the true rural flavor of the story, *The Stealers* was filmed in Mount Vernon, a short distance from New York City. The film did not make Norma Shearer a star, but it led to a modest role in the Norma Talmadge starrer *The Sign on the Door,* a crook melodrama for which director Herbert Brenon had engaged her at twenty-five dollars a day and which was released in 1921. Miss Shearer was paid for eight days' work but her scenes were cut out entirely.

She was next used in *The Leather Pushers* series, which were two reelers in twenty-four episodes produced by the Universal Jewel Company and starring Reginald Denny as a Gentleman Jim type of pugilist. This did nothing much for Miss Shearer either and she was said to have appeared only in two episodes of the series. They were first released early in January of 1922 and concluded in February of 1924. Miss Shearer most likely worked in the early part of the series, since Denny was replaced by Billy Sullivan, following an accident.

The first picture in which she played the feminine lead was a melodrama about the Canadian Northwest called *The Man Who Paid,* opposite Wilfred Lytell, the brother of the noted stage and film actor of the day, Bert Lytell. It had to do with a young Canadian trapper (Lytell) who is falsely accused of embezzlement and serves a prison term. Shearer played his wife, who was also the mother of a little girl.

She was next seen in another one of those melodramatic actioners that contained all the known elements of a blood-and-thunder serial, the kind she used to sit through as a youngster on a Saturday afternoon. This was *The Bootleggers,* in which she was a poor working girl who is unknowingly shanghaied with her sister by a notorious rum runner on his yacht and which culminates in a thrilling climax. The villain of the piece was Paul Panzer, with Walter Miller, a veteran of the serial film, playing the hero: This time Miss Shearer was billed fifth, but her part was an important one nevertheless.

Channing of the Northwest followed, in which she again essayed the feminine lead. The star of the film was Eugene O'Brien, who was highly popular then, and when Miss Shearer was told that she was going to play opposite him she was indeed flattered. O'Brien played a former London

playboy who becomes a member of the Northwest Mounted Police after his fiancée rejects him because she feared he would be disinherited. Miss Shearer appeared as a backwoods girl with whom he found romance. *Channing of the Northwest* was not the usual type of adventure film inspired by the title. It had only a modicum of action, depending largely on picturesque scenery. But it was a good programmer for what it was and Shearer made a pleasing heroine.

During the making of this picture, Miss Shearer recalled an amusing experience with Eugene O'Brien, who was usually very kind to her and had taken her to lunch several times. "Eugene being an actor," she related in a magazine autobiography fifteen years later, "had an enormous yellow roadster that looked as if it had cost $25,000, but which, being all front, had an engine about the size of a peck-basket. In his gorgeous red 'Mountie' costume, Eugene would drive roaring through Forty Second Street, with me, tingling with excitement, beside him. We'd dash up Broadway so everybody could get a good look at this prosperous actor, and then dodge down a side street to a tearoom where they served a very nice lunch for 35 cents.

"The car broke down under the elevated on Sixth Avenue one day, and Eugene, in his stunning costume, had to help a policeman push it to the curb, while hundreds of people stood on the sidewalk and grinned. Eugene's face was redder than his coat, and we jumped quickly into a taxi and left the car to be brought to the studio by a repairman. He was so humiliated he didn't ask me to go with him to lunch anymore."

Miss Shearer's last two films produced in the East were *A Clouded Name*, with Gladden James as her leading man, in which she was the daughter of parents one of whom mysteriously disappears and dies, and *Man and Wife,* a psychological drama about a doctor (Robert Elliott) who marries another woman when his wife (Shearer) is thought to have perished in a fire. Here, Miss Shearer had third billing, while in the former film she had played the lead. Outside of Selznick, Famous Players, Lasky, and Universal, these potboilers were made by independent studios that had only a minimum of prestige and seemed much like stock companies where players alternate in status. Nevertheless, it was excellent training for a young film actress just starting out.

Irving Thalberg, then general manager of the Universal Studios on the West Coast, had contacted its New York Office in the hope of locating Miss Shearer, since he had been trying to get her a contract. She hadn't realized that Thalberg had seen her in *The Stealers* and also in *The Leather Pushers* and was impressed both by her personality and her work, in which he envisioned a future.

Almost simultaneously Miss Shearer received an offer from Louis B. Mayer, at the time an independent producer whose company in Los Angeles was known as the Mayer Company, which was prior to the merger with Metro-Goldwyn in April of 1924. What Miss Shearer didn't know was that Thalberg had left Universal to join Hal Roach, from whom he hoped to arrange a contract for the young Canadian actress, as well as one for himself. Then, when Thalberg was unsuccessful in engineering the kind of terms he wanted with Roach, he joined Mayer as production chief, thereby renewing the original offer made to her.

In New York Miss Shearer signed a six-month contract at a one hundred fifty dollars a week that was optional. Up until now she had been represented by Edward Small, who was instrumental in getting her that amount, in addition to having Mayer pay the Shearers' expenses to California.

Norma, her mother, and Athole arrived on the West Coast early in 1923. When the train pulled into Los Angeles, Miss Shearer was rather disappointed because there wasn't a soul to greet them. Her version of their arrival was as follows: "Having read reams of newspapers and magazine chatter about the gorgeous reception tendered arriving actors and actresses, Mother and I spent hours getting me ready for the greeting, which I felt sure would be waiting for me when the train pulled into the Los Angeles station. But there was no one there — not even a messenger boy from the studios to direct us to our next move. We had to make inquiries as to hotels and find our own way to our first Hollywood home, which was the famous Hollywood Hotel in the heart of the movie city."

The next day, Norma went to see Mayer and Thalberg. The Mayer Co. was on the north end of downtown Los Angeles on Mission Road, on which now stands the administrative and buying offices of a leading department store. Norma's first glimpse of Irving Thalberg when she entered his office gave her the impression that he was the office boy. She soon found out otherwise and couldn't be more surprised. He did look quite boyish and was only twenty-four.

Thalberg had an important part lined up for Norma in *The Wanters,* which John M. Stahl was about to direct for First National, but her screen tests did not impress Stahl and he gave the lead to Marie Prevost, already an established film player. Stahl, however, compensated Miss Shearer with a smaller role in which she received third billing. She was cast as a society girl whose brother (Robert Ellis) becomes enamored of a domestic (Prevost) and later marries her much to the chagrin of his snobbish family. *The Wanters,* when released, was favorably received and Stahl's direction praised.

Thalberg next assigned Miss Shearer a more rewarding part in *Pleasure Mad* for the Mayer Co. Here, she played a headstrong girl who begins to lead a fast and frivolous life when her family comes into sudden wealth.

While working on this picture, Miss Shearer developed a sudden case of fright and self-consciousness, a situation that displeased Reginald Barker, the director, no end. He merely recognized her as an embryonic and was forced into badgering her until her confidence was restored. It seems that she had been a bit too conscientious and in her anxiety forgot what she had learned. This didn't set so well with Thalberg either when Barker reported the incident to him, and he reminded Miss Shearer to be more careful in the future, otherwise he might have to cancel her contract. It was this contract, the one that she had signed in New York, that touched off some argumentative discussions between the budding Hollywood actress and the young executive. She was said to have protested to the point of tears on a few occasions when she disapproved of the parts she was getting, especially when Thalberg remained adamant to her appeals. She felt that it was unfair that other young actresses were being assigned the roles that she should have had. She also told the producer that she didn't have to sign his contract in the first place, that another company had already made her an offer. Thalberg then revealed that he had influenced all of them, and in addition, told her bluntly: "You'll play the parts that are assigned to you and we'll hear no more about it."

Shearer soon curved her dogmatism and prima-donnaish ways and settled down to hard work for the next year and a half. But she still fought for good parts and at the same time harbored a great admiration and respect for Thalberg.

In the months that followed she was loaned out to Warner Bros. for *Lucretia Lombard,* and *Broadway after Dark;* to Iroquois for *The Devil's Partner;* to director-producer Oscar Apfel for *The Trail of the Law;* Fox for *The Wolf Man;* Paramount for *Empty Hands.* None of these films bore any particular distinction, but Miss Shearer profited by them in experience, and eventually audiences grew accustomed to her face and style. Of the lot, *Broadway after Dark* was the most select, though no work of art. Here, she appeared as a waitress who had once committed a petty theft in order to help her invalid mother and then confides her past to a man she trusts who sends her to prison. The direction by Monta Bell, who was to direct Miss Shearer in several films, had style and finesse and afforded the young actress her best opportunity to date of which she took considerable advantage. From Bell, she learned more about technique than from any other director during her silent film career. Bell had once been an assistant to Chaplin, which in itself was a criterion, but he never became as important as he should have been, and today he is hardly remembered, if at all. Miss Shearer was directed by him in six silent films, all of which were potboilers but with sufficient entertainment value.

Lucretia Lombard, filmed prior to *Broadway after Dark,* was a confused and an uneven movie about an influential widow suspected of the death of her invalid husband much older than she and whom a young lawyer falls in love with while engaged to another girl (Shearer). The highlight of the picture was a spectacular forest fire and flood, the latter catastrophe being the cause of Shearer's death. One of the few Shearer silent films available, *Lucretia Lombard* is shown periodically at John Hampton's Silent Movie Theatre in Hollywood. The film's catastrophic climax is highly effective because of the red tints employed to enhance the fire sequence and adds a special glow to Miss Shearer's beauty. But her acting in this indifferent programmer lacked self-assurance, yet her sincerity was evident throughout, and there were moments in it when she conveyed a certain pathos.

Her next film, *The Wolf Man,* in which she appeared opposite John Gilbert shortly before he was to become one of the screen's popular idols, was an adventure melodrama about a socialite who becomes involved with a British peer escaping from England to Canada after killing his fiancée's brother in a drunken rage. The film boasted plenty of action and suspense, particularly the hairbreadth experiences Shearer and Gilbert have in eluding the police. *Blue Waters* and *Empty Hands,* which followed, also had Canadian locales and were mainly dependent on beautiful scenery rather than plot. Again Shearer was the rich girl who discovers that money can't buy love and happiness. In the first, she is attracted to a poor fisherman (Pierre Gendron) in a seacoast village, and in the second she learns what deprivation is really like when she and a rugged mining engineer find themselves stranded in a wilderness following a near-drowning accident.

For Miss Shearer, who was learning her profession the hard way, these minor films were wonderful experience, and whether she enjoyed doing them or not, she benefited from it in the future. They were to be the last of her action-adventure movies. Irving Thalberg had more ambitious plans for her.

In April of 1924, Louis B. Mayer shed his independent producing unit known as the Mayer Co. and formed an alliance with the old Metro Pictures Corp. and Samuel Goldwyn, which officially became Metro-Goldwyn-Mayer and the studio that was to be Norma Shearer's permanent home base for the duration of her career. Their inaugural film was *He Who Gets Slapped,* starring the great Lon Chaney, but because of its special artistic value and star names, among which were Shearer and John Gilbert, it was decided to release the picture in the late fall of that year. The first film to be distributed by MGM was a soap opera called *Broken Barriers* in which Miss Shearer, as a shop girl, has a love affair with an affluent married man (James Kirkwood) whose wife (Winifred Bryson) refuses to grant him a divorce until she finds that he would be useless to her after he has been crippled in an auto accident. The director of this soggy, though fairly good drama was Reginald Barker, the same man with whom Shearer had clashed during the making of *Pleasure Mad,* but by this time she had shown a marked improvement in her acting and was learning how to take direction much better than before.

With *He Who Gets Slapped* finally released in December of 1924, MGM had both an artistic and commercial success. Based on Leonid Andreyev's play of the same name, it had first been produced by the Theatre Guild in New York in 1922 with Richard Bennett as "He," Margola Gilmore as the heroine, Ernest Cossart as the circus manager (the character was completely changed for the film), and Henry Travers as a clown. It was a strange and fascinating story about a former and brilliant scientist who exchanges his noble profession for the sawdust because of his wife's infidelity. Despite the importance of the film, Miss Shearer's role was not particularly inspiring due to the magnetic presence of Lon Chaney, who dominated most of the film, but she made a refreshing and appealing bareback rider Chaney becomes enamored of, while John Gilbert as another circus performer is the handsome rival for her affections. Two other performances that stood out besides Chaney's was Tully Marshall as Shearer's ringmaster father, who is intent on marrying her off to a wealthy baron, and Marc MacDermott as the latter. The direction by Victor Seastrom, whom Mayer had imported from Sweden, was cinematic art at its best. The critics embraced *He Who Gets Slapped* as a film Hollywood should be proud of.

A more rewarding opportunity was afforded Shearer in *The Snob*, in which she appeared with John Gilbert for the third and last time. Monta Bell directed her again, and the result was her best performance to date, as well as Gilbert's. She played a small-town heiress who, in order to avoid disgrace, goes under an assumed name after her father is killed in a roadhouse brawl and soon becomes a school teacher in a university community where she meets a snobbish professor whom she makes a mistake in marrying. *The Snob* was a mature and intelligent film, combining subtle humor and pathos that never overlapped into saccharinity. It was also Monta Bell's directorial triumph and the blossoming of Miss Shearer as an important actress.

Having cast her repeatedly in serious themes, Thalberg decided it was time to give Shearer a chance at comedy, which she had never done. The vehicle he chose was a highly amusing story called *Excuse Me* by Rupert Hughes, which the author had staged in 1915. It concerned an engaged couple who encounter many trials and tribulations in trying to locate a certain minister to marry them before they finally tie the knot. Shearer was the fiancée of a young naval officer (Conrad Nagel) who is suddenly called to duty in the Philippines, which prompts him to propose a hasty marriage so both may spend their honeymoon on the islands. The film was as swift-moving as the express train on which most of the action takes place, with the frenetic pace rarely subsiding. Miss Shearer proved that she was an adept comedienne, while Nagel acquitted himself ably enough in the laugh department, too.

Lady of the Night, which followed, gave her another interesting change in character. Here, she was seen in her first dual role, that of a vivacious gang moll and the refined, cultivated daughter of a prominent judge to whom she sacrifices the man she loves. The role was a challenging one and Miss Shearer managed to bring conviction as well as charm to both parts. *Lady of the Night* was a good romantic drama, interlaced with subtle touches of humor and some poignant moments, most of which was heightened by Monta Bell's sparkling direction.

For the first time in over a year, Shearer was loaned to another company, this being United Artists, where she made *Waking Up the Town,* a rather improbable story about a brash, young inventor (Jack Pickford) who dreams that the world has come to an end shortly after prospering with his invention for an electric power plant. Pickford was the star of the film, in addition to having co-directed it with Vernon Keyes, but Miss Shearer, though she had the feminine lead, was relegated to fourth billing. She appeared as a visitor from out of town who comes to a rural community to visit her grandmother and soon finds herself falling in love with Pickford. Neither the picture nor the part, which was much too conventional and void of any particular color, did anything for her and only demoted her somewhat in prestige, but as usual her charm and appeal was never lost. After *Waking Up the Town* there were no future loanouts for Miss Shearer, even though there were occasional demands for her services at other studios.

It was in *A Slave of Fashion*, a romantic comedy-drama, that Shearer first displayed a glamorous wardrobe that was to stamp her as one of the best-dressed women on the screen. She was

Jean Arthur, Paramount player, was taken from commercial posing by Fox Studios and put under contract. Norma Shearer posed with Miss Arthur her first day on the lot (1925).

the small-town girl who goes to New York in the hope of achieving success and realizes her dreams of luxury while assuming the identity of a woman killed in a train wreck during which she was also a passenger. Gorgeously attired in some of the most stunning creations of that halcyon period, she personified the clothes horse delux and even posed a threat to Lilyan Tashman who then led the fashion parade among female luminaries of the screen. With the boyish bob in vogue at the time, Shearer wore it in this film, which added a special allure and sexiness. She was to adopt the style in subsequent films, establishing something of a trademark with it. Her fans never complained and thought that she looked more sophisticated.

Pretty Ladies, a backstage comedy in which Zasu Pitts and Tom Moore played the leads, found Miss Shearer in a novelty type of role. It was that of a real-life character known as Frances White, a popular vaudeville and musical-comedy star of the day whom she impersonated in a brief cameo that was one of the highlights of the film. Heavily made up and wearing an unusually large chapeau that was flat and round, under which she wore a curved hair-do around the side of her face, and daintily holding a thin walking stick that rested on her half-bare shoulders and body, Shearer was a stunning and vivacious sight to behold. One could only

23

wonder what the result would have been had *Pretty Ladies* been a sound picture instead of a silent one. It was also Joan Crawford's film debut with whom Shearer was to come to grips in a future movie.

A reunion with Lon Chaney and director Victor Seastrom in *The Tower of Lies* was not a particularly happy occasion cinemawise as it had been with *He Who Gets Slapped*. Although the film was quite interesting with its moodiness and psychological overtones, including some excellent photography in a beautiful pastoral setting, it was somewhat heavy-handed with Seastrom overstressing artistry that made the characters appear more or less wooden. As the daughter of a hard-working Swedish farmer (Chaney) who is about to lose his farm because of nonpayment, Shearer manages to save it when she goes to the city to seek employment but upon her return is denounced by a bigoted community as an immoral woman. Despite the mediocrity of the part, it was a much more advantageous one for Shearer than in *He*. Chaney, however, who is still regarded by many as the screen's greatest character actor and its most versatile performer, seemed miscast for a change, as was William Haines as Shearer's childhood sweetheart. The best and truly moving performance in the film was contributed by Claire McDowell as Chaney's devoted wife. There have been periodic revivals of *The Tower of Lies* in recent years, but like most of Shearer's silent films it is still a rarity.

Shearer concluded her 1925 film schedule with an amusing light comedy called *His Secretary* that had her posing as an ugly duckling type of stenographer, pince-nez and all, so that she could ward off the attentions of unwelcome males. Lew Cody, who had been her leading man in *A Slave of Fashion*, played her boss, who makes the mistake of shifting her over to his partner (Willard Louis) after discovering how beautiful she is. Miss Shearer was developing into a good light comedienne.

It was also the year that her brother Douglas, who had become an engineer, came to Hollywood to visit his family and tried to induce Louis B. Mayer to engage him to experiment with what he felt was a future for sound pictures. Mayer discouraged the idea instantly, believing it to be impractical, but two years later when Paramount installed a sound department that was proving successful, Mayer decided to send Douglas Shearer east to work with Bell Laboratories as a highly skilled technician and learn everything he could about sound apparatus. In 1927, when *The Jazz Singer* convinced the industry that sound had a definite future, Shearer was finally appointed by Mayer to organize the sound department for the studio. By 1929, he had become head sound recorder of MGM, a post he was to hold for the next thirty-nine years.

There were three Norma Shearer films released in 1926, none of which won any acclaim, though they were popular enough at the box office. The first, *The Devil's Circus*, was a none-too-credible and complex story about a destitute young girl who becomes involved with an ex-convict and waits for his release from prison, which claims him for burglary once again, meanwhile joining a circus where she almost loses her life in a trapeze accident that was instigated by a jealous rival. The film was Danish director Benjamin Christianson's American debut and it was unfortunate that his initial effort in this country wasn't more auspicious. The circus scenes were effectively staged, and in some they carried much impact and excitement, especially the ones with Shearer at the mercy of a caged lion into whose den she has fallen.

Although it was different in theme, *The Waning Sex* was a better and more civilized film, with Miss Shearer making a welcome return to light comedy. As a clever young lawyer she competed with her legal colleague (Conrad Nagel) in a swimming contest, a larceny case, and a race for the district attorney's office. She lost the first, won the second, and withdrew from the third to marry her opponent. George K. Arthur was very amusing as Shearer's effeminate secretary, while Robert Z. Leonard's direction kept things moving at a spontaneous pace.

Upstage was eighty percent drama in which Shearer was back in the role of a small-town girl who comes to the big city to succeed in the business world, but instead finds herself teaming up with a dancer because he had been smitten by her beauty. She had excellent support from Oscar Shaw, the man responsible for her brief theatrical career, which she decides to give up after discovering how inept she is on the stage.

The year of 1927 was a momentous one for Miss Shearer, regarding both her professional and personal life. The films she was seen in during this period had better-than-usual entertainment value, bordering on gay comedy, melodrama, and romantic drama. In *The Demi-Bride*, a frothy French farce that was sophisticated and racy, she further proved her adeptness as a light comedienne making her one of the most popular in the business, outside of Colleen Moore. Shearer portrayed a naughty French student attending convent school who uses all her wiles to attract a wealthy man about town (Lew Cody), unaware that he is her stepmother's paramour. Despite the flippant nature of the film, it was also witty, with Robert Z. Leonard's direction sparkling like a gem. There was nobody in Hollywood at the time who could play a boulevardier as elegantly as Lew Cody, to say nothing of Adolphe Menjou.

After Midnight, in which Shearer appeared next, was a mediocre, though entertaining film about two sisters working in a cabaret, one as a hard working cigarette girl (Shearer), who redeems a crook (Lawrence Gray) with whom she falls in love, and the other a scheming chorus girl (Gwen Lee), who also earns her living as a prostitute. Monta Bell, who was responsible for the original story, was at the directorial helm again, but it wasn't among his best jobs, nor Miss Shearer's. The acting honors went to Gwen Lee, who was usually identified more with comedy.

Shearer had now reached a pinnacle of success that placed her in the star category, though she was still considered second grade. She was then receiving a thousand dollars a week and had asked Mayer for a revised contract, starting at her present salary that would increase periodically to five thousand within the next five years. Surprisingly, Mayer sanctioned this, but he planned to let Shearer go before that period expired. With Irving Thalberg interceding, however, Mayer had a change of heart and decided not to dispense with the actress's services.

Thalberg, who was then the youngest production executive in the film industry, having been general manager of Universal Studios at the age of twenty-three, shortly before Mayer weaned him away from Carl Laemmle, had fostered Shearer's career every step of the way. He had groomed it as if he were grooming a race horse for the big handicap, and even if the properties he chose for her weren't always the best, they at least bore his indelible stamp of taste and quality in the finished film, which was to be consistent with his future productions at MGM. A firm believer in the star system, he was the originator of it in the Hollywood sphere, establishing such names as Lon Chaney, John Gilbert, Greta Garbo, Ramon Novarro, Joan Crawford, and, when sound came in, Wallace Beery, Robert Montgomery, Marie Dressler, and Jean Harlow. But as far as Norma Shearer was concerned, his plan was to make her a super-star and queen of the studio. Thalberg, one might say, was Pygmalion and Shearer his Galatea.

By now, Thalberg's interest in Miss Shearer had become personal as well, and in January of 1927, they announced their engagement. On September 29 of that year they were married, with Norma shedding her aquiescent anglicanism for Thalberg's Jewish faith. Rabbi Edgar Mangin, who was later to eugolize at the producer's funeral, performed the ceremony and guided the nervous bride through the service. In a press interview some years later she explained her conversion as follows: "When I began to go with Irving, I began to associate with his people. His family are Orthodox Jews and I saw that they found peace and contentment in their religion. I wanted peace and contentment in our marriage. I decided I had no particular religious convictions — that I could find it in the Jewish faith. I loved Irving so much that I wanted our children brought up in the same way he had been."

With *The Student Prince*, which was released a week before their marriage, Miss Shearer had her first prestige film in which she had co-star billing with Ramon Novarro. An endearing operatic favorite with music by Sigmund Romberg, it was originally based on Richard Mansfield's *Old Heidelberg* and was a charming romance about a Teutonic prince (Novarro) and a pretty barmaid (Shearer) at the University that the royal subject was attending. It was sweetness and light for Shearer once again, a role she hadn't played in several years and which she had not forgotten how to portray. With no trace of the sophistication her other parts had not too long ago required, her portrayal of Kathy had dignity, grace, and charm, if not any particualr depth, while Novarro was less flamboyant than usual and more natural than in his past films. But the most important contribution to *The Student Prince* was Ernst Lubitsch, a German director who knew Heidelberg well and its great

Irving Thalberg and Norma Shearer on their wedding day (1927).

Norma Shearer in the early 1930s.

university. His excellent direction enhanced the film immeasurably and also advanced Miss Shearer's career to a large extent. The picture was a box-office success. Remade in 1954 under the same title with Edmund Purdom as the future king and Ann Blyth as Kathy, its only saving grace was the dubbed singing voice of Mario Lanza and an impressive supporting cast.

During 1928, Shearer was seen in three pictures. The first, *The Latest from Paris*, a frothy and amusing comedy spontaneously directed by Sam Wood, had to do with a shrewd traveling saleslady who could outsell her male competitor in the cloak and suit trade while simultaneously fostering the education of her young brother. Ralph Forbes, usually cast as a stuffy type of character, appeared as Shearer's commercial rival and revealed an unexpected ability to play comedy in typical American fashion. Chic and smartly gowned, Shearer added much sparkle to the film and gave a zestful performance. It was the kind of part she seemed to revel in because of its sophisticated aspects and the fact that it gave her a chance to display an elegant wardrobe. In *The Actress*, adapted from Sir Arthur Pinero's *Trelawney of the Wells*, she reverted to simplicity once again as a noted and devil-may-care actress of the mid-Victorian period who is snubbed by the British peerage because of her love for one of the clan (Ralph Forbes) to whom she is engaged. It was also her first costume film and possibly her best performance in silent films. Directing Miss Shearer was Sidney Franklin, whose guidance she was to value above all other directors in the near future. *The Lady of Chance*, a light comedy with melodramatic overtones about the confidence racket, was her last silent picture, which was synchronized and employed a few talking sequences, though she wasn't heard. She appeared as a slick blackmailer who preyed on unsuspecting victims with two other cohorts whom she manages to outwit. Miss Shearer may have been the most beautiful crook to operate, but her respectable mien and gentility were much too obvious in order for her to be convincing as an unsavory character. At any rate, she was her usual pleasing self and so was the film, including some neat performances from Lowell Sherman and Gwen Lee as Shearer's partners in crime.

Once the pressures of studio activity had eased down, the Thalbergs went to Europe on their hon-

Norma Shearer, her mother, Mrs. Edith Shearer, and sister Athole (late 1920s).

eymoon. It has been said that the trip gave Norma a new prospective on life and benefited her career. When she returned she was more sophisticated, which reflected favorably enough on her future screen portrayals.

Awaiting her upon her return was a most unusual wedding gift from Thalberg. It was a portable dressing room on wheels and resembled a stagecoach. Equipped with a refrigerator, a thermos to keep things hot, an ironing board, a dressing table, and a wardrobe to stock clothes, it was built as a trailer and could move anywhere on the studio lot, including location spots. This may have been something of a preview as to Shearer's queenly status at MGM in the years that were ahead.

With sound pictures already in, Miss Shearer's career was at an impasse, since she had never had any stage experience. Her voice posed a problem. How would it record?

At this point, she decided to go to the University of Southern California to have her voice analyzed.

She was said to have had a very pleasant one, a bit high-pitched, perhaps, but not grating to the ears. The voice analysis resulted successfully, while in addition, she aided the university in analyzing and classifying voices of other screen players to evolve the first scientific terminology of the speaking voices. She stood before a microphone—while Professor W.R. Mac Donald and Dean Ray Immel operated the recording instruments. She derived much pleasure from the experience.

Bayard Veiller, who had just sold MGM the rights to his play *The Trial of Mary Dugan*, had been impressed with Shearer's voice experiment and proposed that she play the part of Mary, an ex-Follies girl accused of murdering her lover. The role had originally been played by Ann Harding on the New York stage and had made her a star overnight. It was a highly emotional role and Shearer wanted to do it badly, but Thalberg felt that his wife wasn't quite prepared to undertake such a demanding part, since her dramatic range was limited by the fact that she had played so many genteel characters. Thalberg, apparently, preferred her in the latter, but Veiller, who had also been assigned to direct the film version, had every confidence in Shearer and thought her ideal for Mary, even though it was uncertain as to how her voice would record on the studio apparatus. A talkie test had to be made in order to convice the MGM brass.

Veiller suggested a special rehearsal with Raymond Hackett, who had already been chosen to play one of the leads. It was the cross-examination scene the playwright had selected, probably the tensest scene in the play.

Veiller directed Shearer carefully and gave her as much constructive criticism as he could. After a few more rehearsals, he knew that she was capable of playing the role. Only Thalberg, Louis B. Mayer, and J. Robert Rubin, vice-president and general counsel of MGM remained to be convinced.

Veiller then arranged to have a test of Miss Shearer made in secret after the studio had suspended operations for the day. The electricians, who held the actress in high-esteem, raised no objection to staying overtime and co-operated fully.

Seven executives, including Thalberg, saw the test in the projection room and were pleasantly surprised at the results. Shearer's voice recorded effectively enough and she was signed to play Mary Dugan. It was one of the happiest moments in her life.

While *The Trial of Mary Dugan* was in production during the early part of December of 1928, the studio arranged with the Los Angeles County Jail to have Shearer booked under the name of the character she was portraying in the film. It was all a publicity stunt, but instructional, too, since she was able to get some local color that would lend a certain authenticity to the film. Shearer spent several hours at the jail as an inmate having her fingerprints taken and being escorted through the women's quarters by a special guard. Her fingerprints were eventually enlarged on film so that they could be compared with the fingerprints on the weapon used in the killing.

The Trial of Mary Dugan, MGM'S second talking picture (its first was *The Broadway Melody of 1929*) was released early in June of 1929 and opened at the Embassy Theatre (formerly a newsreel house) in the Times Square area to excellent notices, with Miss Shearer's acting being also highly praised. She revealed a pleasant, low-pitched voice that registered quite effectively, while her emotional scenes were well under control and carried sufficient impact. She was ably supported by such veterans as Lewis Stone, appearing as her defense attorney, and H.B. Warner as a prosecutor; Raymond Hackett as her young lawyer brother and Lilyan Tashman, who was also heard for the first time on the screen, did commendable work, with Bayard Veiller's skillful direction eliciting excitement and suspense. It was a triumph for all concerned, particularly for Miss Shearer, who had finally become a full-fledged star.

Her second talkie was *The Last of Mrs. Cheyney,* an ultra-sophisticated drawing-room comedy based on Frederick Lonsdale's successful stage play in which Gladys Cooper and Gerald DeMaurier had originally appeared in London in 1925. In it, Shearer returned to playing an immoral woman, this time a high-powered crook whose ingenuity and that of her accomplices make it possible to install themselves as house guests among the British aristocracy with the purpose of stealing a valuable diamond from their hostess. She handled the role with aplomb, injecting subtle touches of comedy here and there, which helped to relieve the staticism of the film, since it was virtually confined to one setting as in *The Trial of Mary Dugan*. Although the dialogue was gay and sparkling, the constant talk of the characters obliterated their acting somewhat. Wearing her hair in a sleek, boyish bob, Shearer nonchalantly flourished a long cigarette holder and displayed an extensive wardrobe by Adrian, who was to design her clothes for most of her films. Sidney Franklin again directed her, but his usual artistic work in which he had always had much more cinematic freedom was hindered by the stagey material.

With their first musical, *Broadway Melody of 1929,* already successfully launched, MGM followed it with a novelty in vaudeville form called *The Hollywood Revue* in which practically all of MGM's top personalities made a special guest appearance, each contributing a number, be it a skit, song or dance. One of the highlights of this merry and gorgeously staged show with twenty musical numbers was the balcony scene from *Romeo and Juliet* between Shearer and John Gilbert in a satirical interpretation where both used modern everyday slang that sounded as if it were emanating from the Dead End Kids. As the Master of Ceremonies, Jack Benny made a pleasing if not memorable feature film debut. The critics were not especially entranced with *The Hollywood Revue,* but the public found it an escape, what with the economic turmoil that was to engulf Wall Street shortly and the subsequent depression.

Shearer's next film, *Their Own Desire,* was not exactly in the hit class, nor did she herself elicit any special praise from the press and moviegoers alike. She played a flippant society girl, cynical and neurotic whose parents are on the verge of getting a divorce after twenty-five years of happily married life and who falls in love with the son of the mother her father is having a clandestine affair with. The part was not becoming to Miss Shearer in the least, but a very promising young actor named Robert Montgomery, who played her lover, bore watching, even though his opportunities were rather limited here.

There was much compensation and even rejoicing for Shearer in her following vehicle, *The Divorcée,* based on Ursula Parrott's best-selling novel of the day, *Ex-Wife.* It was the best and most intelligent and mature role she had yet been given, and as Jerry, the divorcee of the title whose marriage disintegrates because of her husband's failure to cope with her principals, she won an

Conrad Nagel presents Norma Shearer with an Oscar for having given the best performance of the year in The Divorcée. *(1930).*

Academy Award. Chester Morris, usually cast as a cocky type of character, was fine as her journalist-spouse who becomes a philanderer. The film, however, suffered a bit from Robert Z. Leonard's antiquated direction, since he adhered to the style of the silent screen. But Miss Shearer's excellent performance overshadowed what faults it had, of which there were few. *The Divorcée* set a new box-office record.

Let Us Be Gay, from Rachel Crother's delightful and frothy stage comedy, saw Miss Shearer back in sophisticated surroundings. Like its predecessor, it was also a theme in which marriage and divorce were the issues at hand, except that here they were treated in a much lighter and humorous vein. Shearer delivered a nice portrayal as a housewife with simple tastes who is forced to divorce her husband (Rod LaRocque) because of his infidelity, then changes her mode of living by becoming a worldy-wise society woman. It was the great Marie Dressler, as an eccentric dowager, who made *Let Us Be Gay* one of the top entertainments of the summer season. Robert Z. Leonard was at the directorial helm once again, but this time his direction was more spontaneous and had sparkle. After this picture had been completed, Miss Shearer took a vacation for several months, and on August 25, 1930, six weeks following its release, she gave birth to her first child, Irving Thalberg, Jr.

Rumors had begun to circulate that she was through with the screen, but these reports only

Norma Shearer poses with one of her children.

served to whet the public's appetite to see her again and again.

Late in 1930, Miss Shearer signed a new long-term contract with MGM at six thousand a week, one of the largest salaries ever paid to a motion-picture actress in that depression-ridden era. Her first picture under this new agreement was *Strangers May Kiss*, from another Ursula Parrott story, which dealt with situations not unlike *The Divorcée*. And like the latter film, it was a good adult romantic drama about a young woman who becomes a lady-gigolo when the man she loves forsakes her. In the mundane character of Lisbeth, Shearer matched her excellent performance in *The Divorcée* as the neglected sweetheart of a globe-trotting newspaperman with whom she could only enjoy brief interludes because of his foreign assignments. Neil Hamilton was capital as the roving journalist, while Robert Montgomery, as the flippant playboy on the loose, remedied Shearer's loneliness, but failed to win her in the end. He had played a similar role in *The Divorcée*. It was *Strangers May Kiss*, though, that made Montgomery a star.

Shearer's next picture was *A Free Soul*, based on a story by Adela Rogers St. Johns, which actually suggested incidents in the life of the author's father, Earl Rogers, a famous criminal lawyer of the twenties who was noted for his flamboyance and actorish mannerisms in a courtroom. (Several years ago Miss St. Johns wrote a fictionalized biography of him called *Tell No Tales*. The character of Rogers was superbly portrayed by Lionel Barrymore, a heavy-drinking but clever attorney who has reared his sensitive, headstrong daughter (Shearer) to be as unconventional as he is by allowing her to be as flighty as she wishes. Her sordid liaison with a notorious gambler (Clark Gable) whom her father has won an acquittal for on a murder charge and the eventual dawning on her of the racketeer's true, vicious personality were the melodramatic ingredients of a pungent and occasionally powerful film. Miss Shearer did very well in the role of Jan, who is smitten by the gangster's swarthy charm, and her emotional scenes were gripping, if a bit overstressed; Gable projected an animal type of magnetism as the hoodlum, and when he molested Shearer by pushing her down on a couch, audiences loved it and cried for more of these caveman tactics; Leslie Howard, a fine and highly intelligent actor,

seemed miscast, lost and even pallid as Shearer's socialite polo player fiancé; some crisp character bits were contributed by James Gleason as the family friend and bodyguard of Barrymore, and Ed Brophy as a staccato-talking henchman of Gable's; but it was Lionel Barrymore who stole every scene in the film that got him an Academy Award as best screen actor of 1931. Most critics expressed no enthusiasm for *A Free Soul*, except for Barrymore's great performance, but they underestimated it at the time, and viewing the film today, it contains much that is worthwhile and has a beginning, middle, and end, which most films have lacked in recent years. Clarence Brown, who so skillfully directed it, praised Shearer for her shading of the character in an interview in the *Los Angeles Times* of August 23, 1931: "To direct Miss Shearer is literally to get an entirely new perspective of picture making. Never before have I seen an actress able to project such delicate shading of drama and always maintain the poise which gives her an individual charm."

It was also Brown who had Shearer disrobe for the first time in her film career in *A Free Soul*. He wanted to achieve a certain eroticism in a scene that takes place in Gable's lavish apartment where she has been living as his mistress and had her seated on a sofa with her thighs and legs fully exposed. It was a slight form of nudity then, but Miss Shearer projected a sexuality that raised the temperature of audiences. And when she motioned Gable with her luminous eyes and low-pitched voice to come to her and put his arms around her it was truly a sizzling cinematic moment for moviegoers of that day. But sex or no sex *A Free Soul* was a box-office winner.

Shearer was glad to return to sophisticated comedy in Noel Coward's classic romp, *Private Lives*, in which she and Robert Montgomery were ex-husband and wife who had remarried, and by coincidence encounter each other while both are honeymooning on the Riviera and staying at the same hotel with their respective new mates. Both made an engaging pair in this madcap farce, playing their roles with a savoir faire that virtually equaled the original stage performances of Noel Coward and Gertrude Lawrence. Despite her absence from comedy for more than a year, Miss Shearer had not lost her light comedic touch and emerged as an even better comedienne. One of the film's highlights was a violent and amusing brawl between Shearer and Montgomery in which they rolled over a sofa and onto the floor, with Shearer finally smashing a phonograph record over Montgomery's head. While this scene was being filmed, Shearer is said to have lost control of her left arm as she was about to strike Montgomery, thereby inflicting a blow that sent the young actor through a screen. Shearer was horrified, but there was no need for a retake. The other newlyweds were played by Reginald Denny and Una Merkel, the latter who seemed rather miscast, mainly because of her southern drawl. Denny, however, as Shearer's stuffy second spouse, was properly cast, since he was an Englishman by birth, though Miss Shearer's slight Canadian speech was noticeable, which might have compensated somewhat for a lack of Anglo-Saxon tones among most of the characters. Except for Miss Merkel, who in more recent years had developed into a fine character actress, the remaining three principal players managed to catch the true essence of Coward's scintillating play. The direction by Sid-

ney Franklin, who was one of Hollywood's most versatile directors, was very deft.

In April of 1932 Shearer relinquished her rights as a Canadian subject and became an American citizen. She said she wanted to show her appreciation to the country that had accorded her screen fame.

Miss Shearer had expressed a fervent desire to do *Strange Interlude*, Eugene O'Neill's powerful drama, and Thalberg, who had planned to film the play, decided to cast his wife in the difficult role of Nina Leeds, a young, frustrated woman who has an illegitimate child by another man because of her husband's impotence and the fear of insanity inherent in his family. For once, Thalberg's choice here was not exactly an astute one, for Shearer lacked genuine dramatic ability to infuse the character with a profundity it so sorely needed. Hers was an intelligent and interesting performance, but the neuroticism of Nina was missing, which made it a surface portrayal. Clark Gable, as Shearer's doctor-lover was not too well cast either and appeared a bit stiff. In the scenes where the two grow old, they aged effectively, if not believably. Robert Z. Leonard, who undertook an almost impossible task in directing the film, was decidedly wrong for it, considering his reputation as a commercial director with a typical Hollywood approach. Fault, however, could not be found in the excellent acting of Alexander Kirkland as Shearer's weak-willed husband, and Ralph Morgan as Charlie, the rejected and mournful suitor of Nina's, both who had appeared in the original stage version. They imbued *Strange Interlude* with depth and sensitivity, making it an absorbing and unusual film. But it was not the commercial success *A Free Soul* and *Private Lives* had been, catering to a select and discriminating audience.

The next vehicle that Irving Thalberg chose for his wife was ideally suited to her talents. This was *Smilin' Through*, the perennial tearjerker based on Allan Langdon Martin's and Jane Cowl's popular stage success of over fifty years ago, which had also been a silent film in 1922 starring Norma Talmadge. It was a charming romantic drama that dripped with sentiment, yet was moving, dignified and genuine in its depiction of genteel English folk and two love stories that bordered between the periods of 1868 and World War I. In the dual role of lovely Irish Moonyean, who is accidentally and

Norma Shearer becomes a United States citizen (1932).

Mary Pickford, Douglas Fairbanks, Sr., and Norma Shearer at Fairbank's farewell party at Pickfair (1932).

fatally shot by a rejected suitor on her wedding day in the early part of the story, and Kathleen, her orphaned niece who has a love affair with the murderer's young son fifty years later, Shearer was perfectly in her element, giving her best performance since *The Divorcée* and *Strangers May Kiss*. It was truly a remarkable transition from a sophisticate to an old-fashioned girl that proved that she was not beyond being versatile. The other double roles were well portrayed by Fredric March and Leslie Howard—the former responsible for the tragedy and as the young American who comes to England to join up for war duty, the latter as the ill-fated young lover of the dead bride and in the twentieth century as the elderly uncle of Kathleen who forbids his niece to have anything to do with the son of the man who killed his beloved. Sidney Franklin rang all the pathos at his command, and as a result the women had a good cry.

Early in 1933, the Thalbergs sailed for Europe, with Irving, Jr., accompanying them, and upon their return in the late Spring, Shearer was ready to begin work on *Riptide*, her first picture in eighteen months. This was to be the first in a series of productions for Thalberg as an independent producer, following his alienation from Louis B. Mayer, with whom he had had a number of disagreements.

Charles MacArthur, one of the best literary talents of Broadway and Hollywood, was assigned to write the screenplay of *Riptide*, but he soon grew disillusioned about the theme. An ultrasophisticated talky triangle comedy-drama, it concerned a young American girl married to a titled Britisher and her romantic involvement with a playboy, also from the States. The husband, who is very much in love with his wife, and she with him, discovers her infidelity and both come to a tense showdown. Shearer was quite believable as the wife whose loyalty is broken because of her husband's suspicious nature, and Herbert Marshall was splendid as the spouse obsessed by jealousy. Robert Montgomery played the correspondent in his usual engaging manner in his fifth and final appearance with Shearer.

Writer MacArthur, however, felt that the situation here stressed Anglo-American relations a bit more than it should and he withdrew from the assignment. He was replaced by Edmund Goulding, a fine English director who had already established a creditable reputation in Hollywood. Goulding's script and direction were highly commendable, but the film was not a commercial success, despite Shearer's popularity.

Shortly after *Riptide* was released, Shearer, in an interview in the *Los Angeles Times* said, "The starting point in many of my portrayals has been idealism. It is that even in several pictures that have been deemed so sophisticated. I can't do the Garbo or the Dietrich thing. I admire them both greatly and wish that I could play such characters as they interpret, but I have to go through a transition to become worldly. Every actress can't be a Garbo or a Dietrich, but many can be sophisticated and it pays."

It isn't generally known, but Shearer was a victim, and still may be, of chronic claustrophobia. In a special interview with Gladys Hall in *Motion Picture Magazine* dated February 1934, Miss Hall, who was once among the top fan-magazine writers, and possibly the most influential, claimed it was the greatest interview Shearer ever printed and the most revealing. To corroborate this unorthodox situation, Miss Shearer appeared before a

34

Gary Cooper's party. Among the guests: Leslie Howard, Norma Shearer, Gary Cooper, Elsa Maxwell, and Lionel Barrymore.

notary public, known as Nancy Smith, on November 20, 1933 and hereby testified that the story contained material never before published in any magazine or newspaper. She signed her name in a notary public seal to this effect. According to Miss Hall this was the compelling mainspring of Shearer's whole life. It partly drove her from Canada to New York. Miss Shearer's statement is as follows: "Sufferer's from the phobia cannot remain in small rooms, cannot ride in subways — trains — cannot go through tunnels — cannot bear the thought of anything but cremation after death — since the confines of the grave would send their restless ghosts a gypsying.

"Claustrophobia is a very real psychosis. There is nothing imaginary about it. I know—because I am a claustrophobiac.

"This phobia, or fear, or whatever you choose to name it is responsible for my whole life—for everything I have ever done and wanted to do.

"Without this phobia I would be a small town woman, living in a small home, doing the family marketing, etc.

"I had to marry a man bigger and more important in every way than I was myself. Only in such a marriage could I live without a sense of being cramped and compressed.

"I had to have freedom of speech, to say the wrong thing, if it came to me, to what I thought at the moment, at any rate. As whenever I am angry or over-excited I tear my clothes off—so, when I get angry or excited or stimulated, do I tear off the clothes of my mind.

"It was the impulse to escape grooves and channels that drove me to New York, and later to the last frontier of the Pacific Coast. It was that impulse, that phobia and nothing else. It was not the thought that I could act. It was not the need for making money. I could have acted on the stage back there. I could have earned a living back there, too. It was the need for more freedom, more scope, more air. It was simply that I was suffering from claustrophobia, though I didn't know it then.

"In New York I once saw the late Evangeline Adams, the famous astrologer, and she told me that I was going far away for my happiness and success. I am free here, as I can be anywhere on earth. There is a sense of enormousness and bigness in California.

"It is possible to use this phobia to great advantage. It is chained like to water falls and has be-

come an inspiring motivating force working in my blood and brain to drive me on ceaselessly, to force me to grow in time and space, to breathe and work more spaciously. And while I can push back walls and escape treadmills and channels, I am safe and reasonably content."

It is possible that Miss Shearer's condition stemmed from childhood and became increasingly manifest as the years went by. Much of this may have been attributed to her love for the outdoors while living in Canada and her decision to have an expansive beach home in Santa Monica facing the ocean where she and her husband had been residing since shortly after their marriage.

Now that Shearer had developed into one of the most skillful actresses in Hollywood, Thalberg had no doubt that his wife was equipped to play almost any type of role. In choosing Rudolf Besier's international stage success, *The Barretts of Wimpole Street*, as her next vehicle he made what was probably his best selection in acquiring a play property. The part of Elizabeth Barrett, an invalid-poetess whose life is unjustly dominated by her tyrannical father, had much idealism and poignancy and was a difficult one to portray because of its physical limitations. And that was why Miss Shearer was hesitant in accepting this plum role, fearing it might limit her, since the character is virtually confined to a chair throughout the story. Her wariness indeed surprised Thalberg, as it did many others at MGM.

Marion Davies, whose films no longer had any box-office assurance, longed to do the part, hoping it would be a comeback for her. She tested for it with William Randolph Hearst backing her to the hilt. But when Shearer learned that Miss Davies was enthusiastic about playing Elizabeth, she changed her mind quickly and decided that she would like to play the part after all. When Shearer had a heart-to-heart talk with the once popular star, Miss Davies soon realized that she would not be too well cast, since the character required a patrician demeanor and beauty that Miss Shearer was fortunate in having. For one thing, Miss Davies was handicapped with a bit of a stutter.

The Barretts of Wimpole Street turned out to be a superb film, with Shearer scoring a personal triumph in it. She dispensed pathos and charm as she had never done before and the critics embraced her performance as they had never done before.

Sidney Franklin's direction was excellent, while Fredric March, as the impetuous Robert Browning, added dash and vigor to his role. But it was Charles Laughton as the pious, unrelenting master of the genteel household to whom most of the acting honors were accorded. His was a magnificent delineation of a man stifled by his own hypocrisy. In 1956, MGM reproduced *The Barretts* with Sidney Franklin directing it again. The cast included Jennifer Jones as Elizabeth, John Gielgud as the straight-laced father, and Bill Travers (much too vigorous and athletic looking) as Browning. For a remake, it was unusually well done, if not as excellent as the original film.

In 1934, during the release of *The Barretts of Wimpole Street*, Norma Shearer and George Arliss headed a poll as England's favorite film players according to 1,250,000 filmgoers. Shearer's popularity in Britain was to reign for a few years to come.

The December issue of *Photoplay* of 1934 quoted Miss Shearer on the subject of sex: "It should figure in every film—never be regarded in terms of vulgarity—it should be approached subtly, suavely."

Asked about the two most varied roles she interpreted from a sex angle, she went on to say: "The girl in *He Who Gets Slapped*, my first role at MGM, and Jan Ashe in *A Free Soul*. In the first, the boy and the girl were two children in love. It was a fresh dawning kind of love, with the timorous gropings and shy responses. But with a very definite undercurrent of young sex.

"The *Free Soul* girl was as close to the primitive

Norma Shearer, Fredric March, Mrs. March, and Irving Thalberg (1935).

elemental sex-surge as any I have ever played. She was wasting no time to build up a romance with Clark Gable.

"In *The Barretts of Wimpole Street*, Elizabeth Barrett was an invalid simply because she had no vitality. She was not ill. I tried to make her vital only from the moment she first saw Robert Browning. From that moment was the urge to walk to see him. He brought her warmth, and life—sex interest. Yet this is not a role that could ever by named sexy. I hate that word."

For almost two years, Shearer was absent from the screen, during which she devoted quite a bit of time to her family and watched over her husband's failing health. Thalberg had been driving himself at the studio.

On June 13, 1935, she gave birth to a daughter who was named Katherine, and shortly following this event, Thalberg was set to produce *Romeo and Juliet*, an ambition he had long nursed since the *Hollywood Revue* skit of Shakespeare's opus, and also the hope of casting his wife as the fateful heroine one day. It was inevitable, of course, that he would, once it was decided to be filmed.

The successful teaming of Shearer and Fredric March in *Smilin' Through* and *The Barretts of Wimpole Street* inspired Thalberg to approach March to undertake the part of Romeo, but the young actor declined the offer, claiming that it would be impossible to avoid a certain swagger with the character. Robert Donat, who had made only one film in Hollywood and preferred working in England, and Brian Aherne, were prospects for the role. After much consideration, Leslie Howard was the final choice, while George Cukor was assigned to direct. Talbot Jennings worked on the script, and Professor John Tucker Murray, an authority on Elizabethan drama, and William Strunk, Jr., were engaged as technical consultants. Miss Shearer had expert coaching from veteran actress Constance Collier, an old hand at the bard, and John Barrymore, to whom Shakespeare was most familiar.

Cukor, in giving direction, said he was hammering at the reality—the simple humanity of the play. "Don't think of it as one of Shakespeare's tragedies," he said. "Just because that's what they taught you at school. These people weren't tragic to themselves. They were in love — that's all — living through the moods all lovers live through — happy part of the time — hopeful most of the time. They didn't know how it was going to end. Play it that way."

Cukor's hopes were apparently fulfilled, for the results were gratifying, if not overwhelming.

On August 20, 1936, *Romeo and Juliet* began a roadshow engagement at New York's Broadway Astor Theatre as it did under the same policy in theatres across the country and abroad. The New York critics proclaimed it a cinematic achievement, but there were mixed reviews in other journalistic corners that didn't exactly indicate that the film was really inspiring. Miss Shearer was an older-than-usual Juliet at the age of thirty-six, but she conveyed a spirit of youthfulness that added a special glow. For this performance, surprisingly enough, she received her fifth Academy Award nomination. Leslie Howard, also aging (he was then forty-seven), made Romeo an intelligent and believable character, if not a vital one. John Barrymore brimmed with vitality, unforgettable as Mercutio, Romeo's scandalous friend.

Miss Shearer had her own special bouquets for Leslie Howard, "I can't think of anyone who could have played it with that inimitable charm and grace and restraint, who could have made it so tender without ever losing his manliness. When he reads the lines, they seem to belong to him, they sound as if no one in the world had ever said them before. You're going to love his Romeo—every woman who sees it is going to love it."

Despite the accolades, the publicity, the imposing cast, and the general fanfare the picture was bestowed with, it was only modestly profitable. It had cost two million dollars to produce.

On September 14, 1936, less than a month after the premier of *Romeo and Juliet*, Irving Thalberg was dead at the age of thirty-seven. His passing was one of the greatest losses the film industry had ever suffered. Like the passing of such screen greats as Lon Chaney, Sr., and Marie Dressler a few years before him, it was the end of an era.

Shortly after the funeral, Miss Shearer went into seclusion and then contracted bronchial pneumonia. Upon recovering she informed the studio that she was planning to retire. Among certain executives and players it was felt that her departure from the screen might reduce MGM's prestige somewhat, both artistically and commercially, even though such luminaries as Garbo, Joan Crawford, Robert Montgomery, William Powell, Clark Gable, Myrna Loy, Robert Taylor, and the Marx Brothers still graced the lot. Others felt she would be wise to relinquish her career while she was still on top. Thalberg had provided his wife with a fabulous estate in the neighborhood of eight million and ten million dollars, which made her not only one of the wealthiest women in the film colony but also in the world.

In the interim, Metro had an investment exceeding four hundred thousand dollars on *Marie Antoinette*, based on Stefan Zweig's book which was scheduled as Shearer's next film. Thalberg had been planning to film it since 1933 when rights were authorized while he was vacationing in Europe and had hoped to produce it prior to *Romeo and Juliet*. Over two months had been spent in preparing the script. But Thalberg was dissatisfied with the way it was progressing and decided to go to work on it himself. Despite the energy he applied to it and some fresh slants he may have added, he felt that it was still in need of much polishing and thought it best to relinquish the project—at least temporarily. A few more postponements were to follow.

Miss Shearer's decision to leave the screen worried Nicholas Schenck and Louis B. Mayer who wanted her badly for *Marie Antoinette,* which had been written to her specifications. They also wished she would go on with her career. But there was too much at stake, with the estate yet to be settled and the fact that she had lost her enthusiasm. An agreement was then reached whereby she would pay a sum of fifty thousand dollars and she would be released from her contract.

A problem posed itself as to the financial settlement concerning Thalberg's heirs that was to come from the Mayer group profits. Thalberg's lawyers, who also represented his partners and Loews Inc., had discovered that a diversity of percentage contracts repeatedly drawn through the years were cryptic. This was debated over for several months. The lawyers for Thalberg insisted that the late producer's estate was entitled to a gross share of the profits. The Mayer group lawyers contended that it should receive nothing. At long length, Nicholas Schenck learned that the company was cold-shouldering Norma Shearer and attempting to do her in. He suspected that it was arousing the ire of Thalberg's friends and soon arranged for a compromise settlement. The Thalberg estate was compensated with a complete allotment of all profits paid to the Mayer group upon the expiration of its contract at the end of 1938. On this basis, which was quite liberal, Miss Shearer resumed her affiliations with MGM and signed a special contract calling for six films over a three-year period at $150,000 a picture. She had been receiving the same amount before Thalberg's death.

Exhausted by it all, Shearer took her children and went to Arizona for an extended rest. When she returned, she felt rejuvenated and about ready to start work on *Marie Antoinette*.

Antoinette was MGM's most ambitious and costly undertaking in years and required painstaking preparation. The research on it was said to be a romance in itself. Top studio technicians were sent abroad to uncover actual possessions of Antoinette, such as her jewels and the jewels belonging to her friends. The late gown designer, Adrian, was credited with unearthing these items and he also discovered material from which he reproduced gowns worn during the reign of Louis XVI. Voluminous biographical data on Louis and the sumptuous courts of that period were compiled, the contents of which were most intimate, revealing particulars related to each of the sixty historical characters to appear in the film.

One of the most interesting and quaintest discoveries was the fact that Louis XV took a bath only seventeen times from the day he was born to the day he died. Another was Louis XVI's life's ambition to set off twenty clocks striking concurrently, and the touching discovery that Antoinette's slippers had holes in them as she knelt before the guillotine.

Hunt Stromberg, who was in charge of production, had talked the French government into permitting his camera unit to photograph the royal chambers in the Palace at Versailles, which was ordinarily prohibited.

An excellent cast was assembled to support Miss Shearer. Tyrone Power was selected to play the handsome Swedish peer who has a brief romance with Antoinette; Robert Morley, who had been brought over from England, was cast as Louis XVI. (The part had originally been offered to Charles Laughton, but commitments in London prevented him from accepting the role.) And John Barrymore made something of a modest comeback in the small, though impressive role of Louis XV. The direction was assigned to Sidney Franklin, who was Shearer's and Thalberg's personal choice.

Shearer's costume fittings were an arduous task in themselves. Her day was said to require fifty-two pounds of wardrobe with a ten-hour working schedule. Her fittings alone took three months. Her diligence in preparing for the part was indeed remarkable. She read and reread Zweig's biography of the queen and was rarely without the book.

In January of 1938, *Marie Antoinette* finally started shooting. For awhile there was much tension on the set that almost unnerved Miss Shearer to the breaking point. But when she saw the first rushes she was greatly consoled.

When everything appeared to be going well on the *Antoinette* set, a situation arose that put a crimp in the proceedings. Sidney Franklin was suddenly taken off the picture by Louis B. Mayer, who was afraid that the gifted director might not bring the picture in on time, since Franklin was usually meticulous and took more time than most directors in striving for visual detail. The removal of Franklin from the production was a great disappointment to Shearer and a blow as well, for she had valued Franklin's guidance these many years. It was he who had brought out some of her best histrionic qualities, with the result that her acting improved immensely. Franklin, who had assisted Thalberg with the script in its early stages, was compensated by Mayer with a producer's job. When informed that W.S. Van Dyke was to replace Franklin, and would she mind, Shearer said it was immaterial to her. She was too tired to care. But then she was also in a quandary. She understood Mayer's concern about lengthening the shooting, which would increase production costs, and therefore she thought it unwise to raise any objection at this time.

Van Dyke, however, was no slouch as a megaphone wielder. He was one of the best and most sought-after directors in Hollywood. His talents, though, did not seem to lie in the direction of such historical subjects as *Marie Antoinette*. He was really better suited for a racy type of film like *The Thin Man* and *Manhattan Melodrama*, or a lusty, romantic spectacle like *San Francisco*, three of his best and most popular films. And, unlike Sidney Franklin, he had a reputation for being brash, temperamental, and rather dictatorial while working on a film. He was known to have walked out on such stars as Clark Gable and Jeanette MacDonald during the making of *San Francisco*. It was feared that he might do the same on Shearer, or, possibly she on him.

An unexpected report then leaked out. Shearer and Van Dyke had clashed. He shot only four takes of her scene. She insisted on a few more. He refused and she finally stalked off the set. It was all exaggerated, of course. The newspapers had gotten hold of the story and the public devoured it. It wasn't long before *Antoinette* became a closed set, particularly to the press.

The tension that had been building up for some time was soon broken when Miss Shearer accidentally lost her footing on the hoop of her gown and pitched forward to the ground while engaged in a delicate scene. The fall was so reminiscent of a Mack Sennett or Hal Roach comedy that it provoked laughter from the entire company, with Shearer joining in. Van Dyke said of her: "She's the sweetest damn woman in Hollywood."

The final results of *Marie Antoinette*, unfortunately, were uninspiring. It was a sumptuous and entertaining production to be sure, and done in the grand manner as only MGM could execute it, but the screenplay by Claudine West, Donald Ogden Stewart, and Ernest Vajda lacked a certain depth and power, though historically it was fairly accurate. The direction, too, was uninspiring and seemed hurried and flamboyant. Van Dyke worked faster than any director and was said to have finished many films ahead of schedule. The acting was good, but not distinguished, with the exception of Robert Morley, who gave a moving performance as a slow-witted monarch Antoinette is forced to marry. As for Miss Shearer, she was competent and sincere, and in one or two scenes, particularly the banishment of the royal family and their awaiting execution on the guillotine, she managed to convey some poignant moments. The critics, if not all of them, were very much impressed with her performance and the film as a whole.

Miss Shearer was expected to attend the opening of *Marie Antoinette*, which had premiered at the Astor in New York City on August 16, 1938, but it wasn't illness that prevented her from attending, as was first reported. Her excuse was this: "I was perfectly well and I looked forward to it with a sort of embarrassed egotism-pride in the picture which I think is wonderful, even if the

The leading lady and leading man, Norma Shearer and Tyrone Power, arrive for the lavish premiere of Marie Antoinette *(1938).*

metropolitan press isn't entirely in accord with me, and embarrassment because it takes something like conceit to ogle one's efforts in company with a theatre audience.

"But I'd been planning to go. I had never before attended the New York opening of one of my pictures and I meant to this time. Then I received a telegram informing me that the Astor was being picketed and would I please not pass through the picket lines. So I didn't. You'll recall in the picture, Marie Antoinette is warned not to go to the opera, but she does anyhow and that's where all the trouble begins. I'm not one to chance trouble."

In September of that year, Miss Shearer recreated her role of the queen on the "Maxwell House Coffee Radio Hour." Said *Variety* in reviewing the program: "Norma Shearer contributed a highly sensitive bit of reading from *Marie Antoinette* — radio a rare appearance for her. She left nothing to be desired. Robert Young, M.C. on the show, did well in the role of the Swedish Count."

At the time *Marie Antoinette* was in release, David O'Selznick was having a problem in casting for the Scarlett O'Hara role in *Gone with the Wind* and Shearer had been mentioned as a likely prospect. Her name, in fact, had come up on several occasions, along with such potentials as Margaret

Norma Shearer was the original choice for the part of Scarlett O'Hara to play opposite Clark Gable's Rhett Butler in Gone with the Wind.

Sullavan, Tallulah Bankhead, Bette Davis, Katherine Hepburn, Paulette Goddard, and Arleen Whelan, an ex-manicurist, while she was in semiretirement between 1936 and 1937. Miss Whelan, despite her lack of prestige, was an interesting possibility.

Then, in August of 1938, Selznick proposed that Miss Shearer accept the Scarlet role, but she did so only on a tentative basis, waiting to see how her fans would react. They weren't for it and deluged her with letters to that effect. Shearer listened to them and immediately withdrew her temporary arrangement with Selznick. She had also been discouraged from undertaking the part by Ed Sullivan, the New York *Daily News* columnist then.

"Anyhow," Shearer was said to have quipped, "Scarlet is going to be a difficult and thankless role. The one I'd like to play is Rhett."

Upon hearing of Miss Shearer's renunciation of Scarlett, Margaret Mitchell, author of the epic novel, commented: "I don't know anybody in the movies that looks like Scarlett. I believe any competent actress can play the part." But British Vivien Leigh, who finally played the southern belle was much more than competent, and as a result won an Academy Award as best screen actress of 1939.

Shearer was next at work on *Idiot's Delight*, based on Robert E. Sherwood's Pulitzer-prize winning play, for which he also wrote the screen adaptation. Her co-star again was Clark Gable, a happy reunion indeed. The film's critical reception was divided. According to some, it was an unusually mature theme by Hollywood standards. The *New York Times,* ordinarily reserved in its judgement on films, cited it as adult and profound, and a better preview of tomorrow's headlines. In it, Shearer portrayed a phony blonde Russian refugee, actually from Omaha, who becomes the mistress of a munitions magnate in order to obtain a passport. But her heart has always been set on Gable, a song and dance man from her hometown, with whom she teams up in an act. The critics thought she was less satisfactory than Gable, but that she did achieve one or two moving scenes. It was further observed that her performance closely resembled that of Lynn Fontanne's, who, with her husband, Alfred Lunt, had delighted audiences in the stage version. Though Shearer was not exactly at her best in *Idiot's Delight*, it certainly did her career no harm, nor Gable's, with the picture

*Norma Shearer, James Stewart, Douglas Fairbanks,
Jr., and Merle Oberon at the opening of* The Ice Follies.

Norma Shearer and Willard George (1923).

Mr. and Mrs. Basil Rathbone and Norma Shearer and Irving Thalberg as they appeared at a masquerade party given by the Rathbones.

doing very well at the boxoffice. The re-teaming of the two stars was further felicitated by the return of their old director, Clarence Brown, who hadn't directed the pair since *A Free Soul*.

In her next film, *The Women*, successfully adapted from Clare Booth Luce's biting comedy-drama about the female species at their deadliest, Miss Shearer seemed more herself as the genteel woman whose marriage was disintegrating because of hussy Joan Crawford and who was the subject of beauty salon gossip vitriolically dispensed by Rosalind Russell and other cats trying to beautify themselves. Ironically enough, Shearer and Crawford were on opposite sides during the making of this film. A certain scene, which was their only one together, needed a line rehearsal where both actresses are supposed to throw each other bits of dialogue. It happened that at this particular moment Miss Crawford was busily engaged with some knitting and the clash of her needles distracted Shearer, who also found it hard to concentrate. She asked Miss Crawford to stop. She refused. Shearer, red-faced, then complained to director George Cukor, to whom she said: "I think Miss Crawford can go home now and you can give me her lines." Cukor, who sympathized with Shearer, ordered Crawford from the set and later reprimanded her in no uncertain terms. Thereafter, both stars avoided each other, but they finished their scene, which obviously must have been dipped in venom.

Miss Shearer, in an MGM publicity release,

Thomas Mitchell, Norma Shearer, and Edward G. Robinson.

45

Norma Shearer visits Robert Taylor on the set of Lady of the Tropics.

shadowed and delivered one of her best performances. In 1956, *The Women* found its way to the screen once again under a new title, *The Opposite Sex.* It was a good remake with June Allyson playing the Shearer role, Joan Collins in the Joan Crawford part, and Dolores Gray as the vicious gossip-monger played by Rosalind Russell. Somehow, it wasn't entirely *The Women* as it had been originally, for there were seven males added to the cast.

On August 21, 1939, it was announced that Miss Shearer would do the Jane Austin classic, *Pride and Prejudice,* with plans to film it in England under George Cukor's direction and with Robert Donat as her co-star. These plans never developed, and in the summer of 1940 *Pride and Prejudice* was released with Greer Garson and Laurence Olivier as the stars and Robert Z. Leonard credited as director. A year before Miss Shearer had turned down Rachel Crother's suc-

made a few observations about the play and film version of *The Women.* She was quoted as follows: "I think women are more romantic than men, but on the other hand, men are more sentimental than women. Women are much better sports nowadays than they used to be. Their feelings are not so easily hurt. They know better how to take it on the chin. They are not as stupidly sensitive as women of another age. Perhaps, along with that, they lack some of the sentimental idealism that Mary Haines had in the picture. When I saw the play in New York, I felt it to be a brilliant observation of women's many faceted personalities. Each character in the picture represents a definite and recognizable type, even the heavy of the film, the gossip who almost wrecks Mary's life."

The Women, released in the late summer of 1939, was a highly entertaining film, which delighted both critics and public alike. Despite the competitive cast, Shearer was not exactly over-

George Raft and Norma Shearer arrive at the preview of Raft's latest starring vehicle, Invisible Stripes *(1939).*

cessful stage play *Susan and God*, a sophisticated comedy-drama about a chastened woman who tries to indoctrinate her friends with religion. Joan Crawford, Miss Shearer's former nemesis, was given the role, after persuading George Cukor that she could handle it. She did, in the usual decorative Crawford manner, but Shearer would have been much better cast in the role that Gertrude Lawrence had played in the stage version.

Since Thalberg's death, Shearer had done very little socially, nor was she keeping company with anybody in particular, with the exception of a few close friends such as Merle Oberon, Sylvia Ashley, the widow of Douglas Fairbanks, Sr., and Charles Boyer and his wife, Pat Patterson.

While vacationing in New York during the 1939 World's Fair, the Boyers invited Shearer to spend an evening with them and meet a certain party in order to make a foursome. It happened to be George Raft, no stranger to Miss Shearer as far as films were concerned. She found him quite likable, and the sleek, dark actor decided he had never met anyone so charming. Shearer and Raft soon became a steady twosome and gave Hollywood plenty to talk about. The film colony anxiously wondered if they had any nuptial plans. But Raft was a married man and on the verge of getting a divorce from Grace Mulrooney, a former actress whom he had wed in 1923. At the time, Raft was also being pursued by Virginia Pine, with whom he had had a recent affair.

Raft disclosed the following statement to the New York *Daily News* dated March 25, 1940: "I am very much in love with Miss Shearer. She is the swellest person I have ever known, and I wish I could tell you we are going to be married soon. If I could make that announcement it would be the happiest day of my life.

"But I do not know what my wife plans to do. There is no talk of a settlement between us at the time, and nothing has happened that changes things from what they have been for a long time." (Whether Raft ever got his divorce is not exactly known, but it is more than likely that he never did.)

To show how he really felt about Shearer, Raft presented her with a five-thousand-dollar-diamond clasp for Christmas, and she reciprocated with a set of initialed cufflinks. It was then rumored that she, too, was in love with him. But with all these exchanges of mutual affection their romance gradually disintegrated. Shearer and Raft

were just not suited to one another, neither from outward appearances or intellectually. Their association, one might say, was somewhat reminiscent of the society girl and the gangster in *A Free Soul*—a beauty and beast type of duo, except that Raft had always been considered one of the nicest guys in Hollywood.

Shearer's contract now called for three more pictures, which she completed in less than two years. The first of these was *Escape*, based on Ethel Vance's taut and gripping novel about the Nazi regime in prewar Germany. Shearer was the American-born countess and a widow living in Germany who aids Robert Taylor, another compatriot of hers, in engineering the escape of his mother from a concentration camp. Conspiring in this, too, was Philip Dorn as a humane prison doctor, while Conrad Veidt was his usual sinister self as a member of the Gestapo and Shearer's lover. Although the acting was on a high level all around, it was Ali Nazimova as the prisoner of the Nazis who gave the film its most eloquent and electrifying moments. She was magnificent. A thriller in the best melodramatic tradition, *Escape* was well received by the critics and was even cited as a potent document rather than entertainment. Actually, it was a combination of both.

Early in December of 1940, Norma Shearer went into Superior Court and won a divorce by proxy for her sister Athole Hawks, whose invalidism had prevented her from appearing in court. The latter charged desertion and the judge granted the decree on this basis, with Mrs. Edith Shearer approving a property settlement as special guardian. It was these proceedings that enabled Mrs. Shearer and her daughter Norma to obtain the divorce for Athole.

As a property settlement Mrs. Hawks was given one thousand dollars a month for three years and one fourth of her husband's salary to forty eight thousand dollars a year. She obtained custody of her children, David Howard, then eleven, and Barbara. Athole and Howard Hawks had been married on March 30, 1928.

In 1941, when Jan Struther's best selling book *Mrs. Miniver* was scheduled for filming, Louis B. Mayer tried to persuade Shearer to play the role of that noble and heroic Englishwoman whose placid family life was shattered by the war, but Shearer declined, preferring to do sophisticated comedies. She feared that the part required too much of an

47

emotional exercise. Possibly what was uppermost in her mind was the fact that Mrs. Miniver was on the brink of forty and had some grown children. It was also a semicharacter role that might have prompted Miss Shearer to think twice about her image. *Mrs. Miniver* was eventually assigned to Greer Garson, a much better choice, since she was English in the first place and which established her as the first lady of the screen, thereby dethroning Shearer, who had reigned as queen of MGM for almost a decade. Miss Garson further won an Academy Award, as did the film itself. The success of *Mrs. Miniver* made Shearer realize how foolish she had been in turning down the part. She later admitted that "Nobody but myself was trying to do me in." But her biggest regret was in passing up *Gone with the Wind*.

Late in 1941, she had her wish and returned to light, sophisticated comedy in *We Were Dancing*, one of the playlets from Noel Coward's international success *Tonight at 8:30,* which was first produced for the stage in 1936. Here, Miss Shearer played an impoverished Polish princess who was reduced to being a professional house guest as was her partner, debonair Melvyn Douglas, also of royal blood. It was a pleasing film, but not much else, with Shearer wearing twenty-four eye-filling gowns designed by Adrian, his last creation at MGM. Of the film Miss Shearer said: "There is one stratum of society that has been neglected in definition. It's country club horsey, wealthy, neither very old, nor very young. It's all bound up in its own interests, and if anyone should ask me briefly what *We Were Dancing* is about, I'd say — 'House Party Society.' " *Marie Antoinette* has remained Shearer's favorite role, but there is more sentiment and nostalgia behind this than anything else.

After finishing *Her Cardboard Lover*, Shearer went to Sun Valley, Idaho, for a vacation with her two children, Irving, Jr., and Kathleen, and there met Martin Arrouge, a well-known skiing instructor of that area. Arrouge had come from a prominent family in San Francisco where he was born of French descent and was a Basque. In addition to being a skier he was also a licensed pilot, a sportscar enthusiast, and a promoter of Squaw Valley, where his father had once grazed sheep.

There was something about Arrouge that reminded Miss Shearer of Irving Thalberg. Not unlike her late husband he was said to be shy, unas-

The wedding of Norma Shearer and Martin Arrouge (1942).

suming, and quite fond of children, except that he was vigorous, more handsome and virile, all of which Thalberg lacked. Shearer's children took to Arrouge quickly enough and he to them. He taught Irving, Jr., and Katherine how to ski, as well as their mother, who wasn't exactly a novice at the sport. It wasn't long before the ex-star and the skier fell in love with each other, and on August 23, 1942, they were married at the Church of the Good Shepherd in Beverly Hills by John O'Donnell, known as the Padre of the film stars. There was a difference of fourteen years between Shearer's and Arrouge's ages—he was twenty-eight and she was forty two. Arrouge, in this case, did not have to provide a wedding ring, since Miss Shearer still possessed the one Thalberg had given her in 1927. However, Arrouge had the ring remodeled with bands of gold welded on either side. Present at the ceremony were Shearer's two children, Sylvia Ashley, and Otto Lang, the skiing champion, who was best man. There was also no need for the couple to look for a new home, for Shearer had not yet given up her Santa Monica beach home, but in later years the Arrouges moved to Beverly Hills, where they currently reside.

The Arrouges had only a brief honeymoon because Miss Shearer was about to go on a bond-selling tour, and though her husband was classified as 3-A, he was attending navigation school in the hope of joining the Ferry Command. Being the sole support of his mother, a resident of Reno, Nevada, Arrouge claimed this exemption.

Many suspected that Martin Arrouge had married Norma Shearer for her money, but both had made a premarital agreement, with Arrouge waiving all rights to the actress's community property from her late husband's estate, which was to be kept in trust for her and her son and daughter. As a skiing instructor, Arrouge received one hundred fifty dollars a week.

Not too long after her remarriage, Miss Shearer's new-found happiness was marred somewhat when the issue of her father's health arose. Andrew Shearer had suffered a mental breakdown as well as a physical setback, and for a while a controversy raged as to whether or not he should be committed to a psychiatric institution.

To resolve the matter, Norma Shearer appeared in court with her brother, Douglas, and announced that she would not oppose a move to have her father removed from the psychopathic ward of the Los Angeles General Hospital. She said: "Father has been ill for nearly four years, and I think he should have the best of care in a private sanitarium. He has been staying at the Miramar Hotel in Santa Monica, but must move because the army has taken over there."

Furthermore, Andrew Shearer was now divorced from his wife, Edith, and had remarried in 1932. Norma's stepmother, Elizabeth, however, opposed her husband's commitment to a sanitarium on the contention that he should remain with her. "My place is by his side," she said, "and obviously that cannot be if he is confined to a sanitarium."

Either way, Andrew Shearer never recovered from his illness, and in 1944 he died at the age of eighty. His first wife, Edith, died in 1958 at a sanitarium in Garden Grove, a suburb of Los Angeles, where she had been a patient since 1951. She was eighty-five.

After four years of professional inactivity, Miss Shearer was again being sought for film roles. Late in August of 1946 it was announced that she was planning a comeback and would return to the screen under a newly signed contract with Enterprise Productions. Her first picture under this agreement was to be produced by David Lewis, who had once been an associate producer of Irving Thalberg's at MGM. The contract with Enterprise called for Shearer's exclusive services for three years, with a one-year renewal period if both parties agreed to the extension—also to have approval of the films in which she appeared, and to be paid by each picture. Three months later, Miss Shearer made the news once more when David Lewis decided that her initial film with Enterprise would be a romantic drama, the type of story that Shearer did best. The script, an original, was to be written by Harry Joe Brown. It seemed an ambitious project, but these plans never saw fruition because Enterprise Productions failed soon after. For Shearer, this would have been an ideal arrangement and it appeared very likely that she would be back on the screen. Three years before, she had rejected another film offer, this time from Bette Davis, who wanted Shearer to play opposite her in *Old Acquaintance*. But this would have meant playing second fiddle to Warner Bros.' first lady, which Miss Shearer probably couldn't bear. The part, that of a writer who becomes highly successful, and which was not in the least thankless, was played by Miriam Hopkins.

Almost immediately following the Coward piece, Shearer began work on *Her Cardboard Lover*, based on Jacques Deval's play in which Leslie Howard and Jeanne Eagles had starred on Broadway in the mid-twenties. It was not as subtle, nor quite as sophisticated as her previous film and resorted to farcical and childish situations that were not in the original comedy. Shearer appeared as a stunning gambling patron to whom Robert Taylor loses over three thousand dollars at baccarat and is unable to settle his losses. She then employs him as both her bodyguard and her deceptive lover in order to avoid George Sanders, the man she is really supposed to be in love with. Released during the summer of 1942, *Her Cardboard Lover* had the right featherweight theme for that time of the season where audiences could relax and forget the heat, but Shearer had descended to what was one of her worst films. Nor was director George Cukor exactly excused in this case after having won such high praise with such distinguished efforts as *A Bill of Divorcement*, *Little Women*, *Dinner at Eight*, and *David Copperfield*, to say nothing of *Romeo and Juliet*. Having been filmed twice already, first as a silent with Marion Davies in 1928, then under a new title *The Passionate Plumber*, with Buster Keaton in 1932, *Her Cardboard Lover* was completely worn out by the time MGM resurrected it again. After this frou-frou, Miss Shearer retired from the screen for good. She was followed by Garbo that same year, who, a few months back, had made a mistake by appearing in *Two-Faced Woman*, also

directed by Cukor, which hurt her prestige, and probably broke her heart, according to Shearer. She said at the time: "After eighteen years, an actress must never lose her ego—without it she has no talent—like a clock without a mainspring."

In 1952, John Merrick, a theatrical producer, offered Shearer the Gertrude Lawrence role in a revival of Moss Hart's stage hit, *Lady in the Dark*, but nothing ever came of it. By this time, it was quite apparent that Miss Shearer was not interested in resuming her career.

On April 21, 1954, Shearer's then eighteen-year-old daughter, Katherine, married Jack Red-

Norma Shearer and her second husband, Martin Arrouge, at Saint-Moritz (1950).

50

Jean Simmons, Stewart Granger, Deborah Kerr, and Norma Shearer arrive for the premiere of Young Bess *(1953).*

dish, twenty-seven, a former University of Utah student and a member of the 1948 Olympic ski teams, and on August 26, 1956, Irving Thalberg, Jr., was wed to Suzanne McCormick of Napa, Calif. But on October 12, 1959, it was reported by the late columnist Danton Walker that the Jack Reddishes had agreed on a property settlement and that an uncontested divorce would follow. She charged cruelty and Reddish's failure to contribute to her support, despite his good salary. Their divorce became final early in January of 1960. Later, Katherine married television star Richard Anderson and has two daughters and a son —

Ashley, thirteen, Brook, eleven, and Deva, nine. Irving, Jr., a Korean war vet, now forty-six, has been teaching philosophy at Oberlin University in Ohio.

Shearer's retirement was not exactly wasted, for she and her husband still indulged in skiing and did a fair amount of traveling. In February of 1956 they went to Europe and didn't return until the early part of July. A few months later, at a party, Miss Shearer discovered Robert J. Evans, a young New York clothing manufacturer and was instrumental in establishing him as a screen actor when Universal was looking for someone to play Irving

Thalberg in *The Man of a Thousand Faces,* a biographical film of Lon Chaney, Sr.*

There was something about Evans, too, that struck a nostalgic note with Shearer, for he bore a slight resemblance to the late producer and appeared to have the same boyish quality, including an amazing capacity for business for one so youthful.

Since that time, Evans had been in demand by different studios and had appeared in several films, in addition to commuting to his business in New York's garment district. These pictures include, besides *The Man of a Thousand Faces*, *The Sun Also Rises*, *The Fiend Who Walked the West* (Evans was the madman), and *The Best of Everything*, with Joan Crawford, in which he played a heel. At this writing, and it is indeed ironic, Robert J. Evans is head of production at Paramount studios, which was acquired some years ago by Gulf Western.

In 1957, Shearer had to give up skiing because of a broken leg, apparently as the result of an accident suffered while active in that sport.

She had been asked on more than one occasion why she retired in 1942. Said she "I believe a movie star should keep them laughing — or crying — for more."

Norma Shearer walks with husband Martin Arrouge (left) and Robert Evans, the young New York businessman whom she discovered to play her late husband, Irving Thalberg, the man who made Lon Chaney a star, in Man of a Thousand Faces.

*Ten years before, Miss Shearer had discovered Janet Leigh at the Sugar Bowl Ski Lodge at Soda Springs in Northern California, where her mother was employed as a receptionist and her father a head auditor. It all came about as a result of a photograph Mrs. Leigh had placed in an album of photos that was usually on the table in the lobby of the resort. A certain photographer had snapped Miss Leigh as she stood at the top of a ski run in the mountains one day, and after the picture was developed, her mother liked it so much that she decided to include it among the other photographs. It happened that Norma Shearer was visiting the lodge for some skiing at the time and chanced to come across Miss Leigh's photograph while thumbing through the album. So impressed was she by the young girl's beauty that she thought it would be a good idea to take the photo with her when she returned to Hollywood. Although Miss Shearer had been in retirement for four years, she was still influential in film circles and lost no time in bringing the photograph to the attention of MGM officials. They, like Miss Shearer, were quite taken by Janet Leigh's unusual prettiness and soon sent for her to arrange a screen test. The test was successful, and within a month Miss Leigh was appearing as Van Johnson's sweetheart in MGM's *The Romance of Rosy Ridge*, a story of Missouri folk during the post-Civil War. After the picture was released the studio put Miss Leigh under contract, and in quick succession she was seen in such films as *If Winter Comes*, starring Walter Pidgeon and Deborah Kerr, *The Hills of Home*, *Little Women*, *Words and Music*, *Act of Violence*, *My Sister Eileen*, *Scaramouche*, Alfred Hitchcock's *Psycho*, *The Manchurian Candidate*, and many others. In recent years Miss Leigh has been more or less inactive in films, having made her last one in 1969. She is now married to Robert Brandt, her fourth husband, a theater executive. To Norma Shearer, Janet Leigh is eternally grateful for her success.

She spoke of her ambitions: "Now that I have leisure, I want to learn to speak French fluently, to play the piano like Horowitz or Van Cliburn and to write a book about life."

During the past several years she was supposed to have been working on her biography for she felt that she had much to relate. However, when Bob Thomas, the well-known biographer of celebrities and member of the Associated Press approached her for help on his book on Thalberg, she refused to cooperate, possibly because of her own project. Thomas's account on Thalberg, as a result, was a good, intelligent piece of work, if not a forceful and pungent one as his *King Cohn* was, but it might have been had Miss Shearer made herself available to him.

Shearer was in the news again when a letter she wrote in 1959 appeared in *Time* magazine in which she attacked Alexander C. Cushing, the millionaire sportsman, for neglecting to mention her husband, Marti Arrouge, as an important asset to the community of Squaw Valley. She said that

Cushing's wit was obvious, but that his memory was short, and that it seemed that he or someone forgot the prologue to the Squaw Valley drama. She went on to say that Arrouge had been the original partner of Wayne Poulsen with whom he supplied the land and Cushing the money—that Arrouge had been a loyal supporter all the way, remaining a stockholder. She regretted that her husband's name had been left out of the cast. Other readers, in support of Miss Shearer, referred to Cushing as an abominable snowman, an old-fashioned American capitalist, and an athletic flop and a snob.

On January 5, 1971, Norma Shearer lost her brother, Douglas, who died at the age of seventy-one. His technical accomplishments had been many through the years at MGM, and he further distinguished himself by winning twelve Academy Awards, the first of which was for sound recording for *The Big House*, the first of the prison films to have dialogue in 1930. He then won two more in the same capacity—for *Naughty Marietta* in 1935 and *San Francisco* in 1936. He retired in 1968, after having held the post of MGM's technical research director since 1955.

In recent years, there has been a scarcity of news on Norma Shearer. Like Garbo, she has withdrawn from public appearances in general, preferring only a small circle of friends whom she regards as her most intimate. She is not by any means a recluse, but rather a very private person. Her thirty-four-year-old marriage to Martin Arrouge, who still promotes California's Squaw Valley, is as happy as ever. About two years ago, while on a shopping tour in Beverly Hills, they were glimpsed by a photographer holding hands. For such an aged couple, this was a most unusual and heart-warming sight.

It is hard to imagine, somehow, that Norma Shearer is seventy-six years old, but that, as records have shown, is her real age. She has been a grandmother twice, yet not the typical matriach who is ordinarily left in the background. According to a certain Hollywood writer who met her quite by accident one day in a Beverly Hills book store a few years ago and who had interviewed her many times when she was a star, the former actress hadn't changed too much, except that she was now a grayish-ashe blonde with her hair cut short in a mod style. Her charm, it was good to report, hadn't diminished either.

For some inexplicable reason, there have been no Norma Shearer film retrospectives as there have with such screen veterans as Garbo, Irene Dunne, and Bette Davis. It is ironic, too, considering that she was one of the most important stars in Hollywood, that her reputation on and off the screen was above reproach, and that her films had enormous appeal from silents to sound. Her career, a brilliant one indeed, should never have been ignored all these years. But then, Miss Shearer still had some loyal fans, both young and old, who had some fond memories of her as the super star she was. As a token of rememberance, a special showing of *Marie Antoinette* was held one fall evening in 1970 at a local Hollywood film society known as Cinema Buffs. An invitation was sent out to Miss Shearer and her husband, but at the time she was gravely ill, according to Mr. Arrouge, who tendered his regrets and that of his wife. It would have certainly done Norma Shearer's heart good to see the large attendance at the screening and to hear the vociferous applause that followed after the picture had ended. To pay her an additional tribute, an album, containing over one hundred affectionate comments about her from members of the group and even non-members, was sent to her home. Mr. Arrouge, in a phone conversation with a representative of the organization, said his wife had been deeply touched. Norma Shearer's wealth is still undiminished, but the wealth she treasures above all is her happy life with Marti Arrouge and the fact that she has not been forgotten, even if film historians tended to overlook her.

II
FILMOGRAPHY

The Norma Shearer Short Films

Voices across the Sea (MGM) (1928)

Running time: 12 Minutes. Released November, 1928

AS THEMSELVES: Ernest Torrence, John Gilbert, George K. Arthur, Joan Crawford, Norma Shearer.

This early talking short was made to commemorate the opening of a new Loew's Theatre in London called The Empire and to plug a new MGM picture. A Transatlantic hook-up was set up, and Ernest Torrence, a popular MGM character actor, acted as M. C., broadcasting the premiere from the stage of the Empire. A telephone is beside him and he picks up the instrument to say hello to certain MGM stars in Hollywood such as John Gilbert, Norma Shearer, Joan Crawford, and George K. Arthur. He is a very amusing M. C. and a sparkling conversationalist. Miss Shearer's voice was said to be pleasing, but Miss Crawford's not quite so admirable. Mr. Gilbert acted in a typical Hollywood manner, using such words as *colossal, amazing,* and *wonderful.* Mr. Arthur needed no introduction as one of Hollywood's best and most popular comedians. He generated sufficient laughter.

(This short subject was shown in conjunction with the MGM feature *Alias Jimmy Valentine* at the Astor Theatre in New York City in November of 1928. It was part talkie and starred William Haines as a safecracker. It was directed by Jack Conway.)

The Stolen Jools (1931) (American title)

The Slippery Pearls (British title)

Produced by the Hollywood Masquers Club
Released by the U.S. in April, 1931 and in Britian in September, 1932 by Butchers Film Service. A Two-Reel Comedy.

AS THEMSELVES: Wallace Beery, Buster Keaton, Edward G. Robinson, George E. Stone, Eddie Kane, Laurel and Hardy, Polly Moran, Norma Shearer, Hedda Hopper, Joan Crawford, Robert Ames, Irene Dunne, Bebe Daniels, Ben Lyon, Loretta Young, Douglas Fairbanks, Jr., Maurice Chevalier, Frank Fay, Barbara Stanwyck, Fifi Dorsay, Warner Baxter, Winnie Lightner, Wynne Gibson, Claudia Dell, Edmund Lowe, Victor McLaglen, El Brendel, Wheeler and Woolsey, Gary Cooper, Charles (Buddy) Rogers, Eugene Pallette, William Haines, Richard Dix, Richard Barthelmess, Charles Butterworth, Louise Fazenda, Lowell Sherman, Fay Wray, Jack Oakie, Joe E. Brown, George "Gabby" Hayes, Mitzi Green, and Members of the Keystone Kops and Members of Our Gang.

A mad-cap satire in which Norma Shearer is the victim of a robbery with every star in Hollywood under investigation by Detective Eddie Kane, except Wallace Beery who happens to be the police station sergeant.

According to Picturegoer, this galaxy of players "made *Grand Hotel* look like a western."

Jackie Cooper's Christmas Party (MGM) (1931)

Running time: 9 Minutes. Released December, 1931

AS THEMSELVES: Norma Shearer, Jackie Cooper, Marion Davies, Lionel Barrymore, Clark Gable, Wallace Beery, Marie Dressler, Polly Moran, Leila Hyams, and Louis B. Mayer.

Jackie Cooper is planning to have a Christmas party for his football team, but his boys are many and there isn't sufficient room in his home. He then appeals to Norma Shearer and the actress arranges with Louis B. Mayer, the head of the studio, for Jackie and his friends to use the sound stage. Hundreds of youngsters come to the party and are given a royal treat. They are graciously served by such MGM luminaries as Marion Davies, Lionel Barrymore, Clark Gable, and Leila Hyams. And guess who is carving the turkey? None other than Wallace Beery, his old sidekick, Marie Dressler, and Polly Moran, who once teamed with Marie in a series of feature comedies, all decked out in chef's attire.

Motion Picture Herald, January 2, 1932:
"The appeal of the stars is wide, and Jackie, of course, is splendid. A very appealing short."

Mister Will Shakespeare (MGM) (1936)

Director: Jacques Tourneur
Script: Richard Goldstone
Narration: Carey Wilson
With Anthony Kemble Cooper as the Bard

A trailer as well as a regular short subject to publicize *Romeo and Juliet,* this initiated a special series called Milestones of the Theatre Miniature. It presents certain highlights in the life of William Shakespeare as a dramatist. Scenes include his long walk to London, fraternizing with his literary cronies at an inn there, then attending performances of someone else's plays, after which he goes to see his own in scenes from *Romeo and Juliet.*
Norma Shearer and Leslie Howard are shown briefly in their scenes as Romeo and Juliet, though they are silent.

Variety, August 19, 1936:
"In short, the short is a nifty builder-upper for Metro's major Shakespearean property and on its own serves as a palatable supplementary film fare which merits a rental all by itself."

Motion Picture Herald, August 1, 1936:

"It is well produced and directed. Anthony Kemble Cooper as Shakespeare gives a thoroughly convincing performance."

The Flapper: *Norma Shearer as an extra (second from left, front row). Sister Athole also worked in the film (third from right, front row).*

The Flapper: *Norma Shearer.*

The Films in Which Norma Shearer Appeared as an Extra

The Flapper (Selznick—1920)

Director: Alan Crosland
Star: Olive Thomas
Support: Warren Cook, Louise Lindroth, Theo Westman Jr., W.P. Carleton, Katherine Johnston, Arthur Houseman.

The Restless Sex (Paramount—1920)

Director: Robert Z. Leonard. From the novel by Robert W. Chambers.
Produced by Cosmopolitan Pictures (W. R. Hearst)

Star: Marion Davies
Support: Ralph Kellard, Carlyle Blackwell, Charles Lane, Robert Vivian, Etna Ross, Stephen Carr, Vivian Osborne, Corinne Barker.

Way Down East (United Artists-1920)

Produced and Directed By D. W. Griffith. By Lottie Blair Parker, based on her play *Way Down East.*
Scenario: Anthony Paul Kelly.
Camera: Billy Bitzer.
Star: Lillian Gish.
Featured and supporting players in order of their appearance: Mrs. David Landau, Josephine Bernard, Mrs. Morgan Belmont, Patricia Fruen, Florence Short, Lowell Sherman, Burr McIntosh, Richard Barthelmess, Vivia Ogden, Porter Strong, George Neville, Edgar Nelson, Mary Hay, Creighton Hale, Emily Fitzroy.

Norma Shearer played an extra part in this magnificent artist's ball production number from The Restless Sex. *Marion Davies was the star and is pictured in the chariot in the background.*

The Stealers (Robertson-Cole — 1920)

CREDITS: Written, produced and directed by William Christy Cabanne. Photography: Georges Benoit. Art director: Daniel Bretino.

Technical director: Thomas O'Neill. Titles: Alfred Carpen. Art titles: Martin, McGuire, and Newcombe. Assistant to Mr. Cabanne: Daniel B. Hogan. Running time: 8 reels. Released September 1920.

CAST: William H. Tooker (Reverend Robert Martin), Robert Kenyon (the minister as a young man), Myrtle Morse (Mrs. Robert Martin), Norma Shearer (Julia Martin), Ruth Dwyer (Mary Forrest), Walter Miller (Stephen Gregory), Eugene Borden (Sam Gregory), Matthew L. Betz (Burt Robinson), Jack Crosby (Raymond Pritchard), Jack O'Brien (the man of the dawn), Downing Clarke (Major Wellington).

STORY OF THE FILM: After finishing her schooling, Julia Martin, a minister's daughter, joins her father at his gospel tent, which has become a site for curiosity seekers, where she officiates at the organ. Julia's predecesser at the organ had been Mary Forrest, who has become a petty criminal and is the sweetheart of Stephen Gregory, a burglar, as well as a pickpocket like Mary. The gospel tent is their prey, which seems to be the ideal spot for them to victimize visitors. Mary is an expert at fleecing people, but one day she meets Raymond Pritchard, a wealthy young man who visits the tent with other rich folk whose pockets she attempts to go through during a service and is foiled by him. Pritchard reprimands the girl for her unsavory deeds and she promises to reform. At the same time she has fallen in love with Pritchard and he with her. A conversation Julia overhears between Mary and Steve in which the former declares that she is through with the gang, bewilders and also shocks Julia. She begins to piece things together and soon discovers that her father is the leader of the crime ring. Years before he had left the pulpit as a result of a mental breakdown, ascribed to his wife eloping seventeen years earlier and abandoning their three-year-old baby. It is Julia, the same child, who is responsible for her father's eventual reformation.

CRITICS' VERDICT:

"In its way, *The Stealers* has somewhat the same strong inspirational sentiment as *The Miracle Man*. There are many resemblances in the underlying thought, but the surface plot is sufficiently different to give newness, and to hold keen interest.

"The cast is an unfamiliar one, but we will look with interest for further appearances of William Tooker, the portrayer of the gang leader and his artful dodger who adds greatly to the humor. The daughter is ably interpreted by Norma Shearer."
Edwin Schallert in the *Los Angeles Times,* March 7, 1921

"It must be confessed that Mr. Cabanne's story resorts often to the convenient, to far-fetched coincidence. He has chosen to shoot at a high mark a theme of *Miracle Man* calibre—and he has scored strongly from a production standpoint, missing only in the strength

The Stealers: *(Top row) Ruth Dwyer, William Tooker, Walter Miller. (Center) Norma Shearer and William Tooker and Ruth Dwyer. (Bottom row) William Tooker, Norma Shearer, Ruth Dwyer, and player.*

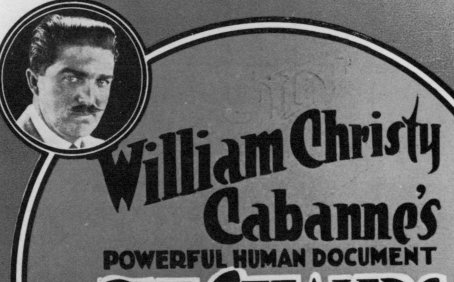

Advertisement for The Stealers.

The Stealers: *Norma Shearer and William H. Tooker.*

The Stealers: *Norma Shearer, Ruth Dwyer, Matthew Betz, William Tooker, Walter Miller, and player.*

and originality of the dramatic incident counted upon to carry over that great message of faith and the wonders it works. Valued as a picture intended for the entertainment of audiences, without attempting comparison, the direction, the acting, which is excellent throughout, and the atmosphere of the offering, should get it over.''
Motion Picture News, October 2, 1920

The Sign on the Door (First National-1921)

Star: Norma Talmadge. Director: Herbert Brenon. (Miss Shearer's face was said to be left on the cutting room floor.)

The Films in Which Norma Shearer Appeared in a Bit

Torchy's Millions (Educational Film Corporation)

Star: Johnny Hines.
Released February 1921
(Information on this two-reeler has been unavailable, though we have one still from this showing Norma and Johnny Hines.)

The Leather Pushers (Universal-Jewel-1922-24)

Director: Harry Pollard
Based on a series of stories by H.C. Witwer (originally in *Colliers*)
Star: Reginald Denny (Did not appear in the entire series)

The Man Who Paid (Producer's Security-Apfel Productions—1922)

CREDITS: Produced and directed by Oscar Apfel. Story and scenario: Marion Brooks. Photography: Alfred Gonfolfi. Running time: 5 Reels. Released March, 1922.

Torchy's Millions: *Norma Shearer and Johnny Hines.*

If You Played the First Series You'll Want These!

"The NEW LEATHER PUSHERS"

A SERIES OF SIX TWO REEL FEATURES.
presented by CARL LAEMMLE
with original cast featuring

REGINALD DENNY

including HAYDEN STEVENSON
MADE FROM THE FAMOUS COLLIER'S WEEKLY STORIES
by H·C·WITWER
directed by HARRY POLLARD

UNIVERSAL JEWEL·

CARVON

LOOK before you BOOK

The New Leather Pushers: *Reginald Denny and Norma Shearer holding hands.*

The Leather Pushers: *Reginald Denny and Norma Shearer.*

CAST: Wilfred Lytell (Oliver Thornton), Norma Shearer (Jeanne, his wife), Florence Rogan (Little Jeanne, their child), Fred C. Jones (Louis Duclos, a trapper), Bernard Siegel (Anton Barbier, his partner), David Hennessy (McNeill, Oliver's storekeeper), Charles Beyer (Guy Thornton, Oliver's brother), Erminie Gagnon (Lizette, nurse girl at Thornton's), Frank Montgomery (Songo, an Indian guide).

STORY OF THE FILM: Oliver Thornton, a young Canadian, has served a prison term for embezzling bank funds, although he is innocent of the crime. To forget this injustice he goes to the wilds of Northern Canada where he soon becomes an agent for a trading company. There he meets Jeanne with whom he falls in love and marries. Eventually a child is born to them and they are very happy for a while until Thornton's prison record becomes known to Louis Duclos, an unscrupulous trapper who had once courted Jeanne. Duclos, still desiring Jeanne, tries to alienate her from herhusband, but fails in his attempts to do so. He then plans to get rid of Thornton and abduct Jeanne, in addition to stealing a deed to a silver mine that Thornton and his brother had come upon. Guy, Thornton's brother, arrives from the city with evidence of his brother's innocence and while both are away fishing, an Indian guide informs them that Jeanne has been kidnapped by Duclos. The brothers rush to the spot where Jeanne is being held, while Duclos, in an encounter with an Indian whom he had doublecrossed, is finally killed by the latter. Jeanne is rescued. Thornton is vindicated of the embezzlement charge for which he was sentenced to prison, and as a result of the silver mine he becomes rich. He considers returning to the city to resume his business career, but he decides to remain in the wilderness where he knows he and his family will be much happier.

CRITICS' VERDICT:

"Wilfred Lytell, as Oliver Thornton, proves an acceptable hero, while Norma Shearer does good work as his wife, the heroine. Miss Shearer's good looks are shown to advantage, and she not only photographs extremely well, but shows no small amount of talent in the portrayal of her part."
Exhibitor's Herald, April 8, 1922

"Wilfred Lytell and Norma Shearer are largely responsible for the realism of the scenes. The star has plenty of energy and nerve, and besides a certain clean-cut attractiveness that should give him wide appeal. Miss Shearer is pretty, and in her emotional scenes, very vivid. The whole production, including the style of direction, and scenic backgrounds, show a sincerity that will be generally appreciated."
Mary Kelly in *Moving Picture World,* March 25, 1922

"Wilfred Lytell is presented as the hero but much better acting opportunities are given Norma Shearer as the factor's wife, all of which she embraces with a poise and skill that stamps this new-comer to the screen as an actress of promise. The girl has beauty and screen personality and she can act. Even in the wild melodrama that many parts of the picture exhibit, she is able to make her work hold attention and her role seem real."
J. S. Dickerson in *Motion Picture News,* April 1, 1922

The Man Who Paid: *Florence Rogan, Norma Shearer, and Erminie Gagnon.*

The Man Who Paid: *A player, Norma Shearer, and Florence Rogan.*

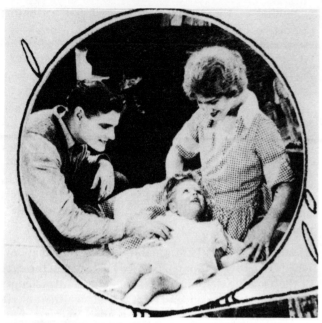

The Man Who Paid: *Wilfred Lytell, Florence Rogan, and Norma Shearer.*

The Bootleggers [F. B. O. (Film Booking Offices)] - 1922

CREDITS: Producer: Al Gilbert. Director: Roy Sheldon. Original story and scenario: Thomas F. Fallon. Photography: Anthony G. Trigili. Running time: 6 Reels. Released April 1922

CAST: Walter Miller (Jack Seville), Paul Panzer (Jose Fernand), Jules Cowles (The Hermit), Hazel Flint (Olive Wood), Norma Shearer (Helen Barnes), Jane Allyn (Alice Barnes), Lucia Backus Seger (Mrs. Murphy).

STORY OF THE FILM: Jose Fernand, an unscrupulous bootlegger, takes a fancy to Helen Barnes, a pretty shopgirl who supports an invalid sister, Alice. Through a ruse with Olive Wood, one of the members of Fernand's bootlegging gang, the latter has her pose as his sister in order to lure Helen and Alice aboard his yacht. Once this is arranged, Fernand manages to get rid of Olive whom he tells to remain at home. After a few miles out at sea, Fernand tries to seduce Helen, and following a brief struggle, she runs to the wireless operator for aid. At that moment, a furious storm comes up and an S. O. S. is made as the ship capsizes and eventually sinks. An ocean liner soon intercepts the signal and proceeds with a search for possible survivors. The only ones are the sisters and Fernand who have been cast upon an unexplored island where they are given refuge by a hermit who appears to be the sole inhabitant. Meanwhile, Helen's fiancée, Jack Seville, a naval officer with the revenue department and in charge of aerial reconnaissance of the Atlantic, learns that she and Alice are in distress and starts to the rescue with his co-pilot by plane. They finally spot the island, and after a forced landing find the girls with Fernand. A fight between Seville and the latter ensues, after which the liner arrives and rescues the party.

CRITICS' VERDICT:

"Norma Shearer is a pleasing figure in the midst of this turmoil. She has beauty, charm and dramatic sincerity. Paul W. Panzer is a good type for the veteran bootlegger, but seems a little apt to overdo in his wicked swagger and fiendish brutality. Hazel Flint is excellent."
Mary Kelly in *Moving Picture World*, April 15, 1922

"If all the bootleggers were as dull and uninteresting as the picture of the name, Volstead would be right. And Pussyfoot Johnson would be out of a job. Much rum running, a sick sister, a working girl, a lover in the revenue service, and a psuedo Spanish villain. The old formula."
Photoplay, July 1922

The Man Who Paid: *A player and Norma Shearer.*

The Bootleggers: *Norma Shearer and Walter Miller in foreground, Paul Panzer and Jules Cowles in background.*

Channing of the Northwest (Selznick) Distributor: (Select — 1922)

CREDITS: Director: Ralph Ince. From a story by John Willard.
Scenario: Edward J. Montagne. Photography: Jack Brown. 5 reels. Released May, 1922.

CAST: Eugene O'Brien (Channing), Gladden James (Jim Farney) Norma Shearer (Jess Driscoll), James Seeley (Tom Driscoll), Pat Hartigan (Sport McCool), Nita Naldi (Cicily Varden), Harry Lee (McCool's man), J. W. Johnston (Buddy), C. Coulter (Channing's uncle).

STORY OF THE FILM: Channing, a London playboy, who is regarded as something of a Don Juan in the eyes of the Picadilly feminine social sphere, is attracted by Cicily Varden, a dancer in a local musical revue. He quickly falls in love with her, but upon learning of his

Channing of the Northwest: *Norma Shearer and Eugene O'Brien.*

nephew's wish to marry the actress, Channing's uncle threatens to disinherit him. Channing breaks the news to Cicily, and she decides that it is best for them to part under the circumstances. Disillusioned, Channing leaves for Canada where he joins the Northwest Mounted Police. Soon, he meets Jess Driscoll, a girl of the wilderness who lives with her father and an adopted brother, Jim Farney.

Channing's first assignment on the force is to investigate the activities of Sport McCool, a dancehall proprietor engaged in smuggling rum. His accomplice happens to be young Farney, whom Channing is searching for. Jess's attempts to mislead Channing, though she is in love with him and he with her, fail when Channing comes upon Farney's horse and is about to arrest him. Before he could, Farney is shot, following an attempt to kill Channing, but instead he shoots McCool. Farney dies as a result of a wound, while Channing and Jess are left to start a new life.

CRITICS' VERDICT:

"The picture works up to a climax that is done with remarkable smoothness and an undercurrent of suspense, the more effective because of its subtlety. There is the scene of the bootlegger hiding in the girl's cabin. Norma Shearer's acting in this rather strenuous situation is exceptionally clever. Her personal charm is a factor that will be recognized, too."
Mary Kelly in *Moving Picture World,* June 17, 1922

"Norma Shearer lends a fragrant charm and emotional capabilities of a high order to the role of the heroine. It is a simple and obvious story on an old theme. And because it is well done it should excite interest for those who never tire of the mounted."
Lawrence Reid in *Motion Picture News,* May 6, 1922

A Clouded Name (Logan Productions) Distributor: Playgoer's Pictures (1923)

CREDITS: Director: Austin O. Huhn. Scenario: Austin O. Huhn. From a story by Tom Bret. Photography: Jean Logan. Length: 4,885 feet. Released February 18, 1923.

CAST: Norma Shearer (Marjorie Dare), Gladden James (Jim Allen), Yvonne Logan (Smiles), Richard Neill (Stewart Leighton), Charles Miller (Sam Slocum), Fred Eckhart (Ben Tangleface).

STORY OF THE FILM: Jim Allen and Marjorie Dare plan to be married when misfortune strikes their families. Marjorie's mother dies suddenly and Jim's father mysteriously disappears. Later, when Marjorie is a guest at Stewart Leighton's country estate, Jim is also a visitor there, but he prefers to avoid Marjorie. While at Leighton's home, Jim meets a precocious

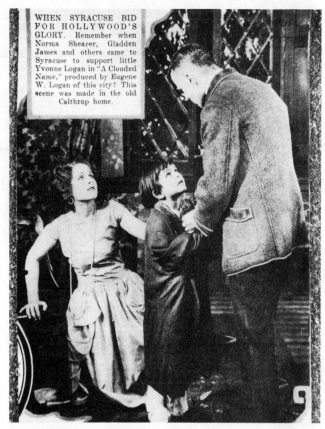

WHEN SYRACUSE BID FOR HOLLYWOOD'S GLORY. Remember when Norma Shearer, Gladden James and others came to Syracuse to support little Yvonne Logan in "A Clouded Name," produced by Eugene W. Logan of this city? This scene was made in the old Calthrop home.

A Clouded Name: *Norma Shearer, Yvonne Logan, and Gladden James.*

youngster named Smiles who is being cared for by Ben Tangleface, an eccentric old man. Leighton has designs over Marjorie and wants to marry her, but his main objective is her money. Marjorie repels Leighton's continued advances on her and during a struggle with him, Jim intervenes and knocks Leighton to the floor.

Ben, whose memory has been obscured by certain events through the years, witnesses the fight between Jim and Leighton and soon pieces things together. He discovers that Leighton had murdered Marjorie's mother and kills him. It is further revealed that Ben is Jim's missing father and Smiles is Marjorie's sister. With these circumstances now clear, Jim and Marjorie are able to resume their marriage plans.

CRITIC'S VERDICT:

"Somewhat lacking in action, this picture will appeal primarily to those who are sentimentally inclined. The story progresses slowly with very little suspense. The picture's most attractive feature is Norma Shearer who imbues familiar situations with considerable interest. She is appealing enough to make one forget at times the obvious trend of the story."
Mary Kelly in *Moving Picture World,* March 3, 1923

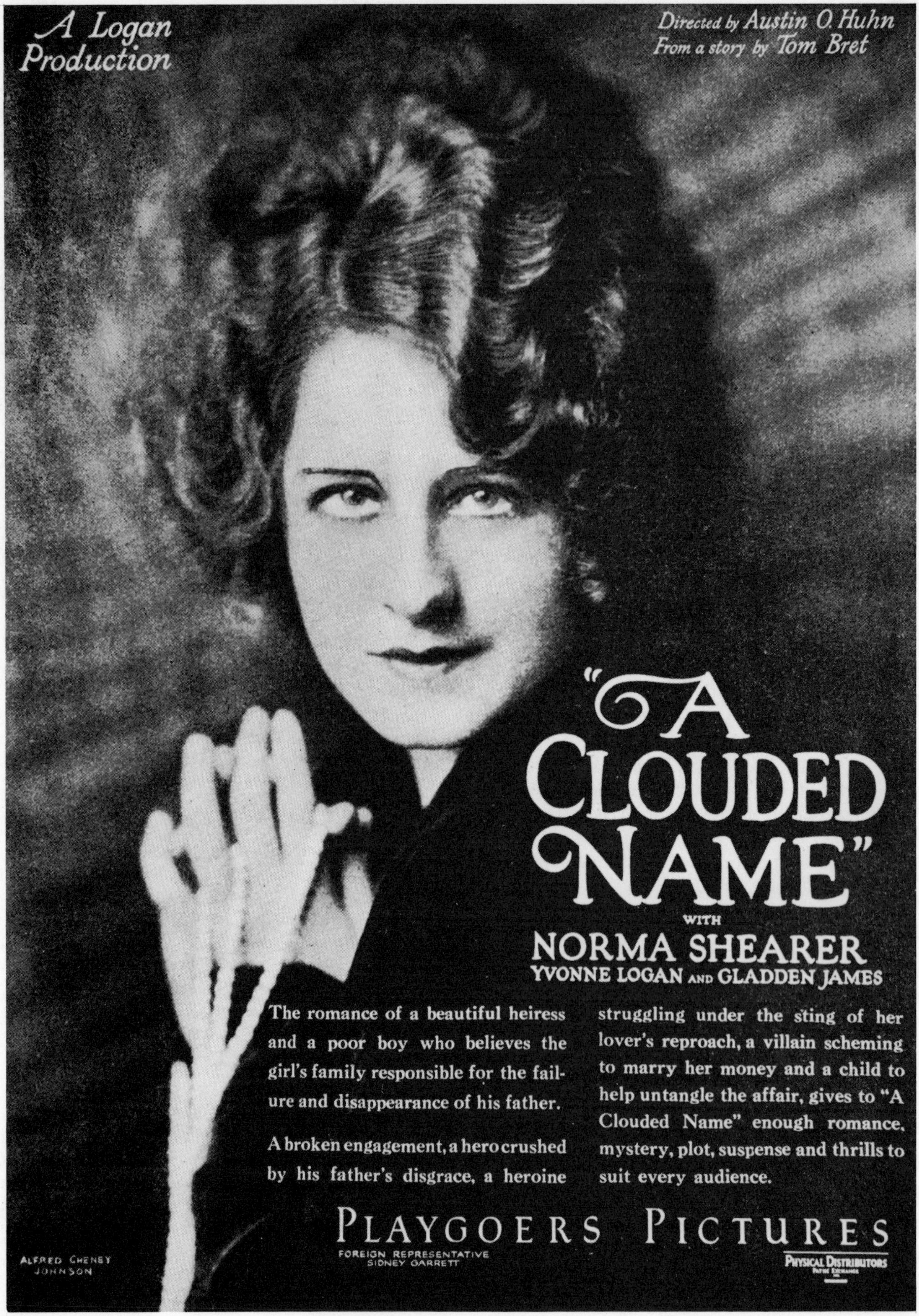

A Clouded Name: *Norma Shearer.*

Man and Wife (Arrow Film Corporation —1923)

CREDITS: Director: John L. McCutheon. Story and adaptation: Leota Morgan. Running time: 5 Reels. Released March 21, 1923.

CAST: Maurice Costello (Caleb Perkins), Gladys Leslie (Dolly Perkins), Norma Shearer (Dora Perkins), Edna May Spooner (Mrs. Perkins), Robert Elliott (Dr. Howard Fleming), Ernest Hilliard (Walter Powell).

STORY OF THE FILM: Dr. Howard Fleming's wife, Dora, has been reported killed in a hotel fire. Grief stricken, Fleming retires to a rural community until he can recover from his sorrow. At a farm he meets and falls in love with Dolly Perkins, whom he soon marries, unaware that Dolly is Dora's sister. Eventually, Fleming is informed that Dora survived the fire, though it had completely affected her mind, causing insanity. Fleming then performs brain surgery on Dora and she becomes sane again. But when she learns of her husband's marriage to Dolly she suffers another mental relapse. Fleming attempts a second operation, but this time the results are fatal. He returns to Dolly and their child, hopeful for a happy future.

CRITICS' VERDICT:
"*Man and Wife* is not a big picture, but it is honest to goodness entertainment and a worthwhile program feature.

"Robert Elliott, Norma Shearer and Gladys Leslie carry off the laurels with Ernest Hilliard, Edna May Spooner and Maurice Costello coming in for their share of credit."
Roger Ferri in *Moving Picture World*, April 28, 1923

"In the cast there is one old star favorite in Maurice

Man and Wife: *Gladys Leslie, Robert Elliott, Edna May Spooner, Maurice Costello, Norma Shearer, and Ernest Hilliard.*

Costello, a stock favorite in Edna May Spooner, and a screen possibility in Norma Shearer.

"From a States Right standpoint at a price, it looks as though it will get some money, although it is rather crudely produced and directed and badly titled and edited."
Variety, June 28, 1923

The Devil's Partner (Iroquois Productions — Independent — 1923)

CREDITS: Director: Caryl S. Fleming
Running time: 5 Reels. Released June 1923.

CAST: Norma Shearer (Jeanne), Charles Delaney (Pierre), (Sergeant Drummond) Henry Sedley (Henri, Jeanne's father), Edward Roseman (Jules Payette).

STORY OF THE FILM: In a Canadian village in the Northwest, Jeanne and her lover, Pierre, are very happy until a sinister smuggler, Jules Payette, kidnaps Jeanne's father and threatens the couple's happiness. Eventually, Payette meets a violent end. Jeanne and Pierre are happy once more.

CRITICS' VERDICT:
"Norma Shearer is always charming. She manages to retain this asset in the portrayal of the hunted heroine. Charles Delaney portrays the youthful lover, while Edward Roseman does his villainous best to make the pursuer hateful.

"Whatever prompted them to call this film *The Devil's Partner* is a conundrum. 'And the Villain Still Pursued Her' would have been far more explanatory."
Variety, October, 1923

"One of the season's crop of films to feel the blighting influence of frost is this absurd and wholly artificial melodrama of the Great Northwest. It is so like hundreds of others that have gone on before that every twist and turn of the plot is known to the picture-goer as soon as he identifies the theme. It is best described as unimportant."
Photoplay, December 1923

Pleasure Mad (The Mayer Company—1923)

CREDITS: Director: Reginald Barker. Based on *The Valley of Content,* by Blanche Upright. Scenario: A.P. Younger. Photography: Norbet Brodine and Alvin Wyckoff. Running time: 8 Reels. Released November 5, 1923.

CAST: Huntley Gordon (Hugh Benton), Mary Alden

(Marjorie Benton), Norma Shearer (Elinor Benton), William Collier, Jr. (Howard Benton), Winifred Bryson (Geraldine De Lacy), Ward Crane (David Templeton), Frederick Truesdell (John Hammond), Joan Standing (Hulda).

STORY OF THE FILM: Hugh Benton is a struggling inventor with a wife and two children who hopes to patent his invention one day. Finally, he achieves success and takes his family to New York after many years in a small town. Eventually, he becomes a millionaire, and soon falls prey to Geraldine De Lacy, a woman much younger than himself, with whom he has an affair. Having divorced his wife, Marjorie, Benton influences his children to go out into the world and experience life. His daughter, Elinor, becomes involved with David Templeton whose forceful attentions she spurns. When Benton finds them together, he shoots Templeton, only wounding him. The latter recovers and confesses that it was he who caused all the trouble, which exonerates Benton, who was on the verge of going to prison had Templeton died. Benton is soon reconciled with his wife and there is a happy family reunion.

CRITICS' VERDICT:
"It is not often that we have to sit through a picture quite as bad as *Pleasure Mad* which is the film feature at the Rivoli this week. According to the producers it was adapted from Blanche Upright's novel *The Valley of Content,* and therefore the exploiters of this dreary film have a catchline, from *The Valley of Content* to *The Whirlpool of Wealth.* The photography is quite fair and the settings are much too good for the story or the way it is told in this photoplay."
Mordaunt Hall in the *New York Times,* January 7, 1924

"Mary Alden, however, as the mother, manages to walk away with that role and gather all the sympathy that there is in the story. Huntley Gordon, as the husband, gives a very convincing performance and registers well. Willie Collier Jr., as the son, scores as a youthful souse and wild kid, but little Norma Shearer manages to put over another wallop for herself in this picture that shows that she can troup. She sure looks like a real find. Winifred Bryson, as the vamp, was there with all the Thedaish stuff, while Ward Crane was the heavy that got walloped behind closed doors. Frederick Truesdale had a minor role."
Variety, January 10, 1924

Advertisement for Pleasure Mad.

Pleasure Mad: *Ward Crane and Norma Shearer.*

Pleasure Mad: *Huntley Gordon and Norma Shearer.*

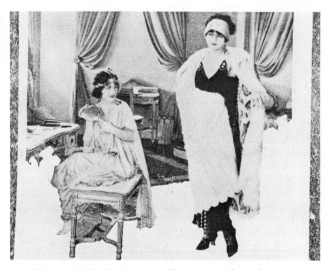

Pleasure Mad: *Norma Shearer and a player.*

73

The Wanters (First National-1923)

CREDITS: Director: John M. Stahl. From a story by Leila Burton Wells.
Scenario: J. G. Hawks, Paul Bern. Photography: Ernest G. Palmer.
Running time: 7 Reels. Released November 26, 1923.

CAST: Marie Prevost (Myra Hastings), Robert Ellis (Elliot Worthington), Norma Shearer (Marjorie), Gertrude Astor (Mrs. Van Pelt), Huntley Gordon (Theodore Van Pelt), Lincoln Stedman (Bobby), Lillian Langdon (Mrs. Worthington), Louise Fazenda (Mary), Hank Mann (the star boarder), Lydia Yeamans Titus (the landlady), Vernon Steele (Tom Armstrong), Harold Goodwin (chauffeur), William Buckley (butler).

STORY OF THE FILM: While visiting his sister Marjorie's home, Elliot Worthington is smitten by Myra Hastings, a domestic who is employed there. He falls in love with her instantly, but his family, fearful of a relationship, discharges Myra. When Elliot meets Myra again he asks her to marry him and she accepts. After their honeymoon he introduces his bride to his relatives, but their hypocritical reaction to the match drives Myra away. She is almost killed by an oncoming train when Elliot arrives in time to release her foot, which has been caught on a track.

CRITICS' VERDICT:

"The production, interior setting and so forth should prove of enough quality to make the picture a suitable program leader within the intermediate houses despite

The Wanters: *Norma Shearer.*

The Wanters: *Gertrude Astor (extreme left), Louise Fazenda (holding pearls), Norma Shearer with hand on Robert Ellis, and Marie Prevost and Huntley Gordon on stairs.*

the patrons will find they've gone up against the same type of story many times previously. Stahl has carried the theme along evenly, though certain deletions might help, as it threatens to hit an upgrade more than once."
Variety, March 12, 1924

"A sympathetic treatment of the plot and characterization coupled with an effective melodramatic climax succeed in saving this story and lifting it above the average program offering.

"The central idea is not new—having served in various guises since it was first introduced. It presents a natural craving for things we cannot have—a craving which affects even the most exclusive circles. Thus is found a reason for the title. While it follows familiar lines it offers moments of interest—having been adequately cast and striking home occasionally with its dramatic touches."

Lawrence Reid in *Motion Picture News,* January 19, 1924

Lucretia Lombard (Warner Brothers—1923)

CREDITS: Producer: Harry Rapf. Director: Jack Conway. Based on a novel by Kathleen Norris. Scenario: Bertram Millhauser, Sada Owen. Running time: 7 Reels. Released December 8, 1923.

CAST: Irene Rich (Lucretia Lombard), Monte Blue (Stephen Winship), Marc McDermott (Sir Allen Lombard), Norma Shearer (Mimi), Alec B. Francis (Judge Winship), John Roche (Fred Winship), Lucy Beaumont (Mrs. Winship), Otto Hoffman (Sandy, Lombard's servant).

Lucretia Lombard: *Norma Shearer, Monte Blue, and Irene Rich.*

Lucretia Lombard: *Norma Shearer and Irene Rich.*

STORY OF THE FILM: Lucretia Morgan, a middle classer, becomes the wife of Sir Allen Lombard, a man much older than herself. The marriage is loveless, and several years later, Sir Allen is an invalid confined to a wheelchair and addicted to drugs. Eventually, he dies from an overdose, his death apparently being a great relief to Lucretia. She soon meets Stephen Winship, a district attorney and both fall in love with each other. Stephen proposes marriage to Lucretia, but his father, Judge Winship, wishes him to marry Mimi, a somewhat impulsive and flirtatious type of young girl who is living with the Winship family. Reluctantly, Stephen does so, but he cannot forget Lucretia, whom he feels he has hurt terribly. During a raging forest fire in which a dam bursts, causing a flood as well, Mimi is caught up in the catastrophe and perishes. Her death reunites Lucretia and Stephen.

CRITICS' VERDICT:

"*Lucretia Lombard,* by the way, has an alternate title, *Flaming Passion,* which is used in those districts where passion is popular. As a matter of fact, the title doesn't make much difference. It isn't a good picture."
Robert E. Sherwood in *Life* magazine, January 10, 1924

"This picture is poorly cut and although it has certain interesting sequences it is not an overwhelming success as an entertainment. Mr. MacDermott and Miss Rich are capable in their respective parts and Monte Blue as Stephen is fairly good."
Mordaunt Hall in the *New York Times,* December 17, 1923

"For some reason, the gentle charm of Kathleen Norris's writing does not translate itself to the screen. Where the book was a success, the celluloid version is

76

flat, which may be blamed, perhaps, upon the inadequate direction. Irene Rich is charming, but Monte Blue fails to register—he and the direction belong together. There is a forest fire, however, that lifts the picture above mediocrity. It is one of the best film fires to date."
Photoplay, March 1924

"The find of the cast is Norma Shearer. She plays a flapper type and then developes a dramatic strain that is above the ordinary. The girl is there in looks as well as screens in an attractive manner."
Variety, December 20, 1923

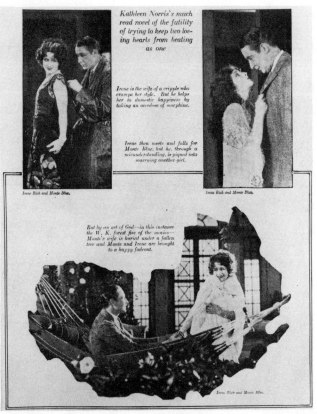

Three scenes from Lucretia Lombard. *Captions on pictures are incorrect. The players are Norma Shearer and Monte Blue.*

The Trail of the Law (Biltmore—Producer's Security Corporation—1924)

CREDITS: Producer and Director: Oscar Apfel. Scenario: Marian Brooks. Released January 25, 1924

CAST: Wilfred Lytell (Fraser Burt), Norma Shearer (Jerry Varden), John Morse (Alvin Varden), Richard Neill (Tom Frost, Alias Steve Merrill), Charles Beyer (Caleb Willis), Herbert Holcombe (Bobby Willis), George Stevens (servant), Baby Florence Rogan (Jerry, four years old).

STORY OF THE FILM: Jerry Varden, a comely, tomboyish type of girl, is living in the backwoods of Maine. The area has become unsafe, and in order to protect herself she poses as a boy by day and in the evening reverts to her own sex when at home. Tragedy had beset her as a child when her mother was killed by a marauder on whom her father had sworn vengeance. The culprit is later revealed as a neighbor who goes under an alias. Upon discovering the identity of the murderer, Jerry's father gives the man a severe thrashing which almost proves fatal. Fraser Burt, a young man from the city, who is in love with Jerry, manages to prevent further bloodshed.

CRITICS' VERDICT:
"Pictorial excellence, adequate direction, good acting and a story very thin, about sums up *The Trail of the Law,* an Oscar Apfel feature, good enough for the minor half of the average double bill. It features Norma Shearer, undoubtedly a comer, and Wilfred Lytell, announced as due to arrive for some time, but who never seems to be able to overtake his older brother. Miss Shearer is appealing even in trousers and cap, but the usual imagination is needed to conceive her palming herself off as a boy."
Variety, January 31, 1924

"When you have seen this piece you will understand why altruistic persons advertise, 'Beware of Imitations.'
Part 1: A country girl is wooed and won by a city chap. Part 2: Because of some rather unquestionable characters in the vicinity, the girl masquerades as a boy during the day. Part 3: For fifteen years Papa has been on the trail of the bad man. Part 4: He gets Him. If this strikes you as interesting, the pleasure is all yours."
Photoplay, April 1924

The Trail of the Law: *Norma Shearer and Wilfred Lytell.*

The Trail of the Law: *Wilfred Lytell and Norma Shearer with players.*

The Trail of the Law: *Norma Shearer and players.*

The Wolf Man (Fox Film Corporation—1924)

CREDITS: Director: Edward Mortimer. From a story by Reed Heustis. Scenario: Frederick Hatton, Fanny Hatton. Photography: Don Short, Michael Farley. Running time: 6 Reels. Released February 17, 1924.

CAST: John Gilbert (Gerald Stanley), Norma Shearer (Elizabeth Gordon), Alma Frances (Beatrice Joyce), George Barraud (Lord Rothstein), Eugene Pallette (Pierre), Edgar Norton (Sir Reginald Stackpoole), Thomas R. Mills (Caulkins), Max Montisole (Phil Joyce), Charles Wellesley (Sam Gordon), Richard Blayden (Lieutenant Esmond), D. R. O. Hatswell (Lord St. Cleve), Mary Warren (English barmaid), Eba Mona (ballet girl).

STORY OF THE FILM: While under the influence of liquor, Gerald Stanley, a young impulsive British peer, believes he has killed his fiancée's brother during a fight. Gerald's older brother, Pierre, also desiring to marry Beatrice Joyce, the girl Gerald is engaged to, makes his kin believe that he had actually murdered Beatrice's brother. Convinced of his guilt, Gerald escapes to Canada, and to avoid arrest he decides to refrain from drinking. Upon hearing that Pierre has married his ex-fiancée, Gerald starts drinking again, and while in a state of intoxication, he meets Elizabeth Gordon, the daughter of a railroad magnate. Desperate, Gerald kidnaps Elizabeth and takes her to his cabin in the wilderness where he proceeds to make love to her. Elizabeth manages to escape from his clutches, but Gerald catches up with her and they board a canoe, in

The Wolf Man: *Norma Shearer, John Gilbert, and Eugene Pallette.*

order to elude their pursuers, for the police are now on Gerald's trail. Caught in the swirling rapids, the canoe capsizes and Gerald saves Elizabeth from drowning. He asks her forgiveness, which she readily grants. Eventually, Gerald is exonerated of the murder of Beatrice's brother and is also saved by Elizabeth from being lynched. Gerald and Elizabeth look forward to a happy future.

CRITICS' VERDICT:
"Just a little program production that seems to start off as though it was going to be a real tale, but does flop before the finish and ends rather abruptly. Judging from the characters programed by the regular press sheet and those shown in the picture, the tale must have been changed materially from the original and revamped after the picture was made."
Variety, April 16, 1924

The Wolf Man: *John Gilbert and Norma Shearer.*

Blue Water (New Brunswick Films Ltd. of St. John, New Brunswick—1924)

CREDIT: Director: David M. Hartford. Based on the book *Blue Water* by Frederick William Wallace. Scenario: Faith Green. Released May 1924.

CAST: Pierre Gendron (Jimmie Westhaver), Jane Thomas (Carrie), Norma Shearer (Lilian Denton). Others: John Dillon, Harlan Knight, Louis D'Arclay, Alice May.

STORY OF THE FILM: A story of Bay of Fundy fishermen. Jimmie Westhaver is raised by his uncle and aunt in a fishing village after his father, a sea captain, wrecks his boat while alone. Jimmie then goes to sea. He has a sweetheart, Carrie, who also leaves their home town and takes up nursing in St. John. There she

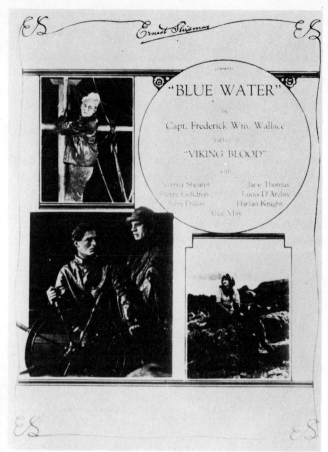

Advertisement for Blue Water. *Courtesy Stills Library, Canadian Film Archives.*

breaks faith with Jimmie and becomes engaged to another man. Jimmie receives this news on his return from a voyage and seeks forgetfulness in drink. He orders his ship to sea and in a terrible storm almost wrecks it. His father's spirit appears to him and sobers him sufficiently to steer his vessel to safety. Another girl, Lilian Denton, is sent to him from the sea and at the end of the film we see the happy couple sailing away on a liner for somewhere in the land of happiness.

Note: Information on this film was practically impossible to track down until I wrote to the Canadian Film Institute, which was kind enough to send me the necessary details such as credits, cast, and a synopsis, all of which are reproduced here. Having checked every available source on the movies, including newspapers and a few Canadian magazines, *Blue Water* never came to light. And it wasn't *Blue Waters* as I thought, but Blue Water. The Film Daily Yearbook listed it as *Blue Waters,* but no review date was mentioned.

I first came across a capsule review mentioned as *Blue Waters* in *Harrison's Reports* and Norma Shearer and Pierre Gendron were listed in the cast, but no

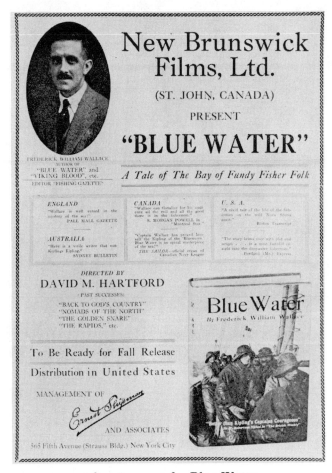

Advertisement for Blue Water.

author, director, other players, etc. According to this review the story had to do with a rich girl who falls in love with a Canadian fisherman, which may be so, but the synopsis that has been sent me differs from what I first saw. What I have here, apparently, is the more factual story, yet the plot if one can call it one, is a bit confused, so I wrote it as I found it, since there were no reviews to check. According to Mr. Peter Morris, the curator of the Canadian Film Institute, *Blue Water* was reviewed in the *Canadian Moving Picture Digest,* May 3, 1924, but no such trade journal exsists here in L. A. or even at the Academy of Motion Picture Arts and Sciences Research Library, USC, U. C. L. A., or the main public library, all of which I've checked. The film seems never to have been released, except on a States Rights basis, and there appear to be no U. S. reviews as I've discovered in my painstaking research on this.

Another story about *Blue Water* is that it had a very limited release and the company which produced it under promoter Ernest Shipman went bankrupt. The company planned to make second film, but it never developed.

I hope this explains why it was so difficult for me to come across a review of *Blue Water.*

Blue Water was completed in late 1922 and was being advertised for release by February 1923, but seems not to have been actually shown before May 1924.

Jack Jacobs

Broadway after Dark (Warner Brothers—1924)

CREDITS: Producer: Harry Rapf. Director: Monta Bell. Based on the play by Owen Davis. Adaptation: Douglas Doty. Photography: Charles Van Enger. Assistant director: Sandy Roth. Running time: 7 Reels. Released May 31, 1924

CAST: Adolphe Menjou (Ralph Norton), Norma Shearer (Rose Dulane), Anna Q. Nilsson (Helen Tremaine), Edward Burns (Jack Devlin), Carmel Myers (Lenore Vance), Vera Lewis (Mrs. Smith, landlady), Willard Louis (''Slim'' Scott), Mervyn Le Roy (Carl Fisher), Jimmy Quinn (Ed Fisher), Edgar Norton (the old actor), Gladys Tennyson (Vera), Ethel Miller (the chorus girl), Otto Hoffman (Norton's valet), Lee Harvey (Tom Devery, the detective), Michael Dark (George Vance). CAMEOS: Fred Stone, Dorothy Stone, Mary Eaton, Raymond Hitchcock, Elsie Ferguson, Florence Moore, James J. Corbett, John Steel, Frank Tinney, Paul Whiteman, Irene Castle, Buster West.

STORY OF THE FILM: Ralph Norton, a wealthy libertine and a popular figure among the Park Avenue smart set, soon tires of the superficiality of his gay strata and retires incognito to a theatrical boarding house where he finds life much more colorful and earthy. There he is attracted to Rose Dulane, an ex-convict employed as a maid. When the proprietor of the resi-

Broadway after Dark: *Adolphe Menjou, director Monta Bell, and Norma Shearer.*

Broadway after Dark: *Norma Shearer*.

Broadway after Dark: *Adolphe Menjou and Norma Shearer*.

dence learns of Rose's prison record he dismisses her and Norton suddenly gets the idea of introducing the girl as his ward to the theatrical profession and the social environment he had just forsaken. Rose is almost framed by a cop in going back to jail until Norton comes to the rescue and takes her out of New York to embark on matrimony.

CRITICS' VERDICT:
"Between Bell and Adolphe Menjou, who plays him, the bachelor boulevardier becomes an absorbing character. Menjou invests him with his usual poise and finesse. Norma Shearer does her best work thus far as the slavy who dons fine feathers, and Willard Louis again makes a subordinate figure, of a down-and-out actor, stand out."
Photoplay, August 1924

"Monta Bell directed this production which makes it unusually good entertainment. Anna Q. Nilsson is attractive as the aggravating blond. Norma Shearer is sympathetic as the heroine, and although he indulges in too much make-up, Edward Burns is acceptable as the callous young schemer. Willard Louis is astonishingly funny as the fat actor in the boarding house."
Mordaunt Hall in the *New York Times,* May 20, 1924.

Broken Barriers (Metro-Goldwyn—1924)

CREDITS: Director: Reginald Barker. Based on the novel by Meredith Nicholson. Scenario: Sada Cowan, Howard Higgin. Photography: Percy Hilburn. Running time: 6 Reels. Released August 18, 1924.

CAST: James Kirkwood (Ward Trenton), Norma Shearer (Grace Durland), Adolphe Menjou (Tommy Kemp), Mae Busch (Irene Kirby), George Fawcett (Mr. Durland), Margaret McWade (Mrs. Durland), Robert Agnew (Bobby Durland), Ruth Stonehouse (Ethel Durland), Robert Frazer (John Moore), Winifred Bryson (Mrs. Ward Trenton), Vera Reynolds (Sadie Denton), Edythe Chapman (Beulah Reynolds), George Kwwa (Chang).

STORY OF THE FILM: When Grace Durland's father goes bankrupt she is forced to leave college and soon becomes a working girl. At a party, she meets Ward Trenton, a married man who is estranged from his wife and who is hopeful that she will grant him a divorce. Trenton has an affair with Grace, which results in love for both, but is complicated by his wife's refusal to

Broken Barriers: *James Kirkwood and Norma Shearer*.

Broken Barriers: *Norma Shearer, James Kirkwood, and players*.

dissolve their marriage. One night, Trenton is highly intoxicated while driving, collides with another car, and is seriously injured. The accident almost cripples him, which makes his wife think that he will never be able to walk again. She starts divorce proceedings, but her husband gradually recovers and he and Grace are finally free to marry.

CRITICS' VERDICT:
"Norma Shearer reveals a steady improvement in her screen work as the girl. She will bear watching. The picture is slightly better than passable film fare."
Photoplay, October 1924

"This production has a happy but disappointing ending which comes with such a jolt that one can hardly believe the picture is finished. There are moments of interest in this film, but the story belongs in the bewildering and quite impossible category."
Mordaunt Hall in the *New York Times,* August 4, 1924

Married Flirts (Metro-Goldwyn—1924)

CREDITS: Director: Robert Vignola. Based on the novel *Mrs. Paramoor,* by Louis Joseph Vance. Scenario: Julia Crawford Ivers. Photography: Oliver T. Marsh. Titles: Frederic and Fanny Hatton. Settings: Charles L. Cadwallader. Film Editor: Frank E. Hull. Running time: 7 Reels. Released October 4, 1924.

CAST: Pauline Frederick (Nellie Wayne), Conrad Nagel (Perley Rex), Mae Busch (Jill Wetherell), Hunt-

Married Flirts: *In foreground front table seated left to right are Hobart Henley, Pauline Frederick, Mae Murray, and Robert Z. Leonard. Visible to the left of Henley's head is Norma Shearer with John Gilbert and May McAvoy.*

ley Gordon (Pendleton Wayne), Paul Nicholson (Peter Granville), Pattison Dial (Evelyn Draycup), Alice Hollister (Mrs. Callender), GUEST STARS: John Gilbert, Norma Shearer, Mae Murray, May McAvoy, Aileen Pringle. Directors: Robert Z. Leonard, Hobart Henley.

STORY OF THE FILM: Desiring to succeed as an author, Nellie Wayne leaves her husband, Pendleton, and decides to go abroad after Jill Wetherell, a notorious vamp, breaks up their marriage. In Europe, Nellie eventually realizes her ambition and becomes a prominent novelist under the pseudonym of Mrs. Paramoor. One day, she is surprised to encounter Jill and Perley Rex, an old friend, whom the former has just married after discarding Pendleton. Nellie then decides to get even with Jill by using her own wiles on Perley, who now wants to divorce Jill. The latter is crushed at her spouse's sudden transference of his affections to Jill but in the end, each forgives the other and the Waynes are back together again.

CRITICS' VERDICT:
"The old theme of the wife who neglects her personal appearance and loses her husband is played upon with variations. Director Robert Vignola does it smoothly and quietly. He is given first aid through a striking performance by Pauline Frederick, who depicts the woman from dowdy-wife to novelist butterfly to a nicety. The author entertains the film company producing her movie. This calls for an interesting behind the screen interlude."
Photoplay, December, 1924

"The picture is filled with gripping moments and there is a climax that puts the feature over with a bang. There is a novelty introduced in the final reels when most of the MGM stars are shown at a banquet and mahjong party. Hobart Henley, May McAvoy, Robert Leonard, Mae Murray, Norma Shearer, John Gilbert, Aileen Pringle and others of equal note are shown in these scenes."
Motion Picture News, October 25, 1924

Empty Hands (Paramount—1924)

CREDIT: Producers: Adolph Zukor and Jesse L. Lasky. Director: Victor Fleming. Original story: Arthur Stringer. Scenario: Carey Wilson. Photography: Charles Edgar Scholnbaum. Running time: 7 Reels. Released: October 13, 1924.

CAST: Jack Holt (Grimshaw), Norma Shearer (Claire Endicott), Charles Clarey (Robert Endicott), Hazel Keener (Mrs. Endicott), Gertrude Olmstead (Gypsy), Ramsey Wallace (Monte), Ward Crane (Milt Bisnet), Charles Stevens (Indian guide), Hank Mann (spring water man), Charles Greer (butler).

STORY OF THE FILM: Having been reared in luxury from the time she was born, Claire Endicott turns out to be spoiled and given to flippancy and coquettishness which displeases her father, Robert Endicott, no end. Claire's flirtatious behavior toward some of her male guests during a party at her home prompts her father to take her to Northern Canada so she can forget her frivolous ways of living for a while and learn how to rough it. While fishing one day from a canoe, Claire is suddenly caught up by the surging rapids and is swept over and lost in an unexplored area. Grimshaw, a young, rugged engineer employed by Claire's father, rescues her and they soon come to an uninhabited valley where they are forced to exist under the most primitive conditions. Faced with starvation, Grimshaw becomes a self-styled Robinson Crusoe and goes about finding what he can to eat for Claire and himself. As time goes on, the two fall in love with each other, and after a few more adventures that almost cost them their lives they are finally located by Endicott and a searching party. Claire is grateful to her father for making her see what a wastrel she has been and she and Grimshaw plan to marry and live in the country.

CRITICS' VERDICT:
"Another variation of the desert island story; with a young engineer and a spoiled daughter of jazz isolated for months in a Northwestern river ravine from which there is no escape. Discarding one piece bathing suits and wearing fur make-shifts cures the spoiled girl of her distorted view of life. Jack Holt is the man who knows the wilderness like an open book and Norma Shearer is the girl."
Photoplay, November 1924

"Miss Shearer's eyes are really beautiful, and, as her hair is not curled according to movie fashion, she is quite pleasing in this film. She seems to be a good swimmer when in the water and is evidently conscious that her ankles are by no means ungainly. Her eye brows deserved at least two words of praise."
Mordaunt Hall in the *New York Times.* August 18, 1924

Empty Hands: *Norma Shearer.*

Empty Hands: *Norma Shearer and Jack Holt.*

Empty Hands: *Norma Shearer and Jack Holt.*

Empty Hands: *Gertrude Olmstead and Norma Shearer*.

Empty Hands: *Jack Holt and Norma Shearer*.

The Snob (Metro-Goldwyn — 1924)

CREDITS: Director: Monta Bell. Adaptation: Monta Bell. From a story by Helen R. Martin. Photography: Andre Bartlatier. Film Editor: Ralph Lawson. Set design: Cedric Gibbons. Running time: 7 Reels. Released November 10, 1924. Presented by Louis B. Mayer.

CAST: John Gilbert (Eugene Curry), Norma Shearer (Nancy Claxton), Conrad Nagel (Herrick Appleton), Phyllis Haver (Dorothy Rensheimer), Hedda Hopper (Mrs. Leiter), Margaret Seddon (Mrs. Curry), Aileen Manning (Lottie), Hazel Kennedy (Florence), Gordon Sackville (Sherwood Claxton), Roy Laidlaw (Doctor), Nellie Bly Baker (maid), Mabel Coleman (registrar).

STORY OF THE FILM: After the death of her wealthy father, who has been killed in a brawl, Nancy Claxton leaves Boston for a small town in Pennsylvania where she obtains a post as a school teacher in a small college. There she meets Eugene Curry, a handsome young instructor whose ambition is to become socially prominent and marry into wealth. To gain his ends, Eugene fawns on anybody whom he believes to be affluent, and as result, virtually forsakes his middle-class family. Nancy, unaware of Eugene's objective, falls in love

The Snob: *Norma Shearer and Phyllis Haver.*

with him and soon they are engaged. Meanwhile, Eugene has set his cap for Dorothy Rensheimer, an heiress, with intentions of marrying her as soon as possible. Nancy suddenly becomes ill and Eugene quickly marries her, thinking she hasn't long to live, yet ignorant of the fact that she, too, is an heiress. Herrick Appleton, a childhood sweetheart of Nancy's and the scion of a prominent Boston family, has decided to relinquish his past as a blueblood and succeed as an artist, but he is still in love with Nancy. Nancy's baby dies in childbirth and she blames Eugene for the miscarriage. Eugene, in a letter to Dorothy, claims that Nancy had tricked him into marriage. When Eugene learns that Nancy is also the daughter of a rich man he asks to be forgiven for his selfishness and philandering. Now recovered, Nancy denounces Eugene as a snob and that she will divorce him and marry Herrick.

CRITICS' VERDICT:
"Check a hit down to the promising Monta Bell, who first revealed his possibilities in *Broadway after Dark*. Bell has developed his dramatic story with fine freshness and originality. *The Snob* is a Helen R. Martin story and there is a Mennonite background. John Gilbert is excellent as the professor and the cast is admirable, particularly Norma Shearer as his wife."
Photoplay, January 1925

"Miss Shearer is restrained and charming, but as Nancy one can't help thinking that she is conscious of all her virtues. Conrad Nagel, as hero, is more pleasing than usual, as he indulges in a variation of expressions and is not as gloomy as in his previous love-sick roles. As for Mr. Gilbert's performance he is too lethargic. A little fire would have made Curry more interesting. Phyllis Haver is capable as Dorothy who powders her face by the hour and worries over flirting and dancing.

The Snob: *Norma Shearer and Conrad Nagel.*

The Snob: *Norma Shearer.*

The Snob: *Conrad Nagel and Norma Shearer.*

This adaptation could have been a really fine screen effort had it been handled by Lubitsch, Chaplin or Buchoweight. As it stands, it is a passing entertainment which ought to be cut in many places to avoid repetition and long-winded close-ups.''
Mordaunt Hall in the *New York Times,* December 15, 1924

"Miss Shearer does especially well with her portrayal of the reserved heiress, adding to her appearance by a performance that bears out the contention this girl both is and has been continuously progressing.''
Variety, December 17, 1924.

He Who Gets Slapped (Metro-Goldwyn — 1924)

CREDITS: Director: Victor Seastrom. Based on the play *He Who Gets Slapped* by Leonid Nikolaevich Andreyev. Adaptation: Carey Wilson, Victor Seastrom. Photography: Milton Moore. Film Editor: Hugh Wynn. Art Director: Cedric Gibbons. Costumes: Sophie Wachner. Presented by Louis B. Mayer. Running time: 7 Reels. Released December 22, 1924.

CAST: Lon Chaney (He Who Gets Slapped), Norma Shearer (Consuelo), John Gilbert (Bezano), Tully Marshall (Count Mancini), Marc McDermott (Baron Regnard), Ford Sterling (Tricaud, a clown), Harvey Clarke (Briquet), Clyde Cook, (a clown), Paulette Duval (Zinida), Ruth King (He's wife), Brandon Hurst (a clown), George Davis (a clown).

STORY OF THE FILM: A brilliant scientist who loves his wife deeply and believes that she has been faithful to him, and who has always trusted his best friend, Baron Regnard, a frequent visitor at his home, loses faith in mankind, which he himself has inspired with his work, when he discovers that the Baron has stolen both his invention and his spouse. Shattered, the husband exchanges his noble profession for a job in a circus where he humbly offers himself as a clown. It isn't long before the ex-scientist wins acclaim as France's foremost clown who is merely billed as He Who Gets Slapped, which remains his sole act because of its great popularity.

A member of the circus is Consuelo, a fetching bareback rider with whom He falls passionately in love. Although Consuelo is fond of He she does not take him seriously and virtually ridicules his romantic approaches. He, however, has a rival for the affections of Consuelo, who is Bezano, a handsome young man and her riding partner in the act, whom the girl loves. Count Mancini, Consuelo's father, is virtually penniless and plans to have his daughter marry Baron Regnard merely because it would enable him to spend his declining years in comfort and luxury, but Consuelo disdains the proposal. When he learns that the Baron has designs on Consuelo, he plans to get rid of both his former friend and also Mancini, whom he considers a threat to his daughter's future, too. He then arranges for Regnard and Mancini to come to his dressing room on a ruse, and there, to the horror of the two men, the clown releases a lion from its cage which claws the Baron and the ringmaster to death, but not before the Baron fatally stabs his one time friend. He dies in Consuelo's arms.

CRITICS' VERDICT:

"Mr. Seastrom has directed this dramatic story with all the genius of a Chaplin or a Lubitsch, and he has accomplished more than they have in their respective works, *A Woman of Paris* and *The Marriage Circle*, as he had, what they did not have, a stirring dramatic story to put into pictures.

"Miss Shearer is charming as Consuelo, and Mr. Gilbert who gave such an excellent account of himself

He Who Gets Slapped: *Norma Shearer, John Gilbert, and Lon Chaney.*

He Who Gets Slapped: *Norma Shearer and Lon Chaney.*

in *His Hour,* is a sympathetic sweetheart. But the player who is entitled to honors only second to Mr. Chaney is Marc McDermott, who takes full advantage of the strength of his role. Tully Marshall is splendid as the scapegoat count.

"For dramatic value and a faultless adaptation of the play, this is the finest production we have yet seen." Mordaunt Hall in the *New York Times,* December 15, 1924

"Lon Chaney, the clown who accepts the kicks and jeers of the multitude, gives an interpretation of surpassing fineness. One of his tender moments with the little bareback rider whom he so hopelessly loves, is memorable. Norma Shearer, too, is delightful in the freshness and gaiety of youth."
Theatre Magazine, February 1925

"The acting is remarkably fine. Lon Chaney does the best work of his career. Here his performance has breadth, force and imagination. Tully Marshall, as usual, gives an outstanding performance, and Norma

Shearer and Jack Gilbert, as the lovers, are delightful." *Photoplay,* January 1925

"He Who Gets Slapped is undoubtedly a fine moving picture. Among those responsible for its success are the author of the stage play, Leonid Andreyev, who provided the producers of the picture with material particularly suited to the screen; Victor Seastrom, who has given it some of his excellent brand of direction; Lon Chaney of the versatile face and skillful pantomime, and the refreshingly different Norma Shearer—not to mention a high class lion, who does his important bit in the denouement."
Alva Taylor in *Liberty Magazine,* December 27, 1924

"Norma Shearer as the little circus rider about whom the love interest revolves is charming and delightful at the same time. She lends the needed touch of youth in the cast. John Gilbert, who plays opposite is fully adequate as the young lover."
Variety, November 12, 1924

92

He Who Gets Slapped: *Norma Shearer and Lon Chaney*.

He Who Gets Slapped: *Marc MacDermott, Tully Marshall, and Norma Shearer.*

He Who Gets Slapped: *Marc MacDermott, Norma Shearer, and Tully Marshall.*

He Who Gets Slapped: *John Gilbert, Norma Shearer, and Lon Chaney.*

He Who Gets Slapped: *John Gilbert, Norma Shearer, and Lon Chaney.*

Excuse Me (Metro-Goldwyn—1925)

CREDITS: Director: Alf Goulding. Original story and scenario: Rupert Hughes. Photography: John Boyle. Assistant director: Nick Grinde. Art director: Cedric Gibbons. Running time: 6 Reels. Released January 19, 1925. Presented by Louis B. Mayer.

CAST: Norma Shearer (Marjorie Newton), Conrad Nagel (Harry Mallory), Renee Adoree (Francine), Walter Hiers (Pullman porter), John Boles (Lieutenant Shaw), Bert Roach (Jimmy Wellington), William V. Mong (Reverend Dr. Temple), Edith York (Mrs. Temple), Gene Cameron (Lieutenant Hudson), Fred Kelsey (George Ketchem), Paul Weigel (Reverend John Wales), Mai Wells (Mrs. John Wales).

STORY OF THE FILM: Lieutenant Harry Mallory, a young naval officer, is engaged to Marjorie Newton, a society girl and hopes to marry her as soon as possible.

His leave is suddenly cancelled when orders come through for him to report for immediate duty in the Philippines. Mallory believes that the Islands would be the ideal place for a honeymoon and he loses no time in proposing to Marjorie, who finally accepts him. After visiting the license bureau there is just about enough time left for them to find a minister and catch a train to San Francisco where they will board a transport for the Islands. Mallory is faced with court martial if he misses his ship.

Having chosen a clergyman somewhat haphazardly, Mallory and his fiancée are dismayed to find, upon calling at the former's home, that he is down with a case of smallpox. Then, on the way to the station, their taxicab is wrecked, which leaves them momentarily stranded. Eventually, they locate another one and soon arrive at the depot. By now, Marjorie has changed her mind about accompanying Harry, but he persuades her to get on board the train with him by telling her that there is sure to be a minister on it. No sooner does Harry mention this than one appears and walks through their car.

After the train has begun to move, Harry frantically begins looking for the minister and upon locating him learns that he is the Reverend Dr. Temple. But the Reverend explains that he is not performing any ceremonies for a while since this is the first vacation he has taken in thirty years. To prove it , he has defrocked his holy attire and is now wearing a stylish suit that makes him look younger. Harry returns to Marjorie, who is waiting in the bridal compartment that some passengers had reserved, thinking they were the expected newlyweds. When Marjorie is told that there are no other ministers on the train she breaks into tears and insists on getting off at once, but the Pullman porter informs her that the next stop isn't until early the next morning. Since they are not as yet man and wife, Harry and Marjorie will not consider spending the night together in the drawing room, and feign a quarrel in order to avoid this, with Harry settling for the washroom.

The following day, at the next station, a young attractive Frenchwoman, whose name is Francine, boards the train with her little son. She is a divorcée and has escaped from her ex-husband and gained custody of the child, but is fearful that the boy might be kidnapped. She recognized Harry whom she had once met in France where he was on duty and decides that he will masquerade as her spouse. Harry's protestations over this, however, don't do him any good, since Francine has a way of inveigling men. When Marjorie finds Harry and the Frenchwoman together she is terribly upset and another quarrel ensues between her and her fiancée. Harry tries to explain that he is merely aiding Francine to shield her identity because she is in danger of losing her son, and after a little while, with Francine interceding, Marjorie is convinced.

The train stops for a brief layover at a village, which

Excuse Me: *Walter Hiers, Norma Shearer, and Conrad Nagel.*

Excuse Me: *Conrad Nagel and Norma Shearer.*

prompts Harry to disembark when he is attracted by a minister's convention there. In desperation, Harry appeals to a clergyman to come on board the train and perform the marriage, but after examining his license he tells Harry that it is only valid in Illinois and not acceptable here. Meanwhile, the train has pulled out and Harry misses it, after attempting to catch up with it. At a nearby airfield he induces a pilot to fly him in the direction of the train that Marjorie is still on, but Harry and the pilot soon notice that the train is about to crash into a bridge that is out. They signal the engineer to stop, and after a few minutes his attention is attracted and disaster is avoided. The plane finally intercepts the train and Harry and Marjorie are flown to San Francisco where they obtain a new marriage license and are married in time to board the vessel to the Islands.

CRITICS' VERDICT:

"Norma Shearer is a charming and beautiful comedienne. We prophesy big things for Norma, for her rise has been very marked and rapid. Conrad Nagel is not handicapped by having to portray too much virtue. Renee Adoree is amusing as a French girl and Walter Hiers shines as a colored porter on the train. Rupert Hughes, himself, must have written the titles, no one else could have done them like that."
Harriette Underhill in *Movie Weekly,* February 28, 1925

"Rupert Hughes' rollicking farce, *Excuse Me* reaches the screen as one of the funniest films of the season. It reminds us of a Harold Lloyd picture in its comedy inventions and assortment of gags. And there isn't a moment that it sags in its diverting incidents and laughs. The picture is played in high-spirited fashion by Bert Roach, Norma Shearer, Renee Adoree, Conrad Nagel, though Walter Hiers as the colored porter is not so successful with burnt cork. It is neatly staged, and certain of responsive laughs."
Motion Picture News, February 7, 1925

97

Excuse Me: *Norma Shearer*.

Excuse Me: *Norma Shearer*.

Excuse Me: *Conrad Nagel and Norma Shearer.*

Lady of the Night (Metro-Goldwyn — 1925)

CREDITS: Director: Monta Bell. From a story by Adela Rogers St. Johns. Scenario: Alice D.G. Miller. Photography: Andre Barlatier. Film Editor: Ralph Dawson. Art director: Cedric Gibbons. Running time: 6 Reels: Released February 23, 1925. Presented by Louis B. Mayer.

CAST: Norma Shearer (Molly and Florence Banning) Malcolm McGregor (David), George K. Arthur (Chunky), Fred Esmelton (Judge Banning), Dale Fuller (Miss Carr), Lew Harvey (Chris), Betty Morrisey (Gertie).

STORY OF THE FILM: A product of the slums, Molly becomes a member of an underworld ring while still in her teens. Her father had also been a lawless character and was sentenced to twenty years in prison during her infancy. Molly is later sent to a penal institution herself and on the same day she is released from the reform school, Florence Banning, a society girl, is graduating

from finishing school. Both, oddly enough, happen to be the spitting image of each other. Molly soon returns to the gang and to her illiterate, though faithful, boyfriend, Chunky, who had been an accomplice of hers.

At a dance, one night, to which she goes with Chunky, Molly is annoyed by a rather brash patron who has been forcing his attentions on her and is rescued from further molestation by David, an enterprising young inventor whose living quarters are adjacent to Molly's. The two become fast friends, with Molly falling in love with David. David wants to sell his safe-opening apparatus to Molly's gang on a percentage basis, but she discourages the idea, suggesting that he interest a group of financiers with his invention. Judge Banning, a prominent figure in social and business circles, is head of the conglomerate, and through him, David is equally fortunate in meeting his daughter, Florence, whose striking resemblance to Molly bewilders him. It isn't long before Florence and David are very much in love, but when Florence learns that Molly had prior claim on David's affections, she insists on

99

breaking up with him. Realizing that David is not in love with her, Molly goes out of his life and marries Chunky, who has loved her all along. Florence and David are reunited and also plan to marry.

CRITICS' VERDICT:

"The make-up of the dance hall girl is something new for Miss Shearer, especially as it is rather exaggerated. She has imbued this character with a great deal of sympathy, and particularly unforgettable is that scene where she visits the room of the man she loves the same evening that he is escorting the other girl to a dance, and offering her proof of his devotion."
Edwin Schallert in the *Los Angeles Times,* March 9, 1925

"Miss Shearer, in this picture, has accomplished one of the most difficult characterizations that fall to the lot of a motion picture actress to portray. That of two girls in two entirely different worlds. This has been done with a clear and well defined contrast, Miss Shearer taking both roles extremely well.

"If you have not had the pleasure of viewing this picture, it would be well worth the time to see it, inasmuch as Miss Shearer is ably supported by Malcolm MacGregor, and the rest of the cast is very good."
E. Merrill Noel in *Film Fun*, August 1925

"Miss Shearer does the best acting she has ever done. She is splendid as Molly, who wears weird clothes and has a flair for imitation aigrette feathers. She is comely, sympathetic and attractively gowned as Florence."
Mordaunt Hall in the *New York Times*, March 2, 1925

"A slight little tale of the romance of two girls of marked resemblance, who fall in love with the same man—with the one from the society circles winning out in the love stakes when the rival, suppressing her feeling in the romance, gives Norma Shearer her opportunity to flash some really inspired acting. It is an intelligent performance, one marked by real understanding and authority. Monta Bell has dressed it up with subtle shafts of humor and human touches. The story shows what good direction can do in giving breadth and color."
Motion Picture, June 1925

Lady of the Night: *Norma Shearer.*

Lady of the Night: *Norma Shearer*

Lady of the Night: *Norma Shearer.*

Lady of the Night: *George K. Arthur, Malcolm McGregor, and Norma Shearer.*

Lady of the Night: *Norma Shearer in a dual role.*

Lady of the Night: *Norma Shearer.*

Lady of the Night: *George K. Arthur and Norma Shearer.*

Waking Up the Town (United Artists—Mary Pickford Company—1925)

CREDITS: Director: Vernon Keyes. Co-director: Jack Pickford. From a story by James Cruze and Frank Condon. Photography: Arthur Edeson, Paul Perry. Running time: 6 Reels. Released April 14, 1925.

CAST: Jack Pickford (Jack Joyce), Claire McDowell (Mrs. Joyce), Alec B. Francis (Abner Hope), Norma Shearer (Mary Ellen Hope), Herbert Pryor (Curt Horndyke), Anna May (Helen Horndyke), George Dromgold (Joe Lakin).

STORY OF THE FILM: In a rural community known as Rainbow Falls, Jack Joyce, a struggling, though overzealous, young inventor, has been trying unsuccessfully to see Curt Horndyke, the town banker, in the hope that he will provide the necessary financial backing for his electric power project that will improve water facilities locally. Jack soon meets and falls in love with Mary Ellen Hope, an out of towner who is visiting her grandparents and who further inspires him in his endeavors.

However tenacious Jack is in his attempts to see Horndyke, they appear to be futile. Jack's luck changes for the better when old Abner Hope, an eccentric and a fanatic on astrology in whose garage he works, and which he also uses as his laboratory, prophesies that the world is about to come to an end and gives the young man eighteen thousand dollars, his life's savings, to spend as he wishes. Immediately, Jack buys an automobile, clothes, and other luxuries he had so long been deprived of and impresses the whole town, including Horndyke. The capitalist finally offers to back the invention and the project is a great success. During a thunder storm, Jack is struck by lightning, but is not seriously injured. He soon dreams that the world, as Abner Hope had predicted, is being destroyed. Upon

Waking Up the Town: *Norma Shearer, Alec B. Francis, and Jack Pickford.*

awakening, Jack finds Mary Ellen beside him.

CRITICS' VERDICT: "Mr. Pickford evidently takes this story seriously himself, as his brew is created much of the time. The narrative is said to have been written by James Cruze and Frank Condon, but they can't be blamed for all that goes on in this production. Miss Shearer is comely and Mr. Francis as the unshorn fanatic is as usual, clever."
Mordaunt Hall in the *New York Times,* March 3, 1925

"*Waking Up the Town* is a nice little picture, even though it doesn't live up to its title. Jack Pickford is the young man who elects himself a committee of one to make the town sit up and take notice and he is successful in that though he does not give as artistic a portrayal as usual. Nor does Norma Shearer delight the eye as she has done in previous productions. To tell the truth their respective roles do not provide much scope for their talents."
Aline O'Brien in *Movie Weekly*, May 2, 1925

Waking Up the Town: *Norma Shearer and Jack Pickford.*

Waking Up the Town: *Norma Shearer and Claire McDowell.*

"We thought the combination of James Cruze and Frank Condon as the authors of the story, with Jack Pickford and Norma Shearer as the leading characters, would result in one of the finest pictures ever made. Perhaps we expected too much, for this turned out to be just an average picture, with a good cast, a few laughs and a movie director's idea of the end of the world."
M.B. in *Photoplay*, June 1925

"Throughout *Waking up the Town* the entire cast of characters is engaged in a mad game called Find the Continuity. They all lose."
Robert E. Sherwood in *Life* magazine, April 23, 1925

Waking Up the Town: Jack Pickford and Norma Shearer.

Waking Up the Town: *Jack Pickford and Norma Shearer.*

Waking Up the Town: *Norma Shearer and Jack Pickford.*

A Slave of Fashion (Metro-Goldwyn—1925)

CREDITS: Director: Hobart Henley. From a story by Samuel Shipman. Scenario: Bess Meredyth, Jane Murfin. Photography: Ben Reynolds. Art director: Cedric Gibbons. Running time: 6 Reels. Released August 23, 1925.

CAST: Norma Shearer (Katherine Emerson), Lew Cody (Nicholas Wentworth), William Haines (Dick Wayne), Mary Carr (Mother Emerson), James Corrigan (Father Emerson), Vivia Ogden (Aunt Sophie), Miss De Pont (Madeline), Estelle Clark (Mayme), Sidney Bracy (Hobson).

STORY OF THE FILM: Katherine Emerson, a small-town girl from the wheat country, is anxious to better herself socially and financially. She finally leaves her home in Iowa and goes to New York in the hope of finding the best of everything. The train on which Katherine is traveling meets with a sudden accident and a woman passenger is killed. The victim's purse is picked up by Katherine who finds among its contents a letter from a wealthy friend inviting her to occupy his elegant New York apartment while he is abroad for six months. This gives Katherine an idea and she decides to masquerade as the invited guest. Once ensconced in her new luxurious surroundings, Katherine proceeds to live it up by wearing the latest styles in dresses, gowns, and other apparel. As a result, she blooms into one of the most stunning women in town. One day, Katherine's parents pay her an unexpected visit and she hastily explains that she has just married Nicholas Wentworth, the tenant of the apartment. Her family is puzzled at the news and also concerned over their daughter living alone. Mrs. Emerson then sends Nicholas a cable to return immediately. Wentworth, however, returns unexpectedly before any word could reach him and is both peeved and rather amused at Katherine's presence. Realizing the predicament she is in he decides to aggravate the situation by humiliating her as much as possible, but he has also fallen in love with her. To ease her conscience, Katherine confesses

A Slave of Fashion: *Norma Shearer.*

A Slave of Fashion: *Norma Shearer*.

A Slave of Fashion: *Lew Cody and Norma Shearer.*

the deception to her mother and father, and as she is about to leave, Nicholas asks her to remain and marry him. Katherine accepts, her dreams finally having come true.

CRITICS' VERDICT:

"Though the central theme is highly preposterous, Hobart Henley, the director, has fashioned so deftly this transparent story that the movie-goer is sure to delight in every foot of the picture. Norma Shearer, who parades the gowns of the hour, is enough scenic beauty for any audience—incidentally, she does well in her share of acting."
Movie, October 1925

"As long as they produce pictures like *A Slave of Fashion* the movie-goer with adult mentality may continue to believe that all's right with the world. It is a question whether the younger generation will get very much worked up over it, though to be sure, there is a series of gowns worn by Norma Shearer which, as we

understand it, ought to make the girls vote with the progressive wing of the party."
Mordaunt Hall in the *New York Times,* July 21, 1925

"Of course little girls who usurp the apartments of wealthy New York bachelors don't usually have such luck. Nevertheless, Norma Shearer makes you believe that even virtue may wear velvet and diamonds. The outlandish comedy is so gaily and adroitly played by Miss Shearer and Lew Cody that it becomes first rate entertainment. Not much fun for the children."
Photoplay, October 1925

"Equipped with an incredibly piffling story, and utterly devoid of any legitimate dramatic interest, *A Slave of Fashion* nevertheless manages to be pretty consistently interesting. It is so because Norma Shearer can engage and hold the attention as successfully as any movie actress now playing; because Lew Cody has developed into a singularly graceful actor, and because Hobart Henley has done an excellent job of direction."
Robert E. Sherwood in *Life* magazine, August 20, 1925

A Slave of Fashion: *Norma Shearer.*

A Slave of Fashion: *William Haines, Lew Cody, and Norma Shearer.*

A Slave of Fashion: *Norma Shearer and William Haines.*

Norma Shearer and Peggy Hamilton, who for fourteen years was Hollywood's fashion arbiter for all motion picture companies and fashion editor for the rotogravure section of the Sunday Los Angeles Times, *on the set of* A Slave of Fashion.

Pretty Ladies (Metro-Goldwyn—1925)

CREDITS: Director: Monta Bell. From a story by Adala Rogers St. Johns. Adaptation: Alice D.G. Miller. Photography: Ira H. Morgan. Running time: 6 Reels. Released September 10, 1925.

CAST: Zasu Pitts (Maggie Keenan), Tom Moore (Al Cassidy), Ann Pennington (Herself), Lilyan Tashman (Selma Larson), Bernard Randall (Aaron Savage), Helena D'Algy (Adrienne), Conrad Nagel (Maggie's dream lover), Norma Shearer (Frances White), George K. Arthur (Roger Van Horn), Lucille Le Sueur, who later became Joan Crawford, (Bobby), Paul Ellis (Warren Hadley), Roy D'Arcy (Paul Thompson), Gwen Lee (Fay), Dorothy Seastrom (Diamond Tights), Lew Harvey (Will Rogers), Chad Huber (Joe Frisco), Walter Shumway (Mr. Gallagher), Dan Crimmons (Mr. Shean), Jimmie Quinn (Eddie Cantor).

STORY OF THE FILM: Maggie Keenan, a tall, willowy, forlorn-looking, though not unattractive, girl, is a featured comedienne in the *Follies*, a popular Broadway show. Maggie is successful at evoking laughter from the audience, but a failure where love is concerned. Possibly because of her homeliness, she doesn't attract the opposite sex too much. During a performance one evening she accidentally falls into the orchestra pit and ruins one of the musician's drums. The victim of this mishap is Al Cassidy, who is also a budding songwriter. At first, Al is quite chagrined over the wreckage of his instrument, but as a result of the accident he and Maggie fall in love. Al is then inspired to compose a special number for the show dedicated to Maggie. The song is a hit, with Al becoming widely

Pretty Ladies: *Lew Harvey, Dorothy Seastrom, Walter Shumway, Dan Crimmins, player, Zasu Pitts, Lilyan Tashman, Ann Pennington, player, Norma Shearer, and Jimmie Quinn.*

Pretty Ladies: *Norma Shearer*.

successful as a composer. Maggie and Al, despite their careers, decide to get married and for a while they are blissfully happy. Al soon reaches the pinnacle of fame as a composer, while Maggie is enjoying motherhood. Selma Larson, the star of the *Follies,* wants Al to write a production number for her and Al goes to Atlantic City to work on it. A temptress, Selma has designs on Al and exercises all her wiles to make him hers and he becomes addicted to her charms. Maggie is now aware that Al has been carrying on with Selma, but she is not bitter and eventually forgives him, with Al realizing how neglectful he has been of Maggie and their child.

CRITICS' VERDICT:

"Here is one of those backstage photoplays with a very commonplace story, and yet it has been made a thoroughly worthwhile film. The external evidence is all to the effect that the directing is what made it. Monta Bell is the director. He deserves the highest praise for this piece of work turned out of his studio."
Mordaunt Hall in the *New York Times*, July 14, 1925

"This picture as far as I can make out was made to glorify Flo Ziegfeld and his Follies. The story isn't much and shows that all that glitters is not gold."
Sally Benson in *Picture Play,* October 1925

The Tower of Lies (Metro-Goldwyn—1925)

CREDITS: Director: Victor Seastrom. Based on the novel *The Emperor of Portugallia* by Selma Ottiliana Louisa Lagerlof. Scenario: Agnes Christine Johnston, Max Marcin. Photography: Percy Hilburn. Titles: Marian Ainslee, Ruth Cummings. Film Editor: J. Haden. Art direction: Cedric Gibbons, James Basevi. Running time: 7 Reels. Released October 11, 1925.

CAST: Lon Chaney (Jan), Norma Shearer (Glory), Ian Keith (Lars), Claire McDowell (Katrina), William Haines (August), David Torrence (Eric).

STORY OF THE FILM: On a Scandinavian farm, Jan is an indefatigable worker who toils in the fields from dawn until dusk, content, yet unhappy because there are no children to fulfill his and wife Katrina's life. Finally, Katrina gives birth to a daughter whom they name Glory. The event makes Jan the happiest man in the village and he begins to lavish much affection on the child. Years pass, and Jan's happiness turns to grief when his best friend who had owned the estate on which he works, suddenly dies and the land is threatened by a new landlord, Lars. The latter soon demands that Jan and the other farmers pay three hundred dollars on their property that is due, otherwise they will be faced with eviction. Glory, now grown up, decides to go to the city

to find work in order to save her parents from being driven from their home and eventually she sends the money on time. Glory's long absence, however, has a shattering effect on Jan, who loses his mind, though he is quite harmless, despite the fact that he believes himself to be the emperor of some mythical country. At length, Glory returns to the farm, a woman of means, but one who has fallen from respectability. No sooner does she arrive than she is beset by the townspeople, who brand her as a prostitute. Humiliated, Glory takes the boat back to the city. On board, she finds Lars, who had been annoying her with marriage proposals and for whom she doesn't care. A sudden catastrophe befalls Lars when he gets caught in the paddle wheel of the boat and drowns. Meanwhile, Jan, desperate that Glory is leaving him again, madly pursues her to the boat, loses his footing on the dock and also drowns. Shortly after the tragedy, Glory, having been redeemed, comes back to the farm to stay and she and August, whom she has known since childhood, and who is the late estate owner's son, marry.

CRITICS' VERDICT:

"Lon Chaney's performance as the grief-crazed Jan is one of the most notable of recent screen portraits. He ceases to be a Hollywood actor and really becomes the poor old peasant, the brother of that unforgettable protagonist, Isak, of Growth of the Soil. Perhaps the most impressive portrayal of the cast, however, is contributed by Claire McDowell in the comparatively brief and simple role of the wife of Jan. The grim old woman, as Miss McDowell plays her, seems less the actor and more the actual person portrayed than any player this reviewer has encountered since Gibson Gowland, who had the leading role in *Greed*. Norma Shearer, as the daughter, has a more conventional role than either Miss McDowell or Chaney, but she acts her scenes admirably. Only Ian Keith, as the melodramatic villian, is unbelievable, and for this the role may be almost as guilty as the actor."
Richard Watts, Jr., in *Theatre Magazine*, December 1925.

"This tale has not been properly analyzed on the screen, for Mr. Seastrom and others must have been able to detect its many failings. Miss Shearer is fair in both senses of the word, but she never permits years to cause any change of her bright countenance. Ian Keith, as the successful wooer, is never in need of a haircut or shave. He looks as if he stepped from a Hollywood ballroom floor to the farm fields of Sweden. Claire McDowell gives a really excellent performance as the mother.

"This is a slow-moving long-faced story, in which Lon Chaney often is stiff and exaggerated. His obvious false whiskers, beard and hair, makes his portrayal

The Tower of Lies: *Lon Chaney and Norma Shearer*.

The Tower of Lies: *Lon Chaney and Norma Shearer*.

during some stages, all the more unconvincing.''
Mordaunt Hall in the *New York Times*, September 28,
1925

''Notwithstanding that *The Tower of Lies* is a sincerely made picture and excellent from the artistic and literary viewpoints, it is too heavy for the picture audiences. When finished the impression left is that one more prostitute has reformed and been forgiven.''
Variety, September 30, 1925

''Norma Shearer makes a fine Glory. In the sequence where she returns from the city wealthy in the wages of sin, she is most effective. The transition is well done.''
Herb Cruikshank in *Exhibitor's Trade Review*, October 10, 1925

The Tower of Lies: *Claire McDowell, Lon Chaney, Norma Shearer, and Ian Keith.*

The Tower of Lies: *Ian Keith and Norma Shearer.*

116

The Tower of Lies: *A player and Norma Shearer*.

The Tower of Lies: *Lon Chaney, Norma Shearer, and William Haines*.

The Tower of Lies: *Norma Shearer*.

His Secretary (Metro-Goldwyn—1925)

CREDITS: Director: Hobart Henley. From a story by Carey Wilson. Scenario: Louis D. Lighton, Hope Loring. Photography: Ben Reynolds. Film Editor: Fran Davis. Titles: Joseph W. Farnham. Art direction: Cedric Gibbons, Richard Day. Wardrobe: Clement Andreani. Running time: 7 Reels. Released December 6, 1925.

CAST: Norma Shearer (Ruth Lawrence), Lew Cody (David Colman), Willard Louis (John Sloden), Karl Dane (janitor), Gwen Lee (Clara Bayne), Mabel Van Buren (Mrs. Sloden), Estelle Clark (Minnie), Ernest Gillen (head clerk).

STORY OF THE FILM: As a spinsterish-looking young woman in mannish attire and spectacles who fails to attract the opposite sex, Ruth Lawrence is a highly efficient stenographer. She is secretly in love with David Colman, a junior partner of John Sloden's, whose wife has purposely selected Ruth in order to prevent her husband from flirting and engaging in romantic capers with the more prepossessing stenos he would prefer. One day she visits her spouse at the office and finds him embracing Clara Bayne, his beautiful blonde secretary. Sloden's wife will forgive him on one condition—that he engage Ruth as his secretary and have her accompany him on a business trip to Washington. Sloden agrees, and later says he would not kiss Ruth Lawrence even for a hundred dollars. When Ruth overhears this remark she immediatly goes to a beauty parlor and undergoes a complete transformation from which she emerges looking radiant. To conform with her newly acquired beauty she buys a stunning wardrobe and soon attracts attention from men wherever she happens to be. Sloden of course, does not recognize her, and when David beholds Ruth he instantly falls in love with her. Ruth decides to play a little trick on David and arranges with the building janitor, an unusually tall, slim, though hefty figure, with a homely face to pose as her husband. When David becomes amorous with Ruth she finally confesses that she was the ugly duckling he had always shunned, but she admits her love for him, too.

CRITICS' VERDICT:
"Norma Shearer gives a splendid performance as Ruth Lawrence, the kind of secretary that only the boss's wife could love. Cotton stockings, sensible shoes, pince nez and all. Without any exaggerated make-up, beautiful Miss Shearer looks plain enough to be a movie critic."
Photoplay, February 1926

"Miss Shearer handles the role of the stenographer with a good deal of thought and earnestness. At times she overdoes the pantomime in her gestures and rattling off long speeches with accompanying expressions. Lew Cody is acceptable as the insincere but plausible man about town. Willard Louis who gave such a splendid account of himself as the Prince Regent in the picturization of Beau Brummel, is very funny as the corpulent Sloden. Gwen Lee, who has a good inning as the bobbed blonde, lends to her part a natural ease, and buoyancy. Karl Dane, the tall corporal of The Big Parade, is cast in a somewhat thankless role, in which, however, he proves the resiliency of his features and the expressiveness of his eyes."
Mordaunt Hall in the New York Times, December 21, 1925

"Again we take off our hats to Norma Shearer. In The Lady of the Night she revealed exceptional ability in character roles as a tough and jazzy girl of the underworld. Now, in the MGM picture His Secretary in which she is starred, she adds to her gallery of achievements an even finer performance as a severely plain, unattractive and old-maidish type of stenographer which stands out even more forcibly by contrast with her portrayal of the stylish beautiful girl in the later reels."
Moving Picture World, January 2, 1926

"Norma Shearer's performance in the early part of

His Secretary: Norma Shearer.

His Secretary: *Norma Shearer, Willard Louis, and Lew Cody.*

the picture was particularly effective because she seemed to depend less on make-up than on a complete change of manner. If her beauty ever faded, and may Providence grant that it won't, she could make a good living as an actress of slavey and spinster roles. But pleasure to the eye is ever more important in pictures than appeal to the mind, so Miss Shearer is hereby given my permission to play beautiful roles exclusively.''
Edwin Schallert in the *Los Angeles Sunday Times*, December 27, 1925

His Secretary: *Lew Cody and Norma Shearer.*

His Secretary: *Norma Shearer*.

His Secretary: *Norma Shearer.*

His Secretary: *Norma Shearer.*

The Devil's Circus (Metro-Goldwyn—1926)

CREDITS: Director: Benjamin Christianson. Story and Scenario: Benjamin Christianson. Photography: Ben Reynolds. Running time: 7 reels. Released February 15, 1926.

CAST: Norma Shearer (Mary), Charles Emmett Mack (Richard Carlstop), Carmel Myers (Yonna), John Miljan (Hugo Lieberkind), Claire McDowell (Mrs. Peterson), Joyce Coad (Little Anita), Buddy (The Dog).

STORY OF THE FILM: Mary, a poor, friendless girl, is befriended by Richard Carlstop, a petty criminal whose specialty is picking pockets. Richard gives Mary refuge in his modest abode and offers to care for her. Mary is now in love with her benefactor, but despite his unsavory way of life she has faith in his redemption. The law soon apprehends Richard and he is sentenced to prison. Destitute, Mary joins a circus, and after being trained by Hugo Lieberkind, a lion tamer, she is ready to perform on a trapeze. The act is the most dangerous in the circus, in which a cage is below, full of bloodthirsty lions. Hugo has become interested in Mary, which infuriates Yonna, his jealous wife. During a performance, Yonna cuts the ropes of the trapeze and Mary plunges into a lion's cage breaking both legs, though she miraculously escapes being clawed by the beasts. Crippled by the fall and destitute once again, she is forced to hawk dolls on the street in order to exist. Meanwhile, Richard has won his freedom and has given up his old way of life by finding work as a shoe cobbler. He is reunited with Mary, and when she tells him of her unpleasant experiences with Hugo, Richard seeks out the latter and threatens to shoot him. He hesitates, however, when he sees that Hugo, a casualty of the war, is blind and begging on the streets. Eventually, Mary is able to walk again and she and Richard finally find happiness.

CRITICS' VERDICT:
"As the girl who's a little too good to be true, Norma is incredibly believable. If she makes you believe in this sap heroine, she can make you believe anything. Charles Mack works hard, but I can never decide whether he is impersonating Dick Barthelmess or John Barrymore. Altogether, Mr. Satan's circus isn't as much fun as some I've been to."
Delight Evans in *Screenland,* June 1926

"Miss Shearer does not convince as the country girl become a circus aerialist. The four year jump in the continuity which picks her up as the cripple shows her face as clear and as fresh as before the accident, and the hardships of the war, a fault on somebody's part if realism were the objective. Of the more important

122

The Devil's Circus: *Norma Shearer*.

The Devil's Circus: *Norma Shearer and Charles Emmett Mack*.

members, Miss Myer's playing impresses as the most genuine.''
Variety, December 17, 1924

"Norma Shearer impersonates Mary and she gives a highly creditable performance of the girl who never appears to have a wrong thought, but who was the victim of tragic circumstances. Charles Emmett Mack figures as the young man who finally changes his ways. Mr. Mack is resourceful in stretches that might drag, and during most of his scenes he is restrained. Sometimes his beckoning and calling appears to be a little overdone, but a scene in which he provided breakfast for the homeless Mary is filled with charm.''
Mordaunt Hall in the *New York Times,* March 29, 1926

The Devil's Circus: *Norma Shearer*.

The Devil's Circus: *Norma Shearer and Joyce Coad*.

The Devil's Circus: *John Miljan and Norma Shearer.*

The Devil's Circus: *Carmel Myers, John Miljan, and Norma Shearer.*

The Devil's Circus: *Norma Shearer and Karl Dane.*

The Waning Sex (Metro-Goldwyn—1926)

CREDITS: Director: Robert Z. Leonard. Based on a story by Raymond and Fanny Hatton. Adaptation and continuity: F. Hugh Herbert. Photography: Ben Reynolds. Film editor: William Le Vanway. Titles: Joe Farnham. Art direction: Cedric Gibbons, Paul Youngblood. Wardrobe: Kathleen Kay, Maude Marsh, Clement Andreani. Running time: 7 Reels. Released September 5, 1926.

CAST: Norma Shearer (Nina Duane), Conrad Nagel (Philip Barry), George K. Arthur (Hamilton Day), Mary McAllister (Mary Booth), Charles McHugh (J.J. Flannigan), Tiny Ward (J.J. Murphy), Martha Mattox (Ellen B. Armstrong).

STORY OF THE FILM: Nina Duane is a clever young lawyer competing with District Attorney Philip Barry in a larceny case, as well as competing in a race for the district attorney's office herself. Philip, however, has never particularly sanctioned women as members of

the bar, but despite his professional differences he is smitten by Nina's beauty and vivacity and asks her to go with him to a dinner party. There, Mary Booth, a flighty widow, inflicts herself on Philip with whom she is infatuated. This amuses Nina very much, and when she visits her colleague's summer home she purposely follows suit where Mary's amours are concerned for the benefit of Philip.

Nina defeats Philip in court, but he triumphs over her in a swimming contest. Mary continues to pursue Philip and again invites him to dinner. Nina is also present that evening and is further amused at Philip's predicament with Mary in trying to make a hasty retreat from her when she becomes too impulsive. The situation becomes even more embarrassing after Mary accidentally spills coffee on Philip's trousers, and as he tries to escape, she feigns a fainting spell. Frantic and embarrassed, and wondering what to do next, Philip suddenly picks up Mary and locks her in a closet. He finally gets away by putting on a pair of pants belonging to Mary's brother. Nina, so as to humiliate Philip more, hides

The Waning Sex: *Norma Shearer*.

Philip's trousers. Later, she denounces Mary for the schemer she is and saves her young brother from a similar fate. Philip forgives Nina and she resigns from her law practice to marry him.

CRITICS' VERDICT:

"Is woman's place in the home or in business? The young district attorney thinks babies are the thing. The pretty lady lawyer thinks different. Since Norma Shearer is the fair Portia the problem becomes darned acute to us. Particularly as Miss Shearer demonstrates gracefully that the modern woman's place is in the one-piece bathing suit. This is pleasant entertainment, proving again Miss Shearer's aptitude for character comedy. Conrad Nagel is the D.A."
Photoplay, December 1926

"A nice picture comedy, *The Waning Sex* made nice and nicer by Norma Shearer. This fresh-looking girl who plays with charm, does a great deal for a picture that has its laugh punches. The film might not stand up so well without this girl, despite the excellent direction by Robert Z. Leonard.

"Conrad Nagel, co-featured, gives a luke-warm performance in a wavering characterization. To plant a domineering point, at the finish, Mr. Nagel wavered continuously."
Variety, September 1, 1926

"Norma Shearer, looking if anything more attractive than ever, does extremely well with the role of Nina. She is evidently a clever swimmer, even though she has not had time to tackle the English channel, and her bathing costume, worn under a frock, is bound to find favor in both masculine and feminine eyes. It is set off with a Turban which does not detract from her good looks, even if it covers her fair hair. The role of Philip is well handled by Conrad Nagel whose talent is unsuited to this style of narrative."
Mordaunt Hall in the *New York Times,* September 21, 1926.

127

The Waning Sex: *Norma Shearer and George K. Arthur*.

The Waning Sex: *Conrad Nagel and Norma Shearer*.

128

The Waning Sex: *Norma Shearer.*

The Waning Sex: *Norma Shearer.*

Upstage (Metro-Goldwyn—1926)

CREDITS: Director: Monta Bell. Original story and scenario: Lorna Moon. Photography: Gaetano Gaudio. Film editor: Frank Sullivan. Assistant film editor: Nick Grinde. Titles: Joe Farnham. Art direction: Cedric Gibbons, Arnold Gillespie. Wardrobe: Kathleen Kay, Maude Marsh, Clement Andreani. Running time: 7 Reels. Released November 7, 1926.

CAST: Norma Shearer (Dolly Haven), Oscar Shaw (Johnny Storm), Tenen Holtz (Sam Davis), Gwen Lee (Dixie Mason), Dorothy Philips (Miss Weaver), J. Frank Glendon (Mr. Weaver), Ward Crane (Wallace King), Charles Meadin (stage manager).

STORY OF THE FILM: Dolly Haven is an attractive, small-town girl with a college degree who comes to New York hopeful of entering the business world as a stenographer, having taken a special course back home She goes to a theatrical agency operated by Sam Davis to apply for a stenog's position, and there meets Johnny Storm, a vaudevillian whom she mistakes for Davis.

Impressed by Dolly's beauty and simplicity, he offers to engage her for his act. Also, Johnny soon learns that Dolly was the winner of a Charleston contest in her home town, which impresses him all the more. Johnny is responsbile for the success of the act, though Dolly is audacious enough to think that she put the show over. As a result, another performer, Wallace King, signs Dolly for his act, while Johnny replaces his former partner with Dixie Mason, a fetching blonde. Success changes Dolly and she becomes egotistical and demanding. Later, Dolly, as a chorus girl, is booked into a theater with Johnny. On the bill is a knife-throwing act in which the parents involved look forward to having their child with them for Christmas. The youngster, who is sitting in the balcony, accidentally falls over the railing and is fatally injured. At that moment, the child's mother is standing against the knife board, while her husband is throwing knives around her. When the mother, Mrs. Weaver, sees the inert form of her child, she disrupts the act and rushes off the stage. Dolly instantly takes her place and emerges unscathed as the target. Johnny, frantic, rushes to her as the curtain falls and promises never to leave her.

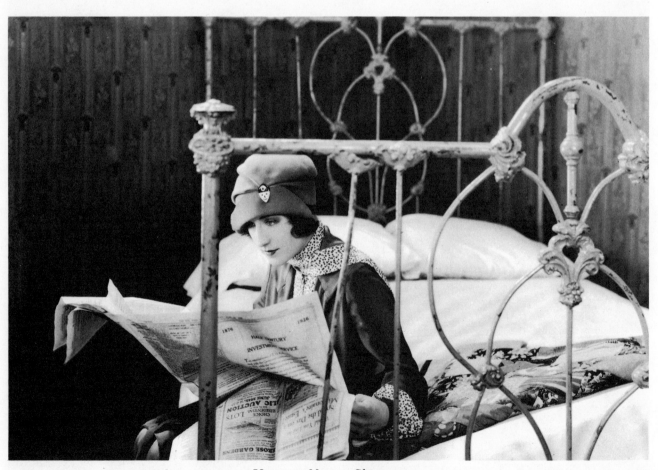

Upstage: *Norma Shearer.*

Upstage: *Oscar Shaw and Norma Shearer.*

CRITICS' VERDICT:

"The uneveness of this photoplay is surprising for it was directed by Monta Bell, who, in the unfurling of screen narratives, has matched his wits against the best producers, and curiously enough, it is occasionally the skipping of necessary detail that excuses an episode to be almost ridiculous. As Norma Shearer and Oscar Shaw render an excellent account of themselves, the falsity of some of the doings of the characters they impersonate, falls upon Mr. Bell's shoulders."

Mordaunt Hall in the *New York Times,* November 15, 1926

"Oscar Shaw is human, appealing, convincing. And we all know Norma. She is particularly good in these impersonations of a stage, circus or vaudeville girl. There is considerable drama, a great many deft touches, reality and compassion. You will have an enjoyable hour or so, guaranteed."
Gladys Hall in *Motion Picture,* February 1927

Upstage: *Oscar Shaw, Norma Shearer, and Ward Crane*.

Upstage: *Norma Shearer*.

The Demi-Bride (Metro-Goldwyn-Mayer—1927)

CREDITS: Director: Robert Z. Leonard. Story and continuity: F. Hugh Herbert, Florence Ryerson. Photography: Percy Hilburn. Film editor: William Le Vanway. Titles: Paul Perez, Terrence Daugherty. Art direction: Cedric Gibbons, Arnold Gillespie. Wardrobe: Clement Andreani. Running time: 7 Reels. Released February 19, 1927.

CAST: Norma Shearer (Criquette), Lew Cody (Philippe Levaux), Lionel Belmore (Monsieur Girard), Tenen Holtz (Gaston), Carmel Myers (Madame Girard), Dorothy Sebastian (Lola), Nora Cecil (School-teacher).

STORY OF THE FILM: Criquette is a French teenager attending convent school who is hungry for life and yearns for a relationship with a man. A saucy young-ster, yet engaging enough to attract men, she decides to pursue Philippe Levaux, a wealthy Parisian who has been having an affair with her stepmother, Madame Girard. Criquette, despite her age, is surprisingly sophisticated and employs all her feminine wiles to entice Philippe into marriage. At first, the boulevardier regards her indifferently and finds her rather obnoxi-ous, but eventually he discovers that he cannot resist her, with Criquette achieving her objective as his wife.

Lola, an ex-sweetheart of Philippe's, visits his apartment one evening, and after having too much to drink, she settles down in Philippe's boudoir for the night. Gaston, Philippe's faithful valet, upon finding Lola in his master's bed, is shocked at the woman's indiscreet behavior and tries to get rid of her. Secretly, he informs Philippe of Lola's presence, but the former is so in love with Criquette that he overlooks Lola's intrusion and forgives her.

CRITICS' VERDICT:
"A very lively French farce has been directed by Robert Z. Leonard with a sure hand, and a humorous eye, which rests not only on each separate scene, but always sees straight through to the end of the picture."

The Demi-Bride: *Norma Shearer and Tenen Holtz.*

The Demi-Bride: *Norma Shearer*.

Which is no ordinary achievement in the handling of these flippant complexities. Each scene is very nicely turned, and the whole is original, utterly ridiculous, and highly entertaining. It's about a not at all timorous little French girl of fourteen or thereabouts who sees what she wants of life over the convent wall, and proceeds to vault. Lew Cody is the unhappy aim of her existence, and he hasn't a chance against the relentless tactics she employs. Norma Shearer makes of this simpering infant as objectionable a child as we've met since Little Mildred. Her performance is clever, consistent, and delightful. Lew Cody's version of the ultra sophisticated Frenchman is rather apathetic, but he gets his effect. It's worth seeing.''
Motion Picture, June 1927

"Norma Shearer's latest starring vehicle, which has set forth on its career under the title of *The Demi-Bride*, is a picture that will not bore anyone with its weight, for it is fare that is decidedly light. There are any number of uproariously funny situations, merged with a story that moves along swiftly and maintains a fine suspense.

"I will not say that it will rank among the more important of Miss Shearer's achievements. It is hardly comparable, for example to *Upstage* and *He Who Gets Slapped*, but it is infinitely superior as entertainment to several of her other efforts.''
Herbert Moulton in the *Los Angels Times,* February 12, 1927

"Despite the box-office draft of the star, Norma Shearer, *The Demi-Bride* is a tedious picture, and all told, just fair.''
Variety, March 23, 1927

The Demi-Bride: *Norma Shearer.*

The Demi-Bride: *Nora Cecil and Norma Shearer*.

The Demi-Bride: *Norma Shearer and Lew Cody*.

The Demi-Bride: *Lew Cody, Norma Shearer, and Dorothy Sebastian*.

After Midnight (Metro-Goldwyn-Mayer—1927)

CREDITS: Director: Monta Bell. Original story: Monta Bell. Scenario: Lorna Moon. Photography: Percy Hilburn. Film Editor: Blanche Sewell. Titles: Joe Farnham. Sets: Cedric Gibbons, Richard Day. Wardrobe: Rene Hubert. Running time: 7 Reels. Released August 20, 1927.

CAST: Norma Shearer (Mary), Lawrence Gray (Joe Miller), Gwen Lee (Maizie), Eddie Sturgis (Red Smith), Philip Sleeman (Gus Van Gundy).

STORY OF THE FILM: Mary and her sister Maizie work together in a night club. Mary sells cigarettes there, while Maizie is a dancer in the chorus who is interested only in having good times and a lot of money which she tries to procure by exerting her charms on the patrons. Mary is the reverse, hard working and sober minded, yet, with a desire for luxuries herself. On the way home from work one night, she is accosted by a young man who tries to sell her a lead pipe for ten dollars. Mary is rather puzzled by this approach, but is not interested in buying the object for which she certainly has no use. The man, who is good-looking and appears intelligent, warns Mary that if she doesn't give him the money she may be harmed. Mary finally yields and takes the pipe. While the robber is counting the money, Mary comes up behind him and brings the weapon down on his head, which renders him unconscious. Fearful that she might have killed him, she helps him up to her room and gives him first aid by sponging his head. After the man regains consciousness Mary learns that his name is Joe Miller, a habitual and petty criminal. Despite Joe's unsavory past, Mary has faith in his redemption and persuades him to reform. Joe has fallen in love with Mary and they decide to get married. Mary deprives herself of many things and eventually accumulates sufficient capital to buy a one thousand

After Midnight: *Gwen Lee and Norma Shearer.*

After Midnight: *Lawrence Gray and Norma Shearer.*

dollar liberty bond, while Joe saves to buy a cab. Oddly enough, Maizie also comes in possession of a liberty bond not unlike Mary's which has been given to her while at a party and which she brings home. Mary, feeling that the efforts have been to no avail, impulsively cashes her bond and spends it on elegant clothes, which she wears to a party she has been invited to. She sees Joe there drinking with her friends and gets drunk. Maizie drives her sister home in a car borrowed from a friend, and during the ride, Mary, who is sitting beside Maizie, begins tampering with the wheel. Maizie loses control of the vehicle and is killed when it swerves over an embankment. Realizing how much at fault they have been, Mary and Joe decide to make a fresh start.

CRITICS' VERDICT:

"In some of the intimate scenes of the two sisters, Mr. Bell manifests a tendency to emulate Erich Von Stroheim and you are constantly made aware that cabaret girls must have silk stockings.

"Norma Shearer takes her role seriously and gives a really fine performance. Lawrence Gray does the best work of his screen career as Joe, and Gwen Lee is capital as the giddy Maizie. This all means that a lot of talent is wasted on a childish yarn."
Mordaunt Hall in the *New York Times*, August 16, 1927

"Norma Shearer plays well, hurt now and then by unflattering photography. Miss Lee, the wild sister, is highly convincing. The ex-crook is handled by Lawrence Gray suitably."
Variety, August 17, 1927

"Monta Bell wrote this around a real cigarette girl in a Hollywood restaurant. Then he directed it with Norma Shearer as the young woman. The story, however, is the old yarn of the heroine who, dazzled by money, is about to slip from the straight and narrow path. This time her sister is killed after a drunken party and everyone reforms. Not worthy of Miss Shearer and Mr. Bell. Mediocre stuff."
Photoplay, October 1927

After Midnight: *Norma Shearer and Gwen Lee.*

After Midnight: *Monta Bell and Norma Shearer on the set.*

After Midnight: *Norma Shearer and Gwen Lee.*

The Student Prince (Metro-Goldwyn-Mayer—1927)

CREDITS: Director: Ernst Lubitsch. Based on Wilhelm Meyer Forster's *Old Heidelberg* and the musical play *The Student Prince*, by Dorothy Donnelly and Sigmund Romberg. Scenario: Hans Kraly. Photography: John Mescall. Film editor: Andrew Martin. Titles: Marian Ainslee, Ruth Cummings. Art direction: Cedric Gibbons, Richard Day. Musical score: David Mendoza, William Axt. Wardrobe: Ali Herbert, Eric Locke. Running time: 10 Reels. Released September 21, 1927.

CAST: Ramon Novarro (Prince Karl Heinrich), Norma Shearer (Kathie), Jean Hersholt (Dr. Juttner), Gustave Von Seyffertitz (King Karl VII), Philippe De Lacy (Heir Apparent), Edgar Norton (Lutz), Bobby Mack (Kellerman), Edward Connelly (Court Marshal), Otis Harlan (Old Ruder), John S. Peters, George K. Arthur (students). Others: Edythe Chapman, Lionel Belmore, Lincoln Steadman.

STORY OF THE FILM: As a royal subject, Prince Karl Heinrich envies the peasantry because they are not restricted by protocol as he is. He yearns to be a part of the masses, to indulge in their fancies, be it sports, drinking beer, or carousing in general, but his freedom is limited, which makes him very unhappy. An old tutor of Prince Karl's, Dr. Juttner, visits him one day and Karl soon forgets his melancholia. Professor Juttner is a warm, simple, and understanding person whose friendship Karl has valued as well as his teachings. Realizing his former student's inhibitions and his dire need for companionship, Dr. Juttner arranges for the young prince to study at the University of Heidelberg, where he will be happier than under the regime of the palace. At an inn frequented by the students, Karl meets Kathie, a barmaid in her father's hostel. Almost

The Student Prince: *Ramon Novarro and Norma Shearer.*

is one who does not choose to repeat on any of his past bright camera ideas. Yet the satirical shafts, the careful attention to telling details, the half-second notes and the keeping within certain bounds, inform the spectator, even though the name of Lubitsch were not emblazoned on the screen, that it is the master from Berlin who has directed this splendid shadow story.

"Ramon Novarro acts the part of the prince after he has reached the University student age. Mr. Novarro is natural and earnest, but a little too Latin in appearance for the role. Norma Shearer is attractive as Kathie. She, however, does not seem to put her soul into the part. She, too, acts very well, but like Mr. Novarro she does not respond as other players have done to Mr. Lubitsch's direction. The ablest acting in this piece of work is done by Jean Hersholt as Doctor Juttner and Gustave Von Seyffertitz as the King. Their efforts in all their scenes reveal their sensitiveness to the direction. Bobby Mack is capital as Kellerman and Edgar Norton gives a fine character study as Lutz, the smileless and haughty servant."
Mordaunt Hall in the *New York Times*, September 22, 1927

"Ernst Lubitsch gets the very best out of his company. Ramon Novarro has a fine part as Prince Karl Heinrich and fills it with a charming sincerity. Norma

immediately they are in love, and for the first time in his life Karl is genuinely happy. He also wins the students over and becomes the most popular at the university, fraternizing with them daily and participating in everything he had always wanted to. But above all, Kathie has become the most precious in his life.

Prince Karl's new found happiness, alas, is short lived when news comes of King Karl's sudden death and the prince is forced to return to the palace to occupy the throne of the late monarch. Now, lonelier than ever, Karl cannot forget Kathie, even though he is to wed a princess he does not love. When the young king returns to Heidelberg for a visit, he finds the once carefree atmosphere completely changed. The students, who had hoisted him on their shoulders as a token of affection, now salute their former colleague, which pains Karl, since becoming a ruler has not lessened his democratic tendencies. He is further saddened upon learning that Dr. Juttner has died, but when he sees Kathie again he momentarily forgets how sad he feels. She is the only one who still accepts him as her equal, and for a little while the two lovers relive the old days—then they part, never to see each other again.
CRITICS' VERDICT:

"In this new offering, Mr. Lubitsch lives up to all that has been written about him. He may be a stylist, but he

The Student Prince: *Norma Shearer.*

141

Shearer is a graceful, tender Kathie; and if the Dr. Juttner is rather younger than we remember his predecessors to have been, he has lost none of his loveableness in the hands of Jean Hersholt. The careful casting and perfect acting of every part, down to the very smallest, give a fine finish to this wholly attractive film.''
Michael Orme in the *Illustrated London News*, February 18, 1928

''This is the best work that Ramon Novarro has ever done. It is comparable with the best work that any one has ever done on the screen. Norma Shearer as the girl gives a performance that is excellent at times, and at other times, a trifle laborious. Jean Hersholt, of course, is perfect.''
Robert E. Sherwood in *Life* magazine, October 13, 1927

The Student Prince: *Norma Shearer.*

The Student Prince: *Ramon Novarro and Norma Shearer.*

The Student Prince: *Norma Shearer and Ramon Novarro.*

The Student Prince: *Norma Shearer and Jean Hersholt.*

The Student Prince: *Ramon Novarro, Norma Shearer, and Jean Hersholt.*

The Latest from Paris (Metro-Goldwyn-Mayer—1928)

CREDITS: Director: Sam Wood. Original story and scenario: A.P. Younger. Photography: William Daniels. Film editor: Basil Wrangell. Titles: Joe Farnham. Art direction: Cedric Gibbons, Arnold Gillespie. Running time: 8 Reels. Released February 4, 1928.

CAST: Norma Shearer (Ann Dolan), George Sidney (Sol Blogg), Ralph Forbes (Joe Adams), Tenen Holtz (Abe Littauer), William Badewell (Bud Dolan), Margaret Landis (Louise Martin), Bert Roach (Bert Blevins).

STORY OF THE FILM: Ann Dolan, a traveling saleslady, is engaged to Joe Adams, another sales executive, despite their business rivalry. Ann, with her remarkable acumen for closing a deal, has always managed to outsell Joe in men's apparel, in addition to fostering her young brother Bud's education at the same time. Joe resents his fiancée paying her brother's way through college and that she must continue to work because of these obligations. Following a quarrel, Ann and Joe break off their engagement and Joe soon becomes attentive to Louise Martin, the daughter of a merchant. When Ann's brother decides that he will now provide

The Latest from Paris: *Norma Shearer.*

The Latest from Paris: *William Bakewell and Norma Shearer.*

for himself and get married, Ann and Joe are happily reunited.

CRITICS' VERDICT:
"A title like *The Latest from Paris* leads one to expect an adventure concerned chiefly with diaphanous periphery. This new Capitol presentation is nothing of the sort, for it is a sketchy idea of a romance between Ann Dolan and Joe Adams, both commercial travelers, who appear to spend most of their time in a place called Summerville.

"Norma Shearer does her best to make her part interesting, and Ralph Forbes, efficient actor though he is, obviously cannot fathom the weird character alloted to him. George Sidney and Tenen Holtz have little opportunity to live up to their natural talents as comedians."
Mordaunt Hall in the *New York Times*, February 27, 1928

"Norma Shearer is ideally cast as Mary Dolan, imparting to the role much sparkle and zest. She appears to advantage, too, in smart tailored clothes.

"Ralph Forbes is excellent as the rival salesman and lover. It is a new type of role for him, appearing as a typical American gogetter. He displays a good sense of comedy."
Marquis Busby in the *Los Angeles Times*, January 27, 1928

The Latest from Paris: *Norma Shearer and Ralph Forbes*.

"Light comedy of no particular importance but with the Norma Shearer name and enough laughs to see it through for program purposes. Productionally the picture doesn't fulfill what the title promotes. Miss Shearer, however looks good all the way, gets a chance to be kittenish here and there and does well with the assignment as a whole. Looks like a good matinee film."
Variety, February 29, 1928

The Latest from Paris: *Ralph Forbes and Norma Shearer.*

The Latest from Paris: *Norma Shearer and Ralph Forbes.*

The Actress (Metro-Goldwyn-Mayer—1928)

CREDITS: Director: Sidney Franklin. Based on Sir Arthur Wing Pinero's *Trelawney of the Wells*. Scenario: Albert Lewin, Richard Schayer. Photography: William Daniels. Film editor: Conrad V. Nervig. Assistant director: Hugh Boswell. Titles: Joe Farnham. Art director: Cedric Gibbons. Wardrobe: Gilbert Clark. Running time: 7 Reels. Released April 28, 1928.

CAST: In the theatrical scenes: Norma Shearer (Rose Trelawney), Owen Moore (Tom Wrench), Gwen Lee (Avonia), Lee Moran (Colpoys), Roy D'Arcy (Gadd), Virginia Pearson (Mrs. Telfer), William Humphrey (Mr. Telfer), Effie Ellsler (Mrs. Mossop). Nontheatrical: Ralph Forbes (Sir Arthur Gower), O.P. Heggie (Vice Chancellor Sir William Gower), Andree Tourneur (Clare De Foenix), Cyril Chadwick (Captain De Foenix), Margaret Seddon (Mrs. Trafalger Gower).

STORY OF THE FILM: The action of the story takes place during the Victorian era. Rose Trelawney, a popular and well-known actress of the day, falls in love with Sir Arthur Gower, an aristocrat, and marries him. Sir William Gower frowns upon his grandson's choice of a commoner, as do Sir Arthur's parents when he introduces his wife to them. They receive her coldly, in addition to making some rather unflattering remarks about Rose's associates in the theater. Having given up the stage for domesticity, Rose soon returns to it, bitter over her in-laws' disapproval of her. This prompts Sir Arthur also to leave and he goes to the theater where Rose is appearing and is cast in the same play. Un-

147

known to both Rose and Sir Arthur, Sir William has a change of heart and finances the production. Rose is also unaware that her husband, of all people, turns out to be her leading man. The play is successful and Rose is finally accepted by the Gower family.

CRITICS' VERDICT:

"*The Actress* is a pleasant little dream for a July evening, a bit sentimental—but having no worrying problems. Miss Shearer plays her part acceptably, even though in one or two spots, she has a tendency to overact."
Mordaunt Hall in the *New York Times,* July 9, 1928

"Though Pinero's brilliant stage production contains a large supply of dramatic and humorous situations transferable to the screen for all of their value, the directorial head of this screen effort has not realized on the possibilities to the fullest extent. As a result, with Norma Shearer unattractive in the early parts of the picture owing to the strange makeup and camera treatment which sharpens and ages her features, the picture cannot be rated a strong draw generally, despite the prominence of the the star, though it should do moderate business in most cases.

"In this house [Capitol Theatre in New York] Miss Shearer's efforts as a comedienne met with light but noticeable returns. It is doubtful if all other audiences will respond even to that extent."
Variety, July 11, 1928

The Actress: *Ralph Forbes and Norma Shearer.*

The Actress: *Norma Shearer and Owen Moore.*

The Actress: *Lee Moran, Roy D'Arcy, Owen Moore, Norma Shearer, and Gwen Lee.*

149

The Actress: *O.P. Heggie and Norma Shearer.*

The Actress: *Owen Moore and Norma Shearer.*

The Actress: *Norma Shearer and Ralph Forbes.*

The Actress: *Norma Shearer and Ralph Forbes.*

A Lady of Chance (Metro-Goldwyn-Mayer—1928-29)

CREDITS: Director: Hobart Henley. Story and dialogue: John Lee Meehan (Talking sequences). Adaptation: Edmund Scott. Photography: Peverell Marley, William Daniels. Film editor: Margaret Booth. Titles: Ralph Spence. Art director: Cedric Gibbons. Gowns: Adrian. Running time: 8 Reels. Released December 1, 1928.

CAST: Norma Shearer (Dolly), Lowell Sherman (Bradley), Gwen Lee (Gwen), John Mack Brown (Steve Crandall), Eugenie Besserer (Mrs. Crandall), Buddy Messinger (Hank).

STORY OF THE FILM: Dolly, better known as "Angel Face," is a notorious blackmailer who victimizes wealthy men by fleecing them out of their capi-tal. Her partners in crime are Bradley, a smooth confidence man, and Gwen, a curvaceous blonde who also knows how to entice unsuspecting victims. One day, Dolly meets Steve Crandall, on whom she excercises her charms. He, of course, cannot resist her either. Believing him to be rich, Dolly marries Steve, but she is sorely disappointed when she finds that he does not reside in a mansion as she thought. Although Steve and his mother live on an estate, they are merely tenants and occupy a rather modest dwelling. Steve happens to be an inventor who is trying to market a cement gimmick, but each time he enthuses over the project, Dolly seems disinterested. He has already fallen in love with her and Dolly is beginning to feel the same way about Steve, yet she is not quite certain that she is in love with him. When Bradley and Gwen learn of Dolly's marriage, they proceed to blackmail her, claiming she owes them a huge sum of money that was actually her cut of the haul. Realizing now that she loves Steve, Dolly returns several thousand dollars to her former associates, having decided to go straight. Finally, Steve receives a lucrative offer for his invention, while Dolly is apprehended and goes back to the reformatory where she had once served time. She is eventually paroled in Steve's custody.

CRITICS' VERDICT:

"Considering her luckless part, Miss Shearer does exceedingly well. As her type of beauty is essentially classical, it cannot be said that she is suitably cast. John Mack Brown is acceptable as Steve. Lowell Sherman's arting of the unscrupulous Bradley is capital."

Mordaunt-Hall in the *New York Times*, January 14, 1929.

"Picture hasn't any action, but extracts some spasmodic good moments from Miss Shearer, who is backed by the smooth working Sherman in a role that is a pushover for him. Brown fits on appearance, wearing a gold football for those who remember, but isn't a heavyweight on histrionics here. Trying to see it from the balcony angle there's not much doubt that Miss Shearer holds this release together. Dolly may be the girl the Flossies like to think they are. If it's anything else, supply your own six letter word."
Variety, January 16, 1929

A Lady of Chance: *Norma Shearer and John Mack Brown.*

153

A Lady of Chance: *Norma Shearer*.

A Lady of Chance: *Lowell Sherman, Gwen Lee, and Norma Shearer*.

A Lady of Chance: *Norma Shearer and Lowell Sherman.*

A Lady of Chance: *Norma Shearer and Gwen Lee.*

The Trial of Mary Dugan
(Metro-Goldwyn-Mayer—1929)

CREDITS: Director: Bayard Veiller (based on his play of the same name). Scenario: Becky Gardner: Photography: William Daniels. Art director: Cedric Gibbons. Film editor: Blanche Sewell. Recording engineers: J.K. Brock, Douglas Shearer. Gowns: Adrian. Running time: 120 mins. Released June 8, 1929.

CAST: Norma Shearer (Mary Dugan), Lewis Stone (Edward West), H.B. Warner (District Attorney Galway), Raymond Hackett (Jimmy Dugan), Lilyan Tashman (Dagmar Lorne), Olive Tell (Mrs. Edgar Rice), Adrian D'Ambricourt (Marie Ducrot), De Witt Jennings (Police Inspector Hunt), Wilfred North (Judge Nash), Landers Stevens (Dr. Welcome), Mary Doran (Pauline Agguerro), Westcott B. Clarke (Police Captain Price), Charles Moore (James Madison), Myra Hampton (May Harris).

STORY OF THE FILM: Mary Dugan, a Broadway show girl, who has been the mistress of a wealthy playboy, is accused of knifing him to death and goes on trial for murder. The man defending Mary is Edward West, who is also a friend of hers, but he virtually refuses to cross examine his witness, which infuriates Mary's young brother, Jimmy, a rising young lawyer. West suddenly decides to withdraw from the case and Jimmy resumes the defense of his sister. In the course of the trial it is revealed that Mary had been the kept woman of several men, so she could acquire sufficient capital for her brother's law education. The trial reaches a climax when Jimmy proves Mary's innocence

The Trial of Mary Dugan: *De Witt Jennings and Norma Shearer.*

156

The Trial of Mary Dugan: *A player, Raymond Hackett,
Wilfred North, and Norma Shearer.*

by his denunciation of West as the murderer and Mary
is acquitted.

CRITICS' VERDICT:
"This film sustained the interest of the audience,
even those who had witnessed Al Woods' clever stage
production, and Miss Shearer gives a performance in
which she reveals herself quite able to meet the requirements of that temperamental device—the microphone."
Mordaunt Hall in the *New York Times*, August 12, 1929

"Norma Shearer, the waxy, ephemeral beauty of a
score of light romances of the screen, invests Bayard
Veiller's skillful lines with a tragic power that frankly
astounded this observer. No cheap histrionics for
her—no spurious assumption of virtue. All in all, we are
prepared to say the *The Trial of Mary Dugan* is the best
talking picture so far made. Perhaps next week there

will be a better one, at the rate they're going, but right
now the best extant, and we felicitate Miss Shearer, Mr.
Veiller and the MGM company, and vote them the
diamond studded microphone with platinum trim-
mings."
A.M. Sherwood Jr. in *Outlook*, April 17, 1929

"Norma Shearer is the young woman known as
Mona Tree who has been loved often and has loved but
once. It is the same Shearer we have been seeing on the
silent screen. She wisely economizes on words in her
debut and she takes for herself a role, at the same time,
that limits her use of gowns and jewels of splendor.
Shearer works hard in her role and she is determined to
put it across."
Douglas Hodges in the *Exhibitor's Herald*, April 27,
1929

"For Norma Shearer the picture is a vindication and

The Trial of Mary Dugan: *Norma Shearer and players*.

a triumph, the former because it validates her claim to stardom in the minds of some of us for the first time, and the latter because in her first talking picture she skillfully combines the technique of both stage and screen and emerges as a definitely compelling actress of greater individuality than she ever revealed in silent pictures.

"Miss Shearer's voice is an extremely natural rather than an elocutionary one, yet it is as expressive as if it had been cultivated to the last degree. From now on she must be recognized as a leader on the audible screen, whose pictures will be awaited with keenest interest." Norbert Lusk in the *Los Angeles Times,* April 7, 1929

"Norma Shearer is the first lady of the talkies. She proves it in *The Trial of Mary Dugan.* With no stage training to give her confidence, Miss Shearer steps quietly into a most difficult role and she handles it like a veteran. Her poise, her voice, her artistry eclipse many actors of long standing. She is truly superb." Delight Evans in *Screenland,* June, 1929

The Last of Mrs. Cheyney (Metro-Goldwyn-Mayer—1929)

CREDITS: Director: Sidney Franklin. Based on the play by Frederick Lonsdale. Scenario: Hans Kraly, Claudine West. Photography: William Daniels. Art director: Cedric Gibbons. Film editor: Conrad V. Nervig. Sound recording: G.A. Burns, Douglas Shearer. Titles: Lucille Newmark. Gowns: Adrian. Running time: 100 mins. Released June 6, 1929.

CAST: Norma Shearer (Mrs. Cheyney), Basil Rathbone (Lord Arthur Dilling), George Barraud (Charles), Herbert Bunston (Lord Elton), Hedda Hopper (Lady Maria), Moon Carroll (Joan), Madeline Seymour (Mrs. Wynton), Cyril Chadwick (Willie Wynton), Maude Turner Gordon (Mrs. Webley), George K. Arthur (Finch Smiles).

STORY OF THE FILM: An adventuress in the grand manner, Mrs. Fay Cheyney, an attractive and vivacious Englishwoman, has been masquerading as a wealthy Australian widow on the continent where her base of operations is Monte Carlo. It seems to be the ideal place to fleece her victims, whether at the gaming tables, or at an elegant hotel, and she soon cultivates the friendship of Mrs. Webley, a wealthy dowager, whose valuable pearl necklace she is after. Despite Mrs. Cheyney's criminal tendencies, she has fallen in love with Lord Arthur Dilling, Mrs. Webley's nephew. As the titled lady she poses as, her retinue includes Charles, a suave, dark young man who engineers the thefts, and a group of other men, all of whom she usually installs as her servants wherever she happens to

The Last of Mrs. Cheyney: *Basil Rathbone and Norma Shearer.*

The Last of Mrs. Cheyney: *Norma Shearer and Basil Rathbone.*

CRITICS' VERDICT:

"The role of Mrs. Cheyney is no mere scenarist's confection. It is strict, precise, exacting. The manner is difficult, the method is more so, the characterization is almost too perfect, by script to admit of perfect portrayal. Yet, perfect portrayal is what Miss Shearer gives it. If you will understand what I mean I say I did not recognize the principal, as Miss Shearer, only as Mrs. Cheyney. Then I will say it. I did not. For Miss Shearer, in my mind as no doubt in yours, is an excellent motion picture actress; whereas Mrs. Cheyney at the Chicago Theatre is an English lady (I seem to be getting a bit diffuse in all this, but I think you are receiving me)."
T.O. Service in *Exhibitor's Herald-World,* July 13, 1929.

"In the portrayals, Miss Shearer averaged well. She evidences a more precise expressiveness facially than she does vocally, and some of her very best scenes are the silent ones. Nevertheless, she measures very well to the majority of the role's requirements, the crispness of her voice being well suited to the repartee portions. She is exceedingly attractive in the role."
Edwin Schallert in the *Los Angeles Times,* July 13, 1929

stop. Having won the unsuspecting Mrs. Webley over with her charm, Mrs. Cheyney becomes a member of London society and is invited to spend the weekend at the matron's country estate. While a guest there she plans to rob the woman of her precious jewel and vacate the premises by dawn with her gang. One night, Lord Dilling catches Mrs. Cheyney with the necklace, which she has just removed from a safe. To Lord Dilling, Mrs. Cheyney has never appeared so radiant and intriguing, which prompts him to make a pass at her. She resists his advances and Dilling threatens to call the police unless she submits to them. Not entirely without principals, Mrs. Cheyney decides to expose herself by confessing the theft to all the guests, whom she asks to be present in her room, leaving them to be judge and jury. After deliberating the matter they find they have no alternative but to call Scotland Yard. At this point, Lord Elton, who is also in love with Mrs. Cheyney, prevents the arrest when he mentions to the group that the former possesses a love letter he had once written to her which could be a source of embarrassment to all concerned if the contents were divulged. The guests then decide to settle a large sum of money on her, but Mrs. Cheyney destroys both the letter and the check that had been made out to her. It is "The Last of Mrs. Cheyney," and she is welcomed back into society as the future Lady Dilling.

The Last of Mrs. Cheyney: *Basil Rathbone, Norma Shearer, and George Barraud.*

"Miss Shearer's work is remarkably good. She talks charmingly and of course, she is goodlooking. The speaking likeness of Mrs. Cheyney makes that resourceful woman of the world a thoroughly engaging person, clever and almost Wildean in her stinging comments to her society companions."
Mordaunt Hall in the *New York Times*, August 12, 1929

"Seriously, *The Last of Mrs. Cheyney* is a praiseworthy entertainment. Norma Shearer is superb as the young lady crook who decides to go straight when she meets Lord Dilling (Basil Rathbone). As for Mr. Rathbone—if I tell you that he is a sort of composite talking picture of John Gilbert and Ronald Colman you may have a faint idea of what to expect. I hope he is here to stay. George Barraud is excellent, and Hedda Hopper lends glamour to the scene. Watson, you may serve the applause."
Delight Evans in *Screenland*, October 1929

The Hollywood Revue (Metro-Goldwyn-Mayer—1929)

CREDITS: Director: Charles Reisner. Dialogue: Al Boasberg, Robert E. Hopkins. Skit: Joe Farnham. Photography: John Arnold, Irving G. Ries, Maxmillian Fabian, John M. Nickolaus. Art directors: Cedric Gibbons, Richard Day. Film editors: William S. Gray, Cameron K. Woods. Songs: "Singin' in the Rain," "You Were Meant For Me," "Tommy Atkins on Parade," by Arthur Freed, Nacio Herb Brown; "Lowdown Rythm" by Raymond Klages, Jesse Greer; "For I'm the Queen," by Andy Rice, Martin Broones; "Gotta a Feelin' For You," by Joe Trent, Louis Alter; "Bones and Tambourines," "Strike Up the Band," "Tableaux of Jewels," by Fred Fisher; "Lon Chaney Will Get You If You Don't Watch Out;" "Strolling Through the Park One Day," "Your Mother and Mine," "Orange Blossom Time," "Minstrel Days," "Nobody But You," "I Never Knew I Could Do a Thing Like That," by Joe Goodwin, Gus Edwards. Score arranged by Arthur Lange, Ernest Klapholtz, Ray Heindorf. Dance ensembles staged by Sammy Lee, George Cunningham. Sound recording: Douglas Shearer, Russell Frank, William Clark, Wesley Miller, A.T. Taylor. Assistant directors: Jack Cummings, Sandy Roth, Al Shenberg. Production Manager: Joe Cohn. Costumes: David Cox, Henrietta Frazer, Joe Rapf. Electrician: Louis Kolb. Produced by Harry Rapf. Running time: 130 Mins. Released September 23, 1929.

CAST: (As themselves) John Gilbert, Norma Shearer, Joan Crawford, Bessie Love, Lionel Barrymore, Cliff Edwards, Stan Laurel, Oliver Hardy, Anita Page, Nils Asther, Brox Sisters, Natova & Co., Marion Davies, William Haines, Buster Keaton, Marie Dressler, Charles King, Polly Moran, Gus Edwards, Karl Dane, George K. Arthur, Gwen Lee, Albertina Rasch Ballet, The Rounders, Biltmore Quartet, Conrad Nagel, Jack Benny.

The Revue: A minstrel number opens the show, followed by the introduction of Jack Benny and Conrad Nagel as masters of ceremonies. Next, Joan Crawford appears and she sings "Gotta a Feelin' For You," accompanied by a special dance number. The Biltmore Quartet then chimes in and finishes the song with her. We are next introduced to Charles King, one of the stars of *The Broadway Medody of 1929*, who sings "Your Mother and Mine," after which Conrad Nagel joins in with "You Were Meant For Me," a song King popularized in *The Broadway Melody of 1929*." Anita Page, a cute blonde, inspires Nagel to sing this number to her. Cliff Edwards, affectionately known as Ukelele Ike, next comes on with his rendition of "Nobody But You," both singing and strumming his uke. Then William Haines, that cleancut young man, known for his flippant and brash type of characters on the screen, does a comedy sketch with Jack Benny. In the midst of this number, Bessie Love suddenly pops out of Benny's pocket in miniature form, while a chorus of male voices sing "I Could Never Do a Thing Like That." This is concluded by a dance specialty. That popular comedy team, Marie Dressler and Polly Moran next appear to evoke chuckles in their singing of "For I'm the Queen," followed by Laurel and Hardy in a skit as magicians. Marion Davies now takes over the spotlight as a cadet, leading a battalion of grenadiers in a tap dance, and singing "Tommy Atkins On Parade" which is then taken up by a male chorus. The first act of the revue is concluded by the Brox Sisters, which includes a song and a dance sequence by an ensemble. Act Two opens with "The Tableau of Jewels," proceeded by "The Dance of the Sea" in which Buster Keaton does a specialty. Next, Gus Edwards sings 'Lon Chaney Will Get You If You Don't Watch Out" and the Natova Company follows with an adagio dance. The show is next highlighted by the appearance of Norma Shearer and John Gilbert in technicolor as they do the balcony scene from *Romeo and Juliet* while Lionel Barrymore tells the pair to speak their lines in modern-day argot. The "Singin' in the Rain" number follows, with Cliff Edwards and a dance ensemble, after which there are two comedy skits. Charles King, Cliff Edwards, and Gus, Marie Dressler, Polly Moran, and Bessie Love join in the technicolor finale of "Strolling Through the Park One Day," with King singing "Orange Blossom Time." Two dance numbers by the Albertina Rasch Ballet proceed this, and the revue concludes with a facsimile of Noah's Ark in which the company is singing "Singin' in the Rain."

The Hollywood Revue of 1929: *Norma Shearer and John Gilbert in a satirical skit of* Romeo and Juliet.

CRITICS' VERDICT:

"*The Hollywood Revue* will afford pleasure to the feminine patrons. It will also make men forget business and children will be glad when their parents make the excuse that they are going to see *The Hollywood Revue* to give the youngsters some fun."
Mordaunt Hall in the *New York Times*, August 15, 1929

"The biggest fall-down among the screen stars is contributed by Norma Shearer and Jack Gilbert in the balcony scene from Romeo and Juliet. They are terrible when they tackle Shakespeare and they are nearly as bad when they try a modern flip version of the love tragedy."
Frederick James Smith in *Liberty Magazine*, September 28, 1929

"It is not the intention of this department to state that *The Hollywood Revue* is as good as Mr. Ziegfeld's best efforts, but we can honestly say that we enjoyed it a great deal more than we have plenty of successful Broadway musical productions."
Harry Evans in *Life* magazine, September 6, 1929

"Results figure to justify the grief packed into this undertaking and as a pioneer it's bound to make every-body do some bed-time mental calisthenics, plus another portion of that at breakfast. If the theatre booths give it an even break nothing can stop it, and if Howard Dietz and Pete Smith will take a tip—make diplomatic requests that the dailies' dramatic men be assigned to review the picture in all spots."
Variety, June 26, 1929

"At the Empire where *The Hollywood Revue* is being shown, it is possible to gaze from 12 am to 12 pm, almost continuously upon a regular galaxy of stars. Stars of such magnitude as Marion Davies, Norma Shearer, John Gilbert, Buster Keaton, shine perhaps most brightly, but the company in which we find them is of almost equal brilliance. Each star it shoots into the limelight to do its turn, is introduced to the audience. There is much gagging around these introductions, and a perpetual clamouring among the cast for the greatest and most startling publicity. All this is part of the fun, but I could not help wondering sometimes whether I was not watching some cinema artists advertising con-ventions. In fact, I got a little bored with the compli-ments and insults which were fired from star to star."
Celia Simpson in the *London Spectator*, November 2, 1929

162

Their Own Desire (Metro-Goldwyn-Mayer—1929)

CREDITS: Director: E. Mason Hopper. Photography: William Daniels. Author: Sarita Fuller. Scenario: James Grant Forbes. Film editor: Harry Reynolds. Titles: Lucile Newmark. Musical score: Fred Fisher, Reggie Montgomery, George Ward. Song: "Blue Is the Night," by Fred Fisher. Art director: Cedric Gibbons. Gowns: Adrian. Sound recording: J.K. Brock, Douglas Shearer. Running time: 75 Mins. Released December 27, 1929.

CAST: Norma Shearer (Lally), Belle Bennett (Harriet Marlett), Lewis Stone (Mr. Marlett), Robert Montgomery (Jack), Helen Millard (Beth), Cecil Cunningham (Aunt Caroline), Henry Herbert (Uncle Nate), Mary Doran (Susan), June Nash (Mildred).

STORY OF THE FILM: Lally Marlett's parents are on the verge of getting a divorce. When she discovers her father's infidelity, she decides to take her mother Harriet on a trip so both can forget their unhappy situation for a while. They go to a resort where Lally meets Jack Cheever, an irresponsible young man who fancies himself as being God's gift to women. Lally and Jack are attracted to each other instantly and soon fall in love. Following a brief courtship, Jack asks Lally to marry him, but she doesn't accept his proposal immediately. Finally, she succumbs to Jack's persistence and promises to become his wife. Lally, however, is unaware that the woman her father is having an affair with is Jack's mother, Beth. Upon learning of this, Lally tells Jack that it would be best for them to part under the circumstances. As a farewell get-together both decide to go on a cruise in a small boat and during the outing a storm overtakes them. The report that Lally and Jack are missing soon reaches Mr. Marlett and Mrs. Cheever and they frantically go in search of their daughter and son with the aid of a searching party. They are all

Their Own Desire: *Norma Shearer and Belle Bennett.*

163

Their Own Desire: *Robert Montgomery and Norma Shearer.*

greatly relieved to find the couple safe, and at this point, Lally's father and Jack's mother realize that their relationship cannot endure any longer and that it was a mistake. Lally's parents are reunited and she and Jack resume their marriage plans.

CRITICS' VERDICT:

"With just a little restraint, this effort at an emotional epic might have been more than a vain attempt. Due to poor direction, the principals emote until both themselves and the audience are exhausted. As a climax, there is a stupendous studio storm and a tailored to box-office ending. Norma Shearer is badly miscast. A little hard to take after *The Last of Mrs. Cheyney.*"
Photoplay, February 1930

"Miss Shearer's spontaneity and pleasing diction are worthy of a more plausible chronicle than that of this current film. Lewis Stone does well by the part of

Marlett; he can't help being discovered in a compromising situation devised by the director. Belle Bennett is sympathetic as Mrs. Marlett and Robert Montgomery at least reveals that he has ability in the role of the irrepressible Jack Cheever."
Mordaunt Hall in the *New York Times,* January 25, 1930

"After *The Trial of Mary Dugan* and *The Last of Mrs. Cheyney* which combined to set Norma Shearer miles ahead of its nearest competitor in my estimation, it was too bad they chose *Their Own Desire.* It isn't, perhaps, a bad picture. It may even be, in a sense, a good picture. But it isn't one-two kick with either of those mentioned, and I'm sorry about it. I hoped Miss Shearer had got away from scripts like this. Belle Bennett, Lewis Stone and Robert Montgomery are others who take the rap with Miss Shearer. None deserve it."
Exhibitor's Herald-World, January 4, 1930

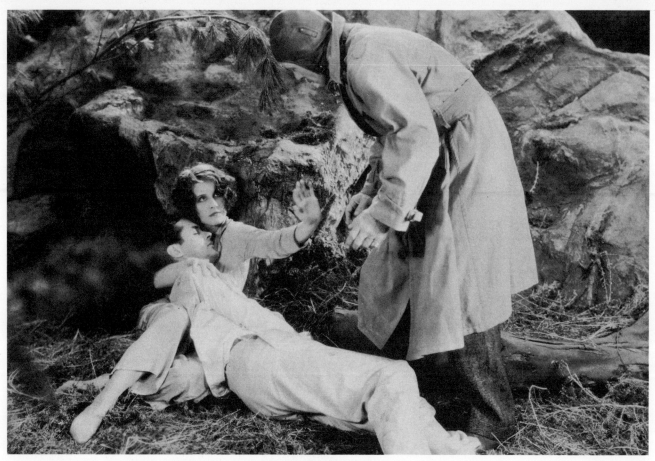

Their Own Desire: *Norma Shearer, Robert Montgomery, and Lewis Stone.*

Their Own Desire: *Norma Shearer.*

The Divorcée (Metro-Goldwyn-Mayer — 1930)

CREDITS: Director: Robert Z. Leonard. Photography: Norbert Brodine. Author: Ursula Parrott. Scenario: Nick Grinde, Zelda Sears, John Meehan. Dialogue: John Meehan. Film editors: Hugh Wynn, Truman K. Wood. Art director: Cedric Gibbons. Gowns: Adrian. Sound recording: Douglas Shearer. Running time: 80 mins. Released April 19, 1930.

CAST: Norma Shearer (Jerry), Chester Morris (Ted), Conrad Nagel (Paul), Robert Montgomery (Don), Florence Eldridge (Helen), Helen Millard (Mary), Robert Elliott (Bill), Mary Doran (Janice), Tyler Brooke (Hank), Zelda Sears (Hannah), George Irving (Dr. Bernard), Helen Johnson (Dorothy).

STORY OF THE FILM: Despite her father's wishes that she marry Paul, with whom she has been having an affair, Jerry Bernard meets Ted, a roving newspaperman at a party and shortly becomes engaged to him. Dorothy, a beautiful young woman who is in love with Paul, offers him surcease by plying him with a few drinks so he can obliterate the memory of Jerry's sudden action. The liquor muddles Paul's brain, and while driving home with Dorothy that night, the car swerves off the road, with Paul suffering a broken arm. Dorothy's face is permanently scarred. A few weeks later Ted and Jerry are wed in church while on the same day Paul and Dorothy tie the matrimonial knot at her bedside in the hospital.

Ted and Jerry have now been married for three years and have been quite happy. On their third anniversary Ted gets an important assignment in Chicago, and just as he is leaving to catch his train, several friends arrive, including Janice, a divorcée, who was once intimate with Ted. Janice's coming infuriates Ted and he berates

The Divorcée: *Robert Montgomery, Norma Shearer, Florence Eldridge, and Chester Morris.*

166

The Divorcée: *Norma Shearer and Conrad Nagel.*

her for it. Jerry soon learns of Ted's liaison with Janice, but Ted tries to explain that Janice never really meant anything to him. Jerry almost believes him, and after Ted has finally left, she attends a party with Don, a young man on the loose who happens to be Ted's closest friend. Jerry is both chagrined and disappointed to find Janice there, too, and asks Don to bring her home. Jerry tells Don that she is lonely and he suggests they make a night of it.

When Ted returns the following week, Jerry confesses to him that she has been keeping company with another man, but Ted refuses to accept this. As a result they get a divorce and Jerry decides to follow the primrose path. She has many affairs, and later has a pleasant reunion with Paul, who has loved her from the start and whose own marriage is in jeopardy since he is not too happy with his wife. He and Jerry go on a trip together and spend an idyllic summer on his yacht. When they return, Paul, after much persuasion, gets Dorothy's consent to divorce him so that he may marry Jerry.

Jerry then learns from her friend, Helen, that Ted is in Paris and quite uncontrollable, what with his nightly drinking provided by American tourists for whom he acts as a guide. At the same time, Dorothy has changed her mind about divorcing Paul and appeals to Jerry to give him up, despite their unhappiness. Paul becomes indignant, but Jerry feels that Dorothy needs him and that she needs Ted, even though he may avoid her. Jerry takes that chance and goes to Paris, where, on New Year's Eve, she and Ted have a festive reunion.

CRITICS' VERDICT:
"M-G-M has taken Ursula Parrot's *Ex-Wife* and made an intelligent, gripping dramatic picture out of it. From the dialogue which, for the greater part is crisp, trenchant and pointed, to the photography which is good throughout, the producers have achieved a first rate reproduction of some of the aspects of modern life, as it is for a few of us and some as it is for almost all of us."
Douglas Fox in *Exhibitor's Herald World,* April 12, 1930

The Divorcée: *Norma Shearer and George Irving.*

"Miss Shearer does all that is possible within the circumstances with her role. Chester Morris also is capable as Ted. Conrad Nagel's is another laudable performance, and Robert Montgomery is scarcely to be blamed for Don's wisecracking and smirking."
Mordaunt Hall in the *New York Times,* May 10, 1930

"The acting throughout is fine, and although Norma Shearer is not so beautiful here as she usually is, she gives more to the part of Jerry than she has ever given to a characterization before. Chester Morris is superb as Jerry's husband and Robert Montgomery as the husband's best friend, is his most attractive care-free self. Conrad Nagel, as the rejected suitor, does a splendid bit of acting in the scene of the motor accident, and that scene, by the way, is one of the most realistic I have ever seen in a picture. It is a breathtaking incident."
Kate Cameron in *Liberty Magazine*, May 24, 1930

"They banned the book *Ex-Wife* from the screen. But it was quite all right to film *The Divorcée* and the strange thing is that whereas the book, although it sold hugely, was not what you might call a classic, the picture is.
"This has turned out to be a problem piece, as neat an essay on marital unfaithfulness as has been made in Hollywood. It sets Norma Shearer at the very top of the

acting class. It gives Chester Morris a chance for another swell performance. The direction is as subtle as the scent of orchids and the clothes are gorgeous. You won't forget this picture and you'll undoubtedly go home and have a good long talk with your spouse. But more important, you'll be amused and held spellbound until the last reel. Don't miss it."
Photoplay, June 1930

Let Us Be Gay (Metro-Goldwyn-Mayer — 1930)

CREDITS: Director: Robert Z. Leonard. Based on Rachel Crother's play. Scenario and dialogue: Frances Marion. Additional dialogue: Lucille Newmark. Photography: Norbert Brodine. Film editor: Basil Wrangell. Art director: Cedric Gibbons. Gowns: Adrian. Sound recording: Karl E. Zint, Douglas Shearer. Running time: 78 minutes. Released August 9, 1930.

CAST: Norma Shearer (Kitty Brown), Rod La Rocque (Bob Brown), Marie Dressler (Mrs. Bouccicault), Gilbert Emery (Townley), Hedda Hopper (Madge Livingston), Raymond Hackett (Bruce), Sally Eilers (Diane), Tryrell Davis (Wallace), Wilfred Noy (Whitman), William O'Brien (Struthers), Sybil Grove (Perkins).

STORY OF THE FILM: After several years of marriage, Kitty has divorced Bob because of his philandering. She goes to Paris to seek a new, if temporary, life and there makes the acquaintance of Mrs. Bouccicault, a wealthy, scheming dowager whose granddaughter, Madge, has serious designs over Bob, though Bruce is her fiancée. Mrs. Bouccicault appeals to Kitty to aid her in dissolving the affair between Bob and Madge and Kitty agrees. Kitty, upon returning from her trip abroad, has changed almost completely in appearance. looking radiant, even vivacious—a woman of the world, since she had always been the homely type and rather unprepossessing, which was one of the reasons Bob resorted to other women. She had, in fact, become much too domestic to excite him anymore. Kitty invites Mrs. Bouccicault to her Long Island home as her weekend guest, including some male friends to liven things up. It is a gay weekend indeed, with Kitty engaging in a few flirtations herself just as Bob had. The men simply can't resist her, nor can Bob, who is also among the guests, but doesn't recognize his ex-wife. Mrs. Bouccicault, however, discourages Kitty's admirers by keeping them away from her as much as possible. She soon arranges for Kitty's and Bob's children to return and the romance between Bob and Madge is finally broken up. Bob, seeing how sophisticated Kitty has become, realizes how foolish he was, and he and Kitty are reconciled.

Let Us Be Gay: *Rod La Rocque and Norma Shearer.*

CRITICS' VERDICT:

"Norma Shearer and Marie Dressler share the honors in this delightfully entertaining version of Rachel Crother's stage play. Miss Dressler is no doubt laugh insurance for any picture. But the role of a belligerent, blustering society dame here alloted her is a perfect vehicle for her brand of humor.

"Norma Shearer as a prim, old fashioned and almost homely wife who later blossoms out in all her modern glory, is a revelation in the art of make up. The excellence of her acting ability has already been demonstrated in her previous pictures and is only strengthened by her superb performance in *Let Us Be Gay*."
Exhibitor's-Herald World, July 26, 1930

"Rachel Crother's brief history of the life that is lived along certain shores of Long Island has come by devious methods to the screen at the Capitol. It has some fairly complete—perhaps more than that—with the dowager and the divorced Browns up to their old tricks.

It is a mirthful affair, eight reels (or is it?) of carefree madness. Then there is an ending—a happy ending. Life continues on Long Island."
Mordaunt Hall in the *New York Times*, July 12, 1930

"Norma Shearer takes the role once played so delightfully by Francine Larrimore and carries it off with grace and point. Her voice matches her personality and records with smoothness and variety. Her scenes with Gilbert Emery have almost the lightness, vivacity and naturalness of life itself. Mr. Rod LaRocque talks in the fashion of a traveling salesman who has about half-finished a course in elocution. His diction is deliberately monotonous and marred by a strong sectional blur. In contrast with the accomplished performance and speech of Gilbert Emery he gives one the impression of being a hastily rehearsed amateur."
Richard Dana Skinner in *The Commonwealth*, July 23, 1930

"No, the story of *Let Us Be Gay*, which ran for more

than a year on the stage in New York, is not a happy accident. It is motivated by a profound knowledge of psychology and is glossed over with clever characterizations, bright dialogue and pleasant uncertainty of the outcome. It could hardly fail even in hands less adroit than those of Miss Shearer and her associates, all of whom rise to the occasion of supporting a gifted star in her best picture.''
Picture Play, October 1930

Let Us Be Gay: *Norma Shearer, Gilbert Emery, and Rod La Rocque.*

Let Us Be Gay: *Norma Shearer and Marie Dressler.*

Strangers May Kiss (Metro-Goldwyn-Mayer — 1931)

CREDITS: Director: George Fitzmaurice. Based on the novel by Ursula Parrott. Scenario and dialogue: John Meehan. Photography: William Daniels. Film editor: Hugh Wynn. Art director: Cedric Gibbons. Gowns: Adrian. Sound recording: Anstruther Mac-Donald. Recording director: Douglas Shearer. Running time: 75 minutes. Released April 4, 1931.

CAST: Norma Shearer (Lisbeth), Robert Montgomery (Steve), Neil Hamilton (Alan), Marjorie Rambeau (Geneva), Irene Rich (Celia), Hale Hamilton (Andrew), Conchita Montenegro (Spanish dancer), Jed Prouty (Harry), Albert Conti (Dr. Bazan), Henry Armetta (waiter), George Davis (waiter).

STORY OF THE FILM: Lisbeth is a young woman of the world whose distaste of stuffy conventions has alienated her from marriage. She loves her freedom and in her travels she meets Alan, a war correspondent, whom she accompanies on business and pleasure trips. They are very much in love, and for Lisbeth, her blissful relationship with Alan is the fulfillment of her life. Alan is sent to Mexico on an assignment and takes Lisbeth with him, who, by now would find it unbearable to be without him. Steve, her childhood sweetheart, who spends most of his time at fashionable cocktail bars getting inebriated and making flippant and witty remarks, has repeatedly made overtures to Lisbeth of his desire to marry her and settle down, but entreaties have usually been met with disdain and refusal. After a few happy months in Mexico, Alan is suddenly called to China to cover an uprising and Lisbeth is left behind for the first time. It's as if the world has just crumbled before her and she soon becomes bitter and disillusioned. She goes to Europe, traveling from city to city where she has numerous affairs, leaving one suitor after another in her wake. Tired of being a self-styled courtesan after several years on the continent, she returns to New York, presumably to marry Steve. About this

Strangers May Kiss: *Irene Rich, Neil Hamilton, and Norma Shearer.*

171

Strangers May Kiss: *Marjorie Rambeau and Norma Shearer.*

Strangers May Kiss: *Norma Shearer and Robert Montgomery.*

Strangers May Kiss: *Neil Hamilton and Norma Shearer.*

time, Alan has also returned, finally intending to ask Lisbeth to become his wife. However, upon learning of her unsavory reputation abroad, Alan decides against proposing to her. Just as Lisbeth is ready to accept Steve, Alan has a change of heart and asks Lisbeth to marry him. She accepts his proposal and together they go off as before, only this time to a more conventional life. As they leave, Steve says resignedly, "I'll be okay. There'll always be a bottle of champagne shining in the window."

CRITICS' VERDICT:

"George Fitzmaurice has made a brisk and good-looking entertainment which goes on its way so gracefully that it leaves little time in examining structural weaknesses in the story and characterizations. Norma Shearer interprets the modern young woman of the piece with all her customary charm and intelligence."
Creighton Peet in *Outlook*, March 25, 1931:

"We girls' love problems have been gone into pretty thoroughly in the past six months, but Norma Shearer's sufferings undoubtedly make the best of the lot. There is something a little forced and melodramatic in Miss Shearer's extreme abandon—but her sufferings are cannily calculated to enthrall the feminine movie audience."
Motion Picture, May 1931

"This is Norma Shearer's first picture since she became a mother and it's her finest picture to date. That's going some, as *The Divorcée* won many of the honors that were floating around last year, but Ursula Parrott develops her characters more logically and Norma's work in some scenes is superb. Rarely has one been as gorgeous as our Norma while treading the primrose path."
Photoplay, May 1931

A Free Soul (Metro-Goldwyn-Mayer — 1931).

CREDITS: Producer: Irving Thalberg. Director: Clarence Brown. Based on the novel by Adela Rogers St. Johns. Scenario and dialogue: John Meehan. Adaptation: Becky Gardner. Photography: William Daniels. Film editor: Hugh Wynn. Art director: Cedric Gibbons. Gowns: Adrian. Musical score: William Axt. Sound recording: Anstruther MacDonald. Recording director: Douglas Shearer. Running time: 91 minutes. Released June 20, 1931.

CAST: Norma Shearer (Jan Ashe), Leslie Howard (Dwight Winthrop), Lionel Barrymore (Stephen Ashe), Clark Gable (Ace Wilfong), James Gleason (Eddie), Lucy Beaumont (Grandma Ashe), Edward Brophy (fast-talking hood).

STORY OF THE FILM: Stephen Ashe, a brilliant but hard-drinking criminal lawyer, has just scored another of his coup de graces by winning an acquittal for Ace Wilfong, a notorious gambler, on a murder charge. In proving his client's innocence, Ashe had produced a hat on which the former's initials were supposedly inscribed and which was left on the site of the killing. The hat, after being clapped on the head of the defendant, is found to be a few sizes too small and he is cleared.

Present during the defense that morning is Ashe's young daughter, Jan, whom he has brought up to be a nonconformist like himself and who is free to do as she pleases. Jan is introduced to the racketeer by her father and is quite intrigued by his virility. Ace is mutually attracted.

At the home of Grandma Ashe on the evening of the same day, a birthday dinner is being given for her. Among those present are Jan and her fiancée, Dwight Winthrop, a socialite polo player to whom she has just become engaged, as well as a few other family members.

The festivities are suddenly interrupted when Ashe, who is highly intoxicated, though in convivial spirits,

A Free Soul: *Clark Gable and Norma Shearer.*

A Free Soul: *Norma Shearer, Lionel Barrymore, and Clark Gable.*

walks in, with Ace Wilfong beside him. Their unexpected appearance startles everybody in the room, except Jan, who is glad to see the gangster again. Ace's presence, however, is frowned upon by the others, and seeing that he is not welcome, he starts to leave. Jan, piqued by this treatment towards Ace, decides to accompany him and goes for a drive in his roadster. Before they know it a car is pursuing them and the sound of a machine gun is heard. Ace quickly swerves his vehicle to the other side of the road, turns a corner, thereby eluding the rival gang. The experience, although it might have cost her her life, exhilarates and excites Jan. She feels that she is just beginning to live. In a little while, she finds herself in Ace's penthouse, under which his gambling headquarters are also located. Jan spends the night with Ace and before long becomes his mistress.

A few weeks later, while Ashe is consuming more than his share of liquor in Ace's gambling establishment, the latter mentions that he would like to marry Jan. Stunned at this sudden announcement, Ashe can only regard his former client with undisguised contempt. He then says to him: "The only time I hate democracy is when one of you mongrels forgets his place. A few illegal dollars and a clean shirt and you move across the railroad tracks. Have your boy bring me something to drink and don't insult your guests."

At that moment, the place is raided by the vice squad and Ashe, though he tries to resist, is propelled by two of Ace's strong-arm men into the gambler's apartment. Another shock awaits the lawyer when he finds Jan, clad in a flimsy gown, with her legs fully exposed, sitting on a sofa. The sight clears his liquor-soaked

brain and Jan goes home with him. She gives him an ultimatum — that if he will stop drinking, she will never see Ace Wilfong again. He promises to do so and both go up to Yosemite where they spend three months, enjoying the fresh, clean air and the wilderness. Ashe has managed to stay on the wagon, but when he and Jan are ready to return home and go down to the depot, he begins to grow restless and stops at a store to purchase a bottle of liquor. When she next sees her father he is quite unsteady on his feet and boarding the train without her. Jan, sacrificing her pride, goes back to Ace, but he is not too receptive towards her, even though he plans to marry her. The idea is revolting to Jan, but Ace is determined to make her his wife at any cost. He then starts to bully her, hurling invectives at her father to whom he refers as a drunken, washed-out bum. When Jan rises to defend this attack, Ace roughly shoves her back. She now sees him for what he is and shortly after he leaves the room, she manages to get away.

The following morning, Ace, looking somewhat disheveled in his evening clothes and very surly, bursts into Jan's apartment and threatens to damage her reputation if she doesn't marry him. A moment later, Dwight Winthrop arrives and also receives a threat from Ace. Winthrop, feeling that Ace has been a menace to society long enough, enters his office that night and shoots him to death as he is sitting behind his desk. Winthrop immediately calls the police and reports the murder as a result of a gambling debt.

On trial for murder, Winthrop refuses to have anybody defend him. Meanwhile, Jan is desperately looking for her father around the waterfront area and finally locates him in a flophouse drunk as ever. The trial has reached its climax when Ashe, perfectly sober now, arrives in court, offering to represent Winthrop, who still does not wish counsel. But despite these objections, Ashe is permitted to take Winthrop on as his client. Jan is called to the witness stand, and though his heart is breaking, Ashe wrings from his daughter the true story of her sordid liaison with Ace Wilfong. In an affecting speech that stuns the courtroom, Ashe admits his own failure in bringing Jan up as he should have and blames himself entirely for the murder. With that, he falls dead. Winthrop is acquitted and he and Jan plan to live in New York where they will start life anew.

CRITICS' VERDICT:

"Talking pictures are by no means elevated by the presentation of a *A Free Soul*, last night's screen contribution put on at the Astor. Nevertheless it should be stated that Lionel Barrymore does all that is possible with his role. In fact, his is the only characterization that rings true, the others being handicapped either through miscasting, the false conception of human psychology or poorly written lines. Norma Shearer

A Free Soul: *Lionel Barrymore and Norma Shearer.*

may be the star of this film, but Mr. Barrymore steals whatever honors there may be.''
Mordaunt Hall in the *New York Times*, June 3, 1931

''Some people may think they have had their money's worth when they have seen Norma Shearer silhouetted in a doorway, wrapped in a skin-tight gold lame negligee, her knee archly kinked, her hair coyly fluffed and her chin in her palm—but I don't. I resent the fact that *A Free Soul* is a preposterous, illogical, over-talkative motionless motion picture, and not even Lionel Barrymore's melodramatic wig-wagging convinced me.''
Creighton Peet in *Outlook*, June 3, 1931

''The picture follows, almost exactly, Adela Rogers St. John's splendid novel of the same name. Lionel Barrymore's performance in the role of a brilliant but heavy drinking criminal lawyer is magnificent.

''Norma Shearer is excellent and handles the part of his daughter perfectly. Her clothes are breath-taking in their daring. But you couldn't get away with them in your drawing room.''
Photoplay, July 1931

''Norma Shearer covers white-hot emotions with the brittle manner of the modern girl in a way that leaves no doubt of her ability as a dramatic actress. Incidentally, she never looked more beautiful. Leslie Howard as the super-civilized polo-player, contrasts with Clark Gable as the handsome brute who appeals to the physical side of the girl's nature.

But the picture honors go to Lionel Barrymore, who does the best acting we have seen on the screen for many months.''
Motion Picture, July 1931

176

A Free Soul: *Norma Shearer, a player, and Lionel Barrymore*.

A Free Soul: *Leslie Howard and Norma Shearer*.

Private Lives (Metro-Goldwyn-Mayer—1931)

CREDITS: Director: Sidney Franklin. Based on the play by Noel Coward. Scenario: Hans Kraly, Richard Schayer, Claudine West. Photography: Ray Binger. Film editor: Conrad V. Nervig. Art director: Cedric Gibbons. Gowns: Adrian. Recording director: Douglas Shearer. Running time: 87 minutes. Released December 12, 1931.

CAST: Norma Shearer (Armanda Prynne), Robert Montgomery (Elyot Chase), Reginald Denny (Victor Prynne), Una Merkel (Sibyl), Jean Hersholt (Oscar), George Davis (bellboy).

STORY OF THE FILM: Armanda, a high-spirited and vivacious young girl, has divorced Elyot Chase and married Victor Prynne, a stuffed shirt, whom she doesn't love. Elyot has also remarried, but he, too, is not in love with his new mate, Sibyl, who, like Victor, is a colorless personality. By sheer coincidence, the two couples are honeymooning at the same hotel on the Riviera and are quartered in adjacent suites. When Armanda and Elyot come face to face with each other one evening on the terrace of the hotel while out for a breath of air, they are both surprised and horrified. Soon, Elyot is quarreling with Sibyl, while Victor is having a spat with Armanda. Elyot and Armanda, realizing that they have been hasty in remarrying, find that they are still in love and plan to elope once again. Leaving Sibyl and Victor to themselves, the pair journey to a mountain retreat where they pretend to have another honeymoon in an Alpine chalet. Armanda's and Elyot's moods are most unpredictable, for, one minute they are in a blissful state, and the next they are exchanging blows, which finally lead to physical ones with the two having a knock-down-drag-out fight in which their abode becomes a shambles. At this point, Victor and Sibyl arrive at the chalet, highly indignant over being deserted by their spouses and engage rooms for the night. The next morning the foursome have

Private Lives: *Norma Shearer and Robert Montgomery.*

178

Private Lives: *Robert Montgomery and Norma Shearer.*

Private Lives: *Robert Montgomery and Norma Shearer.*

breakfast together and much bickering ensues, mostly from Sibyl and Victor, whose tempers begin to flare at each other. In the midst of this, Elyot and Armanda pick up their luggage and sneak out, leaving Victor and Sibyl alone again.

CRITICS' VERDICT:

"In this production directed by Sidney Franklin, Norma Shearer and Robert Montgomery play through the almost actor-proof situations of the comedy with savoir-faire which equals if it does not excel that of their predecessors—author Noel Coward and Gertrude Lawrence."
Time, December 28, 1931

"Well, they've kept them all in—those swell lines of the Noel Coward play. And they're both there—those two grand, impossible delightful characters who kept the show running on Broadway for years. Norma Shearer and Robert Montgomery are excellent as the ex-husband and ex-wife who, having married others, run away with each other. A wild farce idea made snappy by sparkling and at times questionable dialogue. Una Merkel and Reginald Denny play the dull folk who they run away from."
Photoplay, February 1932

"Norma Shearer matches Robert Montgomery's well-known flair for light comedy and after the posey dramatics of late, reveals herself as a charming comedienne."
Motion Picture, February, 1932

"Miss Shearer's own portrayal is in a few isolated scenes better than she has offered—notably, I would say, in the pledging of devotion between herself and her ex-husband when they first meet, and also at moments during their battles. The early portion of the portrayal is almost too brittle, and overemphasis of affectation is also a mark of the impersonation as a whole. This makes the general impression somewhat disappointing."
Edwin Schallert in the *Los Angeles Times*, December 12, 1931

"Norma Shearer's tempestuous performance will simultaneously astonish and delight her admirers. Robert Montgomery, with his American accent well under control, does well in a part which must have held many difficulties for him. The weakest of the cast of five players is Una Merkel, whose diction is faulty and who seems to have been miscast."
John Gammie in *The Film Weekly* (London), February 6, 1932

"Sidney Franklin's direction is excellent and Norma Shearer as Armanda Prynne gives an alert, sharp portrayal. She appears to have been inspired by the scintil-lating dialogue, and taking all things into consideration, it is her outstanding performance in talking pictures."
Mordaunt Hall in the *New York Times*, December 19, 1931

Strange Interlude (Metro-Goldwyn-Mayer — 1932)

CREDITS: Director: Robert Z. Leonard. Based on the play by Eugene O'Neill. Scenario and dialogue: Bess Meredyth and C. Gardner Sullivan. Photography: Lee Garmes. Film Editor: Margaret Booth. Art director: Cedric Gibbons. Gowns: Adrian. Recording director: Douglas Shearer. Running time: 110 minutes. Released December 30, 1932.

CAST: Norma Shearer (Nina Leeds), Clark Gable (Ned Darrell), Alexander Kirkland (Sam Evans), Ralph Morgan (Charlie Marsden), Robert Young (Gordon, as a young man), May Robson (Mrs. Evans), Maureen O'Sullivan (Madeline), Henry B. Walthall (Professor Leeds), Mary Alden (maid), Ted Alexander (Gordon, as a child).

STORY OF THE FILM: When the man she loves suddenly dies, Nina Leeds finds that life holds no future for her. She becomes morbid and apathetic and almost drives herself mad by her grief. In order to save her sanity she leaves home, following the death of her father, Professor Leeds, and takes a job as a nurse in a hospital for the war's wounded. There she meets Ned Darrell, a young, vigorous doctor, who had once treated her father, and Sam Evans, Darrell's best friend. Realizing the state that she is in, Darrell advises Nina to marry Sam and have children, which might be her salvation both mentally and physically. Sam is not as masculine, if at all, like Darrell, but weak-willed and lacks ambition, though he is likable and devoted and worships Darrell.

Nina has an admirer in Charlie Marsden, a well-known novelist, who is gentle, yet smug, and who has a mother complex. After thinking it over, Nina marries Sam, but her love for him is only maternal. Shortly after her marriage, Nina learns from her mother-in-law, Mrs. Evans, that there is a streak of insanity in the family and warns her that she must not have a child by him. Mrs. Evans suggests that if Nina is to bear children, she had better have it by another man. Under these conditions, her son will remain ignorant of his wife's secret, which will prevent his happiness from being destroyed. The revelation is a shattering one to Nina, who eventually offers herself to Ned, although she discovers that she is also in love with him. Their child is born, and Sam believing it to be his, is overwhelmingly happy and loves Nina all the more. The secret between Nina and Ned is kept. When their child, Gordon, reaches boy-

Strange Interlude: *Alexander Kirkland, Norma Shearer, Ralph Morgan, and Clark Gable.*

Strange Interlude: *Clark Gable and Norma Shearer.*

Strange Interlude: *Norma Shearer, Alexander Kirkland, Ralph Morgan, and May Robson.*

hood he develops an instinctive hatred for the doctor, which breaks both Ned's and Nina's heart.

Through the years, Nina, Ned, Sam, and Charlie grow old gracefully. Gordon grows to manhood and is engaged to Madeline, whom he eventually marries. At college, Gordon is considered an outstanding athlete, and during a regatta meet one day on the rowing team he scores a victory. Among the spectators are Nina, Sam, and Ned. Sam is proud and overcome with emotion at what Gordon has accomplished in the race, and during the excitement he suffers a heart attack and dies. With Gordon having married, Nina is left alone. Ned has also gone out of her life, but there is still that faithful old dog, Charlie.

CRITICS' VERDICT:

"In the difficult role of Nina, Norma Shearer lives her lines, gives her greatest performance. It is unquestionably her picture. Clark Gable, as her lover, Darrell, is a new person—intensely sensitive. Alexander Kirkland, as Sam, her husband is convincingly Rotarian. Ralph Morgan, as Marsden, who has a mother complex, is sharply amusing. You won't forget them."
Motion Picture, October 1932

"Norma Shearer takes her place among the great artists of her day. Clark Gable does his finest technical screen work as he ages over a period of forty years. Ralph Morgan, Alexander Kirkland and Robert Young share honors."
Photoplay, September 1932

"Norma Shearer has given several noteworthy performances in recent motion pictures, particularly her portrayal in the film *Private Lives,* but in this present offering she easily excels anything she has done hitherto."
Mordaunt Hall in the *New York Times,* October 15, 1932

Strange Interlude: *Norma Shearer and May Robson.*

Strange Interlude: *Clark Gable and Norma Shearer.*

"Miss Norma Shearer, apparently filled with reverence at the thought of the classic lines she is reciting, but, at the same time, understanding so little about them, makes Nina Leeds, the neurotic heroine, a good, healthy normal, young woman, who ages prettily and isn't bothered much about her tragedies."
Richard Watts, Jr., in the *New York Herald Tribune*, October 15, 1932

"For once Hollywood has dared to produce a picture that deals with life in terms of adult intelligence. But though the courage thus shown deserves every credit, the outgrowth of this courage, the film itself, is hardly a feather in the producer's cap. It confirms faithfully to its Hollywood type of an uninspired crossbreed of the stage and the screen, and it is badly miscast in its two principal parts. Neither the beautiful but cold Norma Shearer, nor the uncouth Clark Gable are the actors for the parts of Nina and Darrell."
Alexander Bakshy in *The Nation*, September 28, 1932

"Norma Shearer is a lovely picture as Nina, but lacks all sense of greatness—as does the altered play itself. Clark Gable, who plays the Ned Darrell, is capable in the earlier scenes, but utterly lacks the ferocious bitterness in the latter part which Glenn Anders seemed to bring from the depths of his soul. Ralph Morgan is an excellent Charles Marsden, but the temper of the screen play has robbed the character of Charlie of its meaning. He now becomes comedy relief."
Richard Dana Skinner in *The Commonweal*, October 5, 1932

Strange Interlude: *Clark Gable and Norma Shearer.*

Smilin' Through (Metro-Goldwyn-Mayer — 1932)

CREDITS: Director: Sidney Franklin. Based on the play by Jane Cowl, Jane Murfin, and Langdon McCormick. Scenario: Ernest Vajda, Claudine West. Dialogue: Donald Ogden, Stewart James, Bernard Fagan. Photography: Lee Garmes. Film editor: Margaret Booth. Art director: Cedric Gibbons. Gowns: Adrian. Recording director: Douglas Shearer. Running time: 97 minutes. Released September 24, 1932.

CAST: Norma Shearer (Moonyean Clare and Kathleen), Fredric March (Kenneth and Jeremy Wayne), Leslie Howard (John Carteret), O.P. Heggie (Dr. Owen), Ralph Forbes (Willie Ainley), Beryl Mercer (Mrs. Crouch), Margaret Seddon (Ellen), Cora Sue Collins (Kathleen, as a child), Forrester Harvey (orderly).

STORY OF THE FILM: It is Moonyean Clare's wedding day and she is marrying John Carteret, whom she has chosen in favor of Jeremy Wayne, a rejected suitor. During the ceremony, Wayne, an erratic and impulsive young man, bursts into the church in a drunken rage, brandishing a pistol, with the intention of killing his rival. Horrified at Wayne's sudden and unexpected appearance, Moonyean steps between her betrothed and Jeremy to avert a tragedy, but the latter misfires and the bullet hits Moonyean. A moment later she dies

Smilin' Through: *Fredric March and Norma Shearer.*

in John's arms, but before she does she promises to come back to him.

Fifty years pass. John Carteret has survived the tragedy, but he is now an embittered old man who is still brooding over the death of his beloved. He adopts Moonyean's orphaned niece, Kathleen, who is a beautiful counterpart of her aunt, and it is she who gives him something to live for, despite his bitterness.

One day, while walking with Willie Ainley, an old friend, Kathleen and he chance upon a rustic old house that seems to have a haunting quality about it. A thunderstorm overtakes them and both take sanctuary in the building. There they find a young man who introduces himself as Kenneth Wayne and is the son of the man who had accidentally shot Moonyean Clare. He has just arrived from America to serve with the British army. Kathleen and young Wayne are instantly attracted to each other and soon fall in love. When Kathleen tells her uncle of her meeting with young Wayne, he forbids her to have anything further to do with him. Kathleen is anxious to know why he feels like this and Carteret relates the tragic happening of fifty years ago. Disappointed, though she hasn't changed her mind about Kenneth, Kathleen promises never to see him again, but only out of respect to her uncle, whom she loves. Kenneth goes to see Kathleen and demands to know why her uncle is opposed to their seeing each other and she tells him the reason. But Kathleen's love for Kenneth is much too deep, as his is for her and she announces to her uncle that she has made up her mind to marry Kenneth that night, since he is leaving for the front the next day. Carteret then asks his niece to leave. Kenneth, realizing that she will be an outcast, decides not to marry Kathleen, and resignedly she goes back to her uncle.

The war is finally over and Kenneth returns wounded. Kathleen rushes into his arms, but Kenneth, although he is as much in love with her as ever, does not exactly respond to her affections. Feeling that he will be a hindrance to Kathleen, he still refuses to marry her, and in a voice that is charged with emotion, tells her that he is through with her. Believing this, Kathleen informs her guardian about Kenneth, and at length his heart begins to mellow. Carteret gives the lovers his blessings, and while playing his traditional game of chess with his old friend, Dr. Owen, a vision of Moonyean appears, as it has in past years. Old John Carteret's eyes begin to fade, and at last he and Moonyean are together for all eternity. Kathleen and Kenneth return to find him dead, but they will go on smilin' through as Moonyean and John have.

CRITICS' VERDICT:

"Gorgeous as is the production, delicate and charming as is every scene, great as the performance is of each

Smilin' Through: *Norma Shearer and Fredric March.*

Smilin' Through: *Norma Shearer and Leslie Howard.*

member of the cast—this is Norma Shearer's picture, and the one adjective that comes to mind upon seeing her is "splendid." That Norma could change so suddenly from the sophisticated heroines which she has been creating lately, to this charming, old-fashioned girl, is a great tribute to her versatility."
Photoplay, November 1932

"Norma Shearer has sprung a surprise on us. Here she has been building up a great reputation as a sophisticate, ever since *The Divorcée* right through to *Strange Interlude*—and now, suddenly, she turns out the season's most romantic picture. Sentimentality is written large all over it, but it makes no apologies for the fact; it justifies itself, with its beauty, its charm, its wistful moodiness—and Norma, I suspect, comes closer to making herself unforgettable than in *Strange Interlude*."
Movie Classic, December 1932

"Miss Shearer is so earnest, so straightforward and touching, so entirely in the proper romantic mood, that you are reminded that she is an effective sentimental player, if hardly an ideal O'Neill heroine."
Richard Watts, Jr., in the *New York Herald Tribune,* October 15, 1932

"Coming very close to being a great motion picture, MGM's *Smilin' Through* is in the nature of a showman's dream come true. Names, story, performances, developements, all are at box-office calibre without question. From the play by Jane Cowl and Jane Murfin and once a silent picture, the production, though tending in the direction of the sentimental, is yet so well developed, so well performed, that there is nothing of saccharinity about it."
Motion Picture Herald, October 22, 1932

"Mr. March is very good, although a trifle too flippant at times. He is, however, far better than the ordinary choice for the role. He does make the character determined and sympathetic. Miss Shearer is no less beautiful than she was in *Strange Interlude*. But here, occasionally, she is almost too careful about her personal appearance. Mr. Howard's performance is splendid, even though his voice belies his disguise of old age. He is, however, so nicely restrained during his scenes that it is a joy to witness his interpretation at all times."
Mordaunt Hall in the *New York Times,* October 15, 1932

188

Smilin' Through: *Norma Shearer and Fredric March.*

Smilin' Through: *O.P. Heggie and Norma Shearer.*

Smilin' Through: *Leslie Howard and Norma Shearer.*

Smilin' Through: *Ralph Forbes and Norma Shearer.*

Smilin' Through: *Norma Shearer*.

Riptide (Metro-Goldwyn-Mayer — 1934)

CREDITS: Producer: Irving Thalberg. Director: Edmund Goulding. Story and scenario: Edmund Goulding. Photography: Ray June. Film editor: Margaret Booth. Art directors: Alexander Toluboff, Fredric Hope. Interior decorations: Edwin B. Willis. Gowns: Adrian. Recording director: Douglas Shearer. Running time: 90 minutes. Released March 23, 1934.

CAST: Norma Shearer (Lady Mary Rexford), Robert Montgomery (Tommy Trent), Herbert Marshall (Lord Philip Rexford), Mrs. Patrick Campbell (Lady Hetty Riversleigh), Ralph Forbes (David Fenwick), Lilyan Tashman (Sylvia), Arthur Jarrett (Percy), Earl Oxford (Freddie), Helen Jerome Eddy (Celeste), George K. Arthur (Bertie Davis), Halliwell Hobbes (Bullard).

STORY OF THE FILM, After a brief affair with Lord Philip Rexford, Mary, a high-spirited American girl, becomes his wife. A child had been born to them prior to their marriage.

Lord Rexford is suddenly called away to America on some important business, but he is unable to take Lady Mary with him. Lonely, she attends a sumptuous party and there meets Tommy Trent, an elegant man about town whom she had once known in New York. Tommy has been in love with Mary for a long time, but his instability had cautioned her about marrying him. Being a romanticist, Tommy still finds Mary irresistible and starts to make love to her. She manages to resist him and goes home. Tommy, drunk, follows her, and in an attempt to enter her boudoir through a terrace, he loses his balance and lands on the ground. Injured, though not too seriously, he is taken to the hospital. The following morning a scandal breaks and the newspapers play up the story.

Lord Rexford, having just returned, is incensed at the publicity involving his wife and Tommy Trent and demands an explanation. She tries to convince him that nothing happened between her and Tommy, but Rexford doesn't believe her and accuses her of infidelity. He decides that it is best for them to separate. Mary

Riptide: *Norma Shearer and Halliwell Hobbs.*

192

Riptide: *Herbert Marshall and Norma Shearer.*

Riptide: *Herbert Marshall and Norma Shearer.*

begins to see Tommy, who has recovered from his accident, and this time they do have an affair. Lord Rexford realizes that he has been unreasonable and pleads with Mary for a reunion. She reveals nothing to him of her ensuing romance with Tommy, but eventually she confesses. Divorce proceedings are begun. As the final arrangements are being made, Lord and Lady Rexford realize how much they care for each other and become reconciled.

CRITICS' VERDICT:

"You will not be disappointed in Norma Shearer's "Comeback" film, her first in over a year, unless you are expecting a new Norma in a highly different role. The star-sophisticate appears in very much the same silken, slightly decadent, and exquisitely accoutered characterization which has won her so much box-office acclaim in the past. In fact, if you'd just dropped in from a year in the stratosphere you would never guess that you, or Norma, had been away at all. And I don't care how you take that. I am, unreasonably I suppose, disappointed in *Riptide*, although it fulfills all the requirements of a smart triangular comedy-drama, and it is beautifully acted by Miss Shearer, Herbert Marshall, as her husband, and Robert Montgomery, as a rather overgrown playboy—oh, so playful—who persists in impersonating the serpent in Norma's Garden of Eden. It must be that some unreasonableness in me that cringes a little at Mr. Montgomery's pat portrayal. Certainly he's amusing enough. Miss Shearer, in those amazing Adrian creations, is always charmingly decorative, and her technique is flawless."
Delight Evans in *Screenland* June 1934

"Norma Shearer is vivid and compellingly convincing as the wife who never dreams of being unfaithful

194

Riptide: *Skeets Gallagher, Robert Montgomery, and Norma Shearer.*

until her husband's insistent suspicions practically force her to be. Miss Shearer has an exceedingly difficult role, and she carries it gallantly and expertly."
Photoplay, May 1934

"Norma Shearer, who had the temerity to absent herself from the screen for eighteen months since she appeared in *Smilin' Through*, is the leading light of *Riptide*, the Capitol's present pictorial attraction. In this film, Miss Shearer and other players, including Herbert Marshall, Mrs. Patrick Campbell and Robert Montgomery, give performances that are emphatically more provocative than the story."
Mordaunt Hall in the *New York Times*, March 31, 1934

"Into the capable hands of Miss Shearer, Mr. Marshall and Mr. Robert Montgomery has been placed a luscious, sloppy gob of whimsical elfishness, and they have done their honest best with it. When Mr. Marshall asks for his little daughter he has to say: 'Do I hear a little mouse somewhere?' And when he speaks to her he calls her: 'Such a very pink little rose.' No dialogue writer should do that sort of thing to any actor, not even to Rudy Vallee or Bing Crosby. If you want to kill an actor, kill him, but don't annoy him."
Cy Caldwell in *New Outlook*, May 1934

Riptide: *Robert Montgomery and Norma Shearer.*

Riptide: *Norma Shearer.*

Riptide: *Robert Montgomery, Norma Shearer, and Herbert Marshall.*

The Barretts of Wimpole Street (Metro-Goldwyn-Mayer — 1934)

CREDITS: Producer: Irving Thalberg. Director: Sidney Franklin. Based on the international stage success by Rudolf Besier. Scenario: Ernest Vajda, Claudine West, Donald Ogden Stewart. Photography: William Daniels. Film editor: Margaret Booth. Art director: Cedric Gibbons. Gowns: Adrian. Recording director: Douglas Shearer. Running time: 110 minutes. Released September 21, 1934.

CAST: Norma Shearer (Elizabeth Barrett), Fredric March (Robert Browning), Charles Laughton (Moulton Barrett), Maureen O'Sullivan (Henrietta Barrett), Katherine Alexander (Arabel Barrett), Una O'Connor (Wilson), Ian Wolfe (Harry Bevan), Marion Clayton (Bella Hedley), Ralph Forbes (Captain Surtees Cook), Vernon Downing (Octavus Barrett), Neville Clark (Charles Barrett), Matthew Smith (George Barrett), Robert Carleton (Alfred Barrett), Ferdinand Munier (Dr. Waterloo), Margaret Seddon (woman bit), George Kirby (coachman), Winter Hall (clergyman), Lowden Adams (butler), Robert Bolder (old man), Flush (Elizabeth's cocker spaniel).

STORY OF THE FILM: Elizabeth Barrett, having been bed-ridden most of her life, and still an invalid, though she is now able to sit up in a chair, is greatly concerned over her brothers and sisters, who have been dominated and ill-treated by their dictatorial father, Edward Moulton Barrett. He has provided his family with security and comfort—even luxuries,—but has denied them the right to live their own lives. Elizabeth, in order to dismiss the oppressiveness from her mind that pervades the household, submerges herself in reading all she can, this being her favorite hobby. Among the works she values above all are those of Robert Browning, the noted poet, whose poems have always inspired her. One day, Browning, an impetuous young man, bursting with vitality, pays Elizabeth a special

The Barretts of Wimpole Street: *Fredric March and Norma Shearer.*

The Barretts of Wimpole Street: *Fredric March and
Norma Shearer.*

visit which brightens her day as it never has before. Browning's warmth, his philosophy, and idealism imbue Elizabeth with a new strength and the will to conquer her invalidism. After he has left, she walks slowly to the window and watches him depart in his carriage.

Although Moulton Barrett does not permit his other daughters to entertain young men, he has extended that privilege to Elizabeth with the understanding that she will never become romantically involved. But Browning's visits become more frequent and now that Elizabeth is able to walk, he takes her for drives. Meeting as they do results in their falling deeply in love. Browning asks Elizabeth to marry him, but she tells him that her father will never consent to it. One night in a showdown with her father, she sees him for what he really is—a tyrannical old man and a hyprocite who has

stifled his own soul. Elizabeth soon informs her sisters and brothers that she is leaving to marry Robert Browning and they are overjoyed. With Elizabeth, the eldest of his daughters, gone, Edward Moulton Barrett feels completely lost for the first time.

CRITICS' VERDICT:
"While Norma Shearer is no more my own conception of Elizabeth Barrett than Fredric March is that of the poet Browning, I, nevertheless, found much of interest in their performances in these roles, they were at least vital, and the slight Canadian accent of the one and the stronger American accent of the latter did not detract from my interest or conviction any more than I think it will from yours.

"As a whole, I found *The Barretts of Wimpole Street*, which is adapted from Rudolf Besier's play and di-

rected by Sidney Franklin, academically interesting and certainly a film not to be missed."
L.C. in *The Picturegoer Weekly*, October 27, 1934

"Norma Shearer, lovely, fragile Norma of *Smilin' Through*, gives a beautiful and sincere performance that will shine brightly in your memory for years and years to come. To me Norma will always be Elizabeth Barrett—and her first weak steps to the window to see the departure of her future husband will always be one of the most memorable scenes in pictures."
Silver Screen, October 1934

"Miss Norma Shearer who has the Cornell part on the screen, is remarkably fine as Elizabeth Barrett, playing with a sensitive skill that makes her performance the best of an interesting cinema career, but somehow, it is Mr. Laughton whose portrayal is transcendent."
The Literary Digest, October 13, 1934

"Miss Shearer is still more lovely to look at than to listen to and Mr. March reels off most of his lines as if he had no great interest in their possible meaning. Only Mr. Laughton may be compared with any members of Miss Cornell's company, but he struggles vainly at times against a direction which tends to make his role a caricature. Yet the play emerges substantially every bit as effective as in its original form and one is confirmed in believing that it would do so even if put on by a high school dramatic society."
William Troy in *The Nation*, October 10, 1934

"Miss Shearer's Elizabeth is a brave and touching piece of acting and she is successful in creating an illusion of a highly sensitive and delicate woman who beats her luminous wings in vain against the chains which bind her. Charles Laughton is, of course superb as the stubborn selfish and pious father. Fredric March makes a healthy and virile Browning, although his per-

The Barretts of Wimpole Street: *Fredric March, Charles Laughton, and Norma Shearer.*

formance will impress the critical as a highly competent job by a versatile actor rather than an inspired portrayal of the great poet."
Andre Senwald in the *New York Times,* September 29, 1934

The Barretts of Wimpole Street: *Fredric March and Norma Shearer.*

The Barretts of Wimpole Street: *Charles Laughton and Norma Shearer.*

The Barretts of Wimpole Street: *Norma Shearer*.

The Barretts of Wimpole Street: *Norma Shearer, Maureen O'Sullivan, and Ralph Forbes.*

Romeo and Juliet (Metro-Goldwyn-Mayer — 1936-37)

CREDITS: Producer: Irving Thalberg. Director: George Cukor. Author: William Shakespeare. Screen adaptation: Talbot Jennings. Musical score: Herbert Stothart. Art director: Cedric Gibbons. Settings: Cedric Gibbons and Oliver Messel. Associates: Frederic Hope, Edwin B. Willis. Costumes: Oliver Messel and Adrian. Dance director: Agnes DeMille. Artistic consultant: Oliver Messel. Literary consultant: Professor William Strunk, Jr., of Cornell University. Photographed by William Daniels, A.S.C. Film editor: Margaret Booth. Recording director: Douglas Shearer. Running Time: 140 minutes. Released April 16, 1937.

CAST: Norma Shearer (Juliet), Leslie Howard (Romeo), John Barrymore (Mercutio), Edna May Oliver (Nurse), Basil Rathbone (Tybalt), C. Aubrey Smith (Lord Capulet), Andy Devine (Peter), Ralph Forbes (Paris), Reginald Denny (Benvolio), Maurice Murphy (Balthasar), Conway Tearle (Prince of Verona), Henry Kolker (Friar Laurence), Robert Warwick (Lord Montague), Virginia Hammond (Lady Montague), Violet Kemble Cooper (Lady Capulet).

STORY OF THE FILM: The families of Romeo and Juliet, the Montagues and the Capulets, have been feuding for generations and their enmity has grown malignant, creating a turbulence and peril that has made the Italian city of Verona uneasy. Because of the hatred that seethes between them, there is always a chance of blood being shed on the street from the point of a sword. Romeo is a Montague, Juliet a Capulet.

Romeo, a scholarly and lovesick young man, has been suffering from melancholia of late because he cannot dismiss Rosaline from his mind, who had been indifferent to his courting. His friends, Mercutio and Benvolio, two adventurous and prankish types of which Romeo is quite the opposite, advise him to forget

Romeo and Juliet: *Henry Kolker, Leslie Howard, and Norma Shearer.*

the fair lady who never loved him. To cure Romeo of his depression, Mercutio and Benvolio invite him to accompany them to a ball the Capulets are giving in the banquet hall of their castle. When they arrive, a dance is in progress, which the lovely Juliet is leading. At that moment, Romeo and Juliet's eyes meet. It is love at first sight. In that instant, Romeo, who has been enraptured by Juliet's beauty, has completely forgotten Rosaline.

The evening's festivities over, Romeo and Juliet bid each other goodnight and go in separate directions. Ensconced in her bedchamber where her loyal nurse is preparing her for the night, Juliet cares nothing about sleep, for she has not recovered from her meeting with Romeo. While she is on the balcony meditating, Romeo suddenly reappears, which surprises and alarms Juliet, who is gravely concerned about the risk her lover has taken, since they are enemies. Juliet then cries out: "O, Romeo, Romeo. Wherefore art thou Romeo? Deny thy father and refuse thy name, or, if thou wilt not, be but sworn my love, and I'll no longer be a Capulet." With-

out fear, Romeo ascends the balcony. The two lovers are in a state of ecstasy. They kiss and embrace, with Romeo promising marriage the next day. Happy as never before, Juliet has her nurse act as a messenger to help them arrange the clandestine wedding.

On the city square the following day, the nurse meets Romeo who mentions his plan to her. He will meet Juliet at Friar Laurence's cell and there the ceremony will take place with the proper rituals.

Several hours have gone by. Juliet tells her parents that she is on her way to confession and had just started out for the priest's cell. Romeo has kept his word that he would meet Juliet and at last they are betrothed.

That night, Romeo climbs Juliet's balcony again, and there, they engage in passionate lovemaking as before. But their happiness is short-lived when their families clash once again. It seems that Tybalt, Juliet's cousin, had resented Romeo's presence at the ball and took it as an insult, thereby seeking revenge on the Capulets.

On the way to the house of Capulet, Tybalt encoun-

Romeo and Juliet: *Leslie Howard and Norma Shearer.*

ters Mercutio and reproaches him for consorting with Romeo, a Montague. Angry words are exchanged between the two men, who are about to draw their swords when Romeo, having just come from the Friar's approaches the would-be combatants and stops them. Incensed, Tybalt insults Romeo, but the latter amazes his friend by not defending himself. Loving Juliet as he does, Romeo cannot bring himself to harm a relation of hers. Mercutio, believing his friend Romeo to be a coward, proceeds to attack Tybalt, sword in hand, and a duel ensues. Romeo tries to stop the fight because of his concern for Mercutio, but it is too late. Mercutio has been fatally wounded by Tybalt, who quickly leaves the death scene. Grief-stricken at the demise of his friend, Romeo seeks out Tybalt and kills him in a spectacular duel. The law is now in full pursuit of Romeo. Meanwhile, Juliet has learned of the fatal encounter between her husband and her cousin and is shocked at the murder of her kinsman. She both denounces and condones

Romeo for his act, but her love for him obliterates any other feelings.

Romeo finds sanctuary at Friar Laurence's where he is informed of his exile. He hastens to Juliet to say farewell and they have a reunion on the balcony. Dawn has already broken. Juliet is reluctant in making Romeo leave and she kisses him goodbye. That morning, her parents find her alone, weeping. They believe her tears are for Tybalt and can only admire their daughter's compassion. Despite Juliet's grief, Lord Capulet suddenly announces that he has chosen a husband for her. It is Paris, a courageous and virtuous young man with whom Juliet has had a past association. Appalled at her father's selection, Juliet pleads with him to spare her from marrying Paris, but he threatens to throw her into the streets if she doesn't do as he orders. Juliet has no one to comfort her except her nurse, who nevertheless thinks that she should respect her father's wishes. In a dilemma, Juliet appeals to Friar Laurence, who advises

Romeo and Juliet: *Edna May Oliver and Norma Shearer.*

her to tell her parents that she is willing to marry Paris but the night before the marriage she must drink a secret potion that will put her in a trance resembling death and will last forty-two hours. Her parents, believing her to be dead, will arrange her funeral, place her on the ceremonial bier, and transport her to the family tomb. Meanwhile, he, Friar Laurence, will get word to Romeo that this ceremony is only a mock funeral. Then he will speed to the vault and be there when her sleep breaks, in order that he may carry her off to Mantua and security.

Regardless of the danger it involves, Juliet is quite agreeable to the plan, but she is also apprehensive that the sleeping potion may never awaken her. Having no alternative she drinks the potion, which takes immediate effect and simulates death.

News soon reaches the palace of Juliet's death and she is greatly mourned. In the interim, Romeo has learned of Juliet's passing, but has received no word from Friar Laurence that her death is only a mock one. This breaks Romeo's heart and he desires but one thing—to join his beloved in an eternal sleep. He hastens to an apothecary and buys a phial containing poison, then starts for Verona to Juliet's tomb beside which he will die upon taking the deadly liquid. At the entrance he is startled at meeting Paris, and unaware of the reason for the latter's presence, he challenges him to a duel. A moment later Paris is dead. At the funeral bier, Romeo intones his final farewell to Juliet who is lying there so peacefully. He then swallows the poison and dies. At that moment Juliet awakens to find both her lover and Paris dead. Her grief is too much. Life is now meaningless to her. Death is her only resignation. She picks up a dagger and fatally stabs herself. At last Romeo and Juliet are reunited for all eternity.

CRITICS' VERDICT:

"The movies have finally done it. They have made a

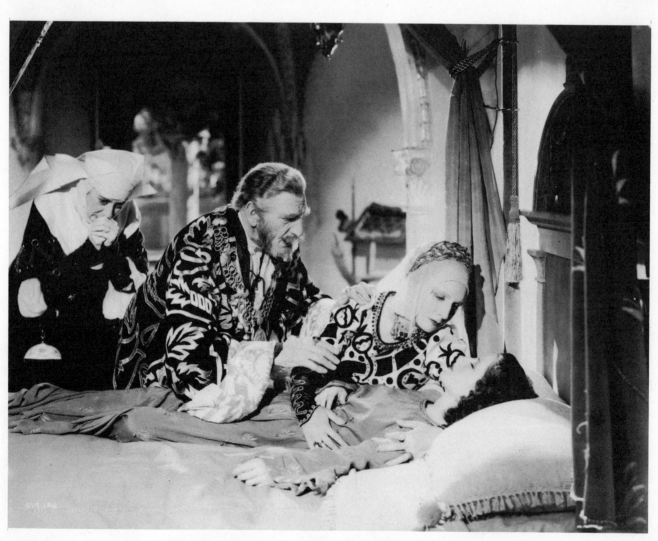

Romeo and Juliet: *Edna May Oliver, Sir Aubrey Smith, Violet Kemble Cooper, and Norma Shearer.*

Romeo and Juliet: *Leslie Howard and Norma Shearer.*

screen version that is not only excellent in itself, but a decided improvement over a legitimate presentation. Shakespeare has become a bore to so many high school and college students (through no fault of his own) that it is a positive pleasure to report on Irving Thalberg's MGM, has made out of *Romeo and Juliet*. It is beautiful, it is authentic, it is moving, and when all is said and done, it is still Shakespeare."
Scholastic, September 19, 1936

"Critics consider *Romeo and Juliet* a triumph of motion picture art, very possibly one of the finest pictures ever made in Hollywood. The most acidulous [critics] admitted Miss Shearer's Juliet to be a triumph, garlanded Leslie Howard for a curbed disciplined performance of Romeo. Also, they delighted in the Mercutio of John Barrymore. *Romeo and Juliet* is Hollywood's best joust with Shakespeare to date. Skilled performances, knowing delivery of the famous lines, an acute sense that cheers would be grudged, jeers easy, combining to set alight the talents of all concerned."
The Literary Digest, August 15, 1936

"Metro the magnificent has loosed its technical magic upon Will Shakespeare and has fashioned for his *Romeo and Juliet* a jeweled setting in which the deep beauty of his romance glows and sparkles and gleams with breathless radiance. Never before in all its centuries has the play received so handsome a production as that which was unveiled last night at the Astor Theatre. All that the camera's scope superb photography and opulent costuming could give it has been given it here. Ornate, but not garish, extravagant, but in perfect taste, expensive, but not overwhelming, the picture reflects greatly upon its producers and upon the screen as a whole. It is a dignified, sensitive and entirely admirable Shakespearean—not Hollywoodian production.

"Miss Shearer was not at her best in the balcony scene. With more pleasure and with a sense that this memory will endure the longer, do we recall Miss Shearer's tender and womanly perverse Juliet during her farewell scene with Romeo before his flight to Mantua. Bright, too, with recollection of her surrender to uncertainty, fear and suspicion before swallowing the potion, and of that scene in which she finds her lover

207

Romeo and Juliet: *Leslie Howard and Norma Shearer.*

Romeo and Juliet: *Norma Shearer.*

Romeo and Juliet: *Leslie Howard and Norma Shearer.*

dead beside her in the tomb, Miss Shearer has played these, whatever her earlier mistakes, with sincerity and effect.''
Frank S. Nugent in the *New York Times*, August 21, 1936

"With rare good taste and surprising resourcefulness the screen has translated Shakespeare's *Romeo and Juliet* into a distinguished and beautiful photoplay. The singing measures of the tragedy have been framed into sumptuous pageantry. The acting, always effective, rise at times to genuine brilliance. You will find it the cinema's most successful and engaging obeisance to the Bard. Of all the splendid performances in the film, that of Mr. Barrymore's is outstanding. Miss Shearer is remarkably good. She is inclined to coyness at the start, but from the balcony scene on she plays with simple intensity and profound assurance. In her most ambitious role she does the finest acting of her career. As Romeo, Leslie Howard is almost too restrained, although he conspires with Miss Shearer to make the lover's meeting incidents of haunting beauty. The screen version of *Romeo and Juliet* has flaws, but they are trivial when weighed against the beauty and compelling power of the production.''
Howard Barnes in the *New York Herald Tribune*, August 21, 1936

"Mr. Irving Thalberg, producer, showman, and visionary, has evolved a picture that should be timeless as the story it tells, gives him top billing in this magnificent effort. It is a picture born to be re-issued. It seems to this humble reviewer that, once seen, it must be seen again. The superb acting throughout of a cast of picture favorites is another thing that you'll want to view again and again—everything about the production will make you proud to be a movie fan. There isn't anyone we can think of who will not love it, who will not wonder why Shakespeare has been so long neglected or viewed with such pedantic awe.''
Helen Gwynn in the *Hollywood Reporter,* July 16, 1936

"On *Romeo and Juliet* in the screen version I can only report that if you like a play as it stands, and do not require something far and indefinable and somehow beyond, you will like it; if not, not. The picture is done well, but it seems little more than that. Norma Shearer is rather unappetizingly made up, but neither bad nor good and (surprisingly enough) usually content with just being in there trying; Leslie Howard has grace, intelligence and a flair for lines, but the sophomorics of Romeo are too much for him and there are times when that sensitive horse's face of his, wrapped in these disguises must lead to unfortunate giggles. But as Mercutio John Barrymore is the real study. I hardly know what to say about it, but am sure there will never be seen on the boards so much scenery chewing and rub-

ber face trickery until the day they put 'Lear' into Billy Minsky houses.''
Otto Ferguson in *The New Republic*, September 2, 1936

"The whole thing should have value as a reference film for students of the Elizabethan drama. Vulgarians may overlook the fine points and see it in somewhat the usual costume piece done on a rather bigger than average scale. The picture clearly belongs to Norma Shearer as Juliet. Actually, for once, we see a Juliet who is a girl. Miss Shearer never seems desperate, and though her eyes well so richly with tears, seems hardly either terrified or tragic, never inelegantly tense. Her first encounter with Romeo is a delightful scene. Leslie Howard appears to be an intelligent, well-bred, and not quite well Romeo. He is possibly a little chilly in the role. It's in the later and tragic scenes that Mr. Howard is at his best, and there is a good deal to be said for a Romeo who isn't the violent gallant so much as the mournful romantic, which is the kind of Romeo Howard probably intended. I think the studio has been overwhelmed by Shakespeare, and has rendered the film somewhat cumbersome, removed the possibilities of something fresh and exciting. This is a good sensible presentation of *Romeo and Juliet*. But it won't be one you'll hark to when you are discussing the movies as a great art.''
John Mosher in the *New Yorker,* August 22, 1936

"Miss Shearer may well glory in the character of her performance. It has youth and charm, and she reveals an expertness and efficiency in her reading of the lines which will long stand as a beacon. Leslie Howard's Romeo, while not the ideal fulfillment is still in the truest sense a beautiful and intelligent rendition.''
Edwin Schallert in the *Los Angeles Times,* October 1, 1936

"Mr. Howard is at first a trifle stiff, though always consummately elegant in his movements, but as he proceeds he becomes more elegant and imaginative and he is excellent in his tragic passages. Miss Shearer, on the other hand, is at her best in her simplest passages at the beginning of the play, and when she attempts high tragedy she ceases to be the young Juliet. Mr. John Barrymore's Mercutio is, it must frankly be admitted, disasterously casual, and he entirely ruins the speech about Queen Mab by paying no attention at all to the poetry. Miss Edna May Oliver's reading of Juliet's nurse is perhaps overemphatic, and with too much by-play, but then she is not allowed to make many of the best of the nurse's remarks, and her portrait is certainly remarkably competent.''
The London Times, October 14, 1936

"Mr. John Barrymore is inclined to weigh down his merry Mercutio with whimsical arabesques, though he

Romeo and Juliet: *Henry Kolker, Norma Shearer, and Ralph Forbes.*

dies in a line of superb scorn, and the nurse of Miss Edna May Oliver emphasises the comic rather than the comforting aspects of the character. These two parts seem to me to be overacted, whereas Mr. Leslie Howard and Miss Norma Shearer, though a gracious and poetic pair of lovers, are a shade too carefree, too reticent. They bring to their passion and their grief a hint of precise preparation and a circumspection alien to the youth of Romeo and Juliet. They preserve a poise, even in despair which takes from their tragedy something of its poignancy. But whilst opinion may be divided on the acting, the production, admirably directed by Mr. George Cukor, must be universally recognized as one of the major achievements of the screen."

Micheal Orme in the *Illustrated London News*, October 31, 1936

Marie Antoinette (Metro-Goldwyn-Mayer—1938)

CREDITS: Producer: Hunt Stromberg. Director: W. S. Van Dyke II. Based on Stefan Zweig's biography. Screen play: Claudine West, Donald Ogden Stewart, Ernest Vajda. Photography: William Daniels. Film editor: Robert J. Kern. Art director: Cedric Gibbons. Musical score: Herbert Stothart. Montage: Slavko Vorkapich. Dances: Albertina Rasch. Wardrobe: Adrian. Recording director: Douglas Shearer. Running time: 160 minutes. Released: August 26, 1938.

CAST: Norma Shearer (Marie Antoinette), Tyrone Power (Count Axel de Fersen), John Barrymore (King Louis XV), Gladys George (Mme. DuBarry), Robert Morley (King Louis XVI), Anita Louise (Princess De-Lamballe), Joseph Schildkraut (Duke of Orleans), Henry Stephenson (Count de Mercey), Reginald Gardiner (Comte D'Artois), Peter Bull (Gamin), Albert Van Dekker (Provence), Barnett Parker (Prince De Rohan), Cora Witherspoon (Mme. De Noailles), Joseph Calleia (Drouet), Ivan F. Simpson (Sauce), George Meeker (Robespierre), Marilyn Knowlden (Princess Theresa), Scotty Beckett (Dauphin), Henry Daniell (LaMotte), Alma Kruger (Empress Marie Theresa), Leonard Penn (Toulan), George Zucco (Governor of Conciergerie), Ian Wolfe (Herbert), John Burton (LaFayette), Mae Busch (Mme. La Motte), Cecil Cunningham (Mme. De Lerchenfeld), Brent Sargent (St. Pre), Tom Rutherford (St. Clair), Ruth Hussey (Mme. DePolignac), Victor Killian (guard in Louis's cell), Charles Waldron (Swedish Ambassador), Walter Walker (Benjamin Franklin), Zeffie Tilbury (dowager at birth of Dauphin), Lawrence Grant (old nobleman at birth of Dauphin), Claude King (Choisell), Frank Elliott (King's Chamberlain), Herbert Rawlinson (Goguelot), Wade Crosby (Lanton), George Houston (Marquis De St. Priest), Moroni Olsen (bearded man), Barry Fitzgerald (peddler), Kathryn Sheldon (Mrs. Tilson), Lionel Royce (Guillaume), Lyons Wickland (Laclos), Anthony Warde (Marat), Olaf Hytten (Boehmer), Rafaela Ottiano (Louise, Marie's maid), Guy Bates Post (Convention president), Gustav von Seyffertitz (King's confessor), Nigel De-Brulier (Archbishop), Howard Lang (Franz), Mary Howard (Olivia), Ramsay Hill (Major Domo), Jack George (orchestra leader), Thomas Braidon (lackey), Denis d' Auburn (Beuregaard), Frank Campeau (lemonade vendor), Harts Lind (nurse), Theodore von Eltz (officer in entrance hall), Frank Jaquet (keeper of the seal), Harry Davenport (Monsieur de Cosse), Jacques Lory (French peasant), Bea Nigro (woman at the opera), Hugh Huntley (man in opera gallery), Harold Entwistle (old aristocrat at opera), Guy D'Ennery (minister at King's Council), Edward Keane (general), Frank McGlynn, Jr. (soldier with rude laugh), Esther

Marie Antoinette: *Tyrone Power and Norma Shearer.*

Howard (streetwalker), Inez Palange (fish wife), Frank Arthur Swales (chimney sweep), Dick Alexander (man with pike), Billy Engle (man with goblet), Alonzo Price (second guardsman), Erville Alderson (passport official), Duke R. Lee (coach driver), Ben Hall (young man with lantern), Neil Fitzgerald (first councillor), Harry Stubbs (second councillor), Ben Hendricks (national guard), George Kirby (priest), Corbet Morris (La Rue), Trevor Bardette (first municipal), John Butler (second municipal, Alan Bridge (official in passport office), William Steele (footman), Helene Millard, Dorothy Christy, Frances Millen, Mimi Olivera (ladies in waiting to DuBarry), Luana Walters, Greta Granstedt, Ann Evers, Ocean Claypoole, Claire Owen, Roger Converse, Phillip Terry, Vernon Downing (bits in gaming house), Buddy Roosevelt, Lane Chandler (revolutionary officers), Carl Stockdale (national guard).

STORY OF THE FILM: Marie Antoinette, a young, vivacious, and beautiful Austrian princess of the House of Hapsburg, falls victim to a marriage that is not of her choosing. The man selected as her husband to be is Louis August, Dauphin of France, who is later to become Louis XVI. Marie, upon meeting him, is most disillusioned when she sees what a pathetic figure he is and her heart goes out to him. Louis, unfortunately, is a misfit, a dull, slow-witted, and stupid clod who appears to have the mentality of an immature boy.

The matrimonial alliance established, Marie becomes the Dauphine of France. On their wedding night, Louis confesses to Marie that he had no wish to marry, but like his bride, the choice was not his. Antoinette, hated by Madame DuBarry, pleads with her husband to help her because she needs him. She asks him to assert his position on their behalf, but Louis, a subject of ridicule in court circles, fears that to carry out his wife's wishes could only cause trouble.

212

Marie Antoinette: *Joseph Schildkraut and Norma Shearer.*

At a gambling party, Antoinette meets Count Axel De Fersen, a handsome young nobleman to whom she is instantly attracted and he to her. She engages in a little flirtation with the count, which her friends observe with amusement, but her coquetry fails to make an impression. Present at the gathering is DuBarry, who takes the opportunity to insult Antoinette, whom she feels dislikes meeting her, but Marie tells the woman that this is not true and that even royalty likes an occasional roll in the gutter.

The next day Antoinette goes to the Austrian Embassy for aid and there meets Count De Fersen. He declares his love for her, having always loved her. She tells him that for the first time she is really in love and would renounce the throne, since it has become meaningless to her.

Denied a husband's love, even the advice of trustworthy friends, Antoinette soon emerges as the gayest and most frivolous woman in France, reckless in her abandon to derive as much pleasure out of life as she can. She gambles excessively, is seen at the wildest parties, and becomes generally engulfed in a whirlpool.

After returning from one of her gay parties with the Princess de Lamballe and Mme. de Polignac, Antoinette is met by Count Mercey, Austria's ambassador to France, who had arranged her marriage to the Dauphin, and who is now the bearer of an important message from Maria Theresa, Empress of Austria. Mercey informs Antoinette that her reputation is in jeopardy, for without an heir she faces exile. She must further acquiesce publicly Du Barry's standing.

Antoinette is summoned by the King who tells her that she must leave France. Du Barry has purposely used the pretext that Antoinette is childless so that she may have her banished with the king's support. When the Duke d'Orleans, who had pledged to stand by An-

Marie Antoinette: *Robert Morley and Norma Shearer.*

toinette, learns that the king is deporting her, he immediately forsakes her.

King Louis XV dies suddenly as the result of smallpox and Antoinette becomes Queen of France. Despite her love for Count Fersen, she is bound by duty to the monarchy and bids him farewell. Her efforts to strengthen the decaying monarchy prove futile, for the revolution is about to encompass them, which is the beginning of the end.

Antoinette's greatest joy now is her two children, her young son, the Dauphin, and Princess Theresa, both of whom will one day ascend the throne. The Queen has also learned to love her husband, but it is not the kind of love she had for Count Fersen. She has, nevertheless, been a good and loyal wife, in spite of her frivolity and her interludes with Fersen.

With the revolution quickly approaching, the king and queen find themselves in desperate straits and appeal to the Duke d'Orleans for aid, but he refuses to help the couple and suggests that the king abdicate.

The queen, realizing that the populace is starving, has decided to deprive herself and her family of all luxuries. When a jeweler presents a valuable diamond necklace to her that is considered the most priceless gem in France and attempts a sale, the Queen does not buy it. The necklace is later stolen by jewel thieves and the Queen is accused of purchasing the diamond. Before long, an angry Paris mob storms into the Palace of Versailles and invades the apartments of the king and queen. They are helpless and are forced to vacate the premises. Traveling incognito as visiting Russians in order to prevent themselves from arrest, their destination is Varennes, where they will go into exile. The slightest blunder on the part of the king when his coach is stopped for passport examination can mean doom. It is a suspenseful and harrowing journey for the royal family. The king, who has blundered all his life, finally does make a slip while being questioned by authorities on the highway and he and his family are apprehended and taken to the Prison La Force where Louis and Antoinette are sentenced to die on the guillotine. It is a heart-breaking moment when Antoinette's husband

214

Marie Antoinette: *Barnett Parker, Robert Morley, and Norma Shearer.*

and children are torn from her, but her tearful pleas to have them stay with her a little longer is in vain.

As Marie Antoinette awaits her end, her whole life begins to take shape, from childhood until the fateful present. She then goes bravely to the guillotine, not realizing that the only man she is being mourned by is Count Fersen, in whose heart she will remain until he dies. The drums are heard in the distance, announcing Marie Antoinette's death, as Fersen stands alone, his head bowed. He wears a ring on his finger that Antionette had once give him, and on it is inscribed: "Everything leads me to thee."

CRITICS' VERDICT:

"Based on part on the book by Stefan Zweig, Marie Antoinette in the films is most sympathetic, and it is not meant to be an historic study of the Queen of her times. If Norma Shearer is lovely as the princess, and there can be no doubt of it, she is even more beautiful as the

Queen Mother who suffers in prison when her husband and children are torn from her. The weakness of the film is the love story that is thrown in, Marie's affair with the Swedish Count De Fersen. Tyrone Power is convincing enough as the nobleman who chivalrously falls in love with the Queen; however, Miss Shearer forgets that she is no longer Juliet, and somehow these extra love scenes detract from the main theme. Don't be discouraged by the slow moving first half of this super-colossal Hollywood production. Excitement comes when the revolution starts."
Philip Hartung in *The Commonweal*, August 26, 1938

"For all its great length, this filming of history moves with pace, power and absorbing interest. Norma Shearer does the best work of her career as the little Austrian dropped into a mad, fantastic maelstrom. She is at once appealing, lovely and believable. The performance of Robert Morley is superb as the dullard Louis

Marie Antoinette: *Mae Busch, Anita Louise, Olaf Hytten, and Norma Shearer.*

XVI, even if he isn't history. Tyrone Power, we regret to report, lacks color as the one flash of romance in the tragic Queen's life.''
Beverly Hills in *Liberty Magazine*, August 27, 1938

''Marie Antoinette is one of the historical colossals where the pageant is actually secondary to a rather fresh story of love and personal tragedy, tied to history, mainly through the costumes and sets. Robert Morley makes a grand figure of the slow and tortured Louis XVI; Norma Shearer carries the main pattern; Joseph Schildkraut and John Barrymore are good in their separate ways.''
Otis Ferguson in *The New Republic*, August 31, 1938

''Metro-Goldwyn-Mayer has lavished all its production resources on *Marie Antoinette*. The result is the most sumptuous historical spectacle of the year. It is far more than a sad story of the death of kings. A poignant portrayal of the title role by Norma Shearer and the equally fine characterization of the doomed Louis by Robert Morley gives eloquence and dramatic power to

what might have been merely an elegant costume show. The tragedy is far better than the romance. The excellent Tyrone Power is ill at-ease in the part of Count Axel De Ferson and he stays pretty much a grand opera figure throughout the production.''
Howard Barnes in the *New York Herald Tribune*, August 17, 1938

''Actually the whole picture belongs to the ancient school of things. Big crowds, fancy clothes, and the lovers—they are all in here, and I guess they have their enduring appeal. Long as it is — the two hours and three quarters, you know the action holds up well. One is impressed by the sudden boldness with which Miss Shearer portrays the final tragedy and without any nonsense whatsoever becomes the woman on the guillotine. That guillotine moment is director Van Dyke's most courageous detail—an ending to be commended in a film of an old fashion, big, costly, perhaps negligible.''
John Mosher in *The New Yorker*, August 10, 1938

216

Marie Antoinette: *Joseph Schildkraut, Robert Morley, and Norma Shearer.*

Marie Antoinette: *Robert Morley, Scotty Beckett, Maryilyn Knowlden, Anita Louise, and Norma Shearer.*

Marie Antoinette: *Norma Shearer*.

Marie Antoinette: *Scotty Beckett and Norma Shearer*.

Marie Antoinette: *Norma Shearer*.

"Signaling the triumphant return to the screen of Norma Shearer, and destined to win universal acclaim as one of the most impressive and spectacular film offerings of all times, this lavish production has been beautifully and painstakingly mounted and motivated and should record staggering grosses in its deluxe and first run engagements everywhere. It approaches the ultimate in production in every department."
Box-Office, July 30, 1938

"The splendors of the French revolution in its dying days have not simply been equalled, they have been surpassed by Metro-Goldwyn-Mayer's film biography, *Marie Antoinette.* It's the Queen's story and Miss Shearer seems to have been stuck with it as much as anybody. Her sincere efforts to breath life into a weak script and to discount a marked unsubtlety of direction by personal histrionics are everywhere apparent, and it would not be fair to assume that any other screen ac-

tress could have made this particular Antoinette more real than she has done. As a whole, the script must be blamed for what, with the history of an era to draw from, is a surprising ineptitude of characterization."
B.R. Crisler in the *New York Times*, August 17, 1938

"Miss Shearer returns to the screen for her first part since she played Juliet two years ago. Her performance is lifted by skillful portrayal of physical and mental transitions through the period of a score of years. Gaiety and frivolity are followed by impressive fortitude towards the end of the film where she stands with her back to the wall fighting for the lives of her children. Her moments of ardor with Fersen (Power) are tender and believable. Despite handicaps of the artificialities of costumes she maintains character. In every respect Miss Shearer shows progress as an artist and reveals certain capabilities heretofore kept from view."
Variety, July 13, 1938

219

Marie Antoinette: *Tyrone Power and Norma Shearer.*

Marie Antoinette: *Joseph Schildkraut, Tyrone Power, Anita Louise, Norma Shearer, and Reginald Gardner.*

Marie Antoinette: *Norma Shearer*.

Marie Antoinette: *Norma Shearer and Tyrone Power*.

Marie Antoinette: *Norma Shearer*.

Marie Antoinette: *Norma Shearer*.

Marie Antoinette: *Tyrone Power and Norma Shearer.*

Marie Antoinette: *Tyrone Power and Norma Shearer.*

Idiots' Delight (Metro-Goldwyn-Mayer—1939)

CREDITS: Producer: Hunt Stromberg. Director: Clarence Brown. Based on the play by Robert E. Sherwood. Screen play by Robert E. Sherwood. Photography: William Daniels. Film editor: Robert J. Kern. Art director: Cedric Gibbons. Gowns: Adrian. Recording director: Douglas Shearer. Running time: 105 minutes. Released January 27, 1939.

CAST: Norma Shearer (Irene Fellara), Clark Gable (Harry Van), Edward Arnold (Archille Weber), Charles Coburn (Dr. Waldersee), Joseph Schildkraut (Captain Kirvline), Burgess Meredith (Quillery), Pat Paterson (Mrs. Cherry), Skeets Gallagher (Donald Navadel), Peter Willes (Mr. Cherry), William Edmunds (Dumptsey), Fritz Feld (Pittatek), Edward Raquello (Chiari), Paula Stone (Beulah Tremoyne), Virginia Dale (Francine Merle), Joan Marsh (Elaine Messiger), Bernadene Hayes (Edna Creesh), Frank Orth (Benny Zinsser), George Sorel (Major), Hobart Cavanaugh (Frueheim, theatre manager), Adolph Milar (Fellara), Clem Bevans (Jimmy Barzek), Claire McDowell (Mother), Emory Parnell (5th Avenue cop), Robert Middlemass (hospital commandant), Evelyn Knapp (nurse), Joe Yule (comic), Mitchell Lewis (Indian), Eddie Gribbon (cop), Jimmy Conlin (stagehand), Buddy Messinger (usher), Charles Judels (Greek restaurant owner), Paul Panzer (Greek chef), E. Alyn Warren (clerk, Grand Hotel), Frank Faylen (Ed), Frank M. Thomas (Bert), Gary Owen (news stand man), Lee Phelps (train announcer), Francis McDonald (Flight Captain).

STORY OF THE FILM: Harry Van, a former vaudevillian, finds that bookings have become scarce after returning from the war. Unable to get back into show business he becomes a hawker of patent medicines, spieling his wares on the street. Eventually, at an Omaha theater, Madame Zulieka, a clairvoyant, engages him as her assistant for her mind-reading act. Zulieka, however, has a strong penchant for liquor, and one evening, during a performance she becomes inebriated and fumbles the act. Irene, a vivacious and pretty

Idiot's Delight: *Clark Gable and Norma Shearer.*

Idiot's Delight: *Edward Arnold and Norma Shearer.*

acrobat on the bill, cues Zulieka so loudly from the wings that the audience hears her and the curtain is rung down.

Backstage, in Harry's dressing room, Irene, who has always admired Harry, finally tells him so and apologizes for ruining the show. They go to supper, at Irene's suggestion and later Irene comes to Harry's hotel room where she begins to fabricate stories of her past as a Russian countess. Harry knows that this isn't true, but Irene has become irresistible to him. The next morning they bid each other goodbye.

Years pass. Harry is again successful as a song-and-dance man, in addition to organizing a dance troupe known as Les Blondes with which he travels widely. On their way to Geneva, the train is halted at the frontier and no one is permitted to cross the border, for there have been rumors of war. Later, at the Monte Lodi Hotel in the Alps, where Harry and his company are registered, there arrives a prosperous looking couple in

the person of a blonde Russian countess and Achille Weber, a munitions tycoon. The sight of the countess makes Harry wonder, as she bears a striking resemblance to Irene. Her liaison with Weber, whose prescence has created a strain, is unexplained, except for his wealth and prestige which she shares.

Irene, feeling gay, invites Mr. and Mrs. Cherry, a young couple, to have a drink with her and tries to impress them by romanticizing her past. To Harry, who seems very much amused, this has a familiar ring, since he has memories of a hotel room in Omaha where he heard similar tales.

Meanwhile, more guests have arrived who were stopped at the frontier. They include two men, Quillery, a dedicated pacifist, and Dr. Waldersee, a research scientist. For the moment, Quillery, who is usually discreet, forgets himself and engages in a heated discussion about the futility of war with the quiet and reserved Mr. Cherry, which makes the latter and his wife feel uncomfortable But it is only talk and nothing serious comes of the controversial issue.

Irene has grown tired and bored with Weber and soon denounces him as a war-monger who has promoted destruction everywhere. Weber, cut to the quick, decides that Irene is no longer any good to him, and fearing an air attack he manages to escape and leaves her behind with her passport, for which he had refused the responsibility. But to Irene, his departure is quite a relief.

To relieve the tension of the war clouds that are gathering, Harry decides to entertain the guests by giving a special show with his Les Blondes. In the midst of their singing and dancing, word comes that an air raid is taking place, but the show continues.

Harry is almost sure of Irene's identity, but she denies ever having met him. Now that he feels certain that it is she, he is reluctant to leave with his girls and the other guests who are frantically hurrying to catch the last train across the frontier. Before joining the others, Irene finally reveals her true identity to Harry and that she was the girl that he had been in love with in Omaha. The train departs—with Les Blondes, but Harry is not on it. As Harry and Irene drink a toast to the future, the bombs begin to fall and they begin singing "Onward Christian Soldiers."

CRITICS' VERDICT:

"Mr. Clark Gable does his best, but Miss Norma Shearer adds to the heavy saturated ennui the weight of a far too powerful personality. Over-acting could hardly go further. The programme is saved by one of the best Disneys for years — the adventures of Pluto with a rubber seahorse, coy, flippant and aerated."
Graham Greene in *The Spectator*, April 21, 1939

Idiot's Delight: *Peter Welles, Pat Patterson, Norma Shearer, and Clark Gable.*

Idiot's Delight: *Norma Shearer and Clark Gable.*

Idiot's Delight: *Norma Shearer and Clark Gable.*

"Clark Gable's hard-boiled hoofer is a fine characterization. Norma Shearer plays a difficult and purposely exaggerated role to the hilt and perhaps a little farther. With an extra credit for its worthy intention, *Idiot's Delight* is refreshingly intelligent entertainment."
Newsweek magazine, February 6, 1939

"Miss Shearer is even more pretentious than her pretentious part."
Franz Hoellering in *The Nation,* February 18, 1939

"For all that it has lost, the final punch of the *Idiot's Delight*, the MGM version, directed by Clarence Brown, is within its special limits an important, unusual and engrossing picture. Gable's exceedingly clever portrayal helps to make it that and Miss Shearer disclosed a maximum of skill in her impersonation of a peculiarly fantastic heroine. The two will undoubtedly enjoy an abundance of popular success, Gable, doubtless the greater."
Edwin Schallert in the *Los Angeles Times*, February 2, 1939

"It is seldom that a play makes such an intelligent movie as does *Idiot's Delight*. Norma Shearer and Clark Gable come through in grand style in the roles made famous by the Lunts. This is a strong and bitter condemnation of a civilization tottering on the verge of war."
The Commonweal, February 17, 1939

The Women (Metro-Goldwyn-Mayer — 1939)

CREDITS: Producer: Hunt Stromberg. Director: George Cukor. Based on the play *The Women* by Clare Boothe. Screen Play: Anita Loos, Jane Murfin. Photography: Oliver T. Marsh, Joseph Ruttenberg. Film editor: Robert J. Kern. Musical score: Edward Ward, David Snell. Art director: Cedric Gibbons. Associate: Wade B. Rubottom. Set direction: Edwin B. Willis. Gowns and fashion show: Adrian. Hair stylist: Sidney Guilaroff. Recording director: Douglas Shearer. Running time: 132 Minutes. Released September 1, 1939.

CAST: Norma Shearer [Mary (Mrs. Stephen Haines)], Joan Crawford (Chrystal Allen), Rosalind Russell [Sylvia (Mrs. Howard Fowler)], Mary Boland (the Countess De Lave), Paulette Goddard (Miriam Aarons), Phyliss Povah [Edith (Mrs. Phelps Potter)], Joan Fontaine [Peggy (Mrs. John Day)], Virginia Weidler (Little Mary), Lucile Watson (Mrs. Morehead), Florence Nash (Nancy Blake), Muriel Hutchison (Jane), Esther Dale (Ingrid), Ann Morris (excercise instructress), Ruth Hussey (Miss Watts), Dennie Moore (Olga), Mary Cecil (Maggie), Mary Beth Hughes (Miss Trimmerback), Virginia Grey (Pat), Marjorie Main (Lucy), Cora Witherspoon (Mrs. Van Adams), Hedda Hopper (Dolly De Peyster).

STORY OF THE FILM: Mary Haines, happily married to Stephen Haines, a prominent New York businessman (he and other males never appear—they are only discussed), has become the main topic of malicious beauty salon gossip, including other gathering places of the elite, concerning her drifting marriage of which she is completely unaware. Having always been loyal to her husband, and a loving mother besides, who lavishes much affection on her daughter Little Mary, Mary can easily claim the distinction of being a model wife. Her friends, however, are a predatory lot—a pack of hypocritical cats whose meows register more than just a

The Women: *Norma Shearer and Virginia Weidler.*

The Women: *Phyllis Povah, Rosalind Russell, Norma Shearer, Joan Fontaine, and Florence Nash.*

purr, and who drip with venom in their daily exchange of prattle. Among this coterie is Sylvia, whom Mary has known since childhood and who simply thrives on being nasty. She is usually the first to dispense the latest gossip and is the most effusive of her set, but she is also the slyest. The other cats are not quite as subtle, but have equally sharp claws.

While having her nails manicured one day at a salon where she is known, Mary learns from Olga, who is attending her, that her husband is having an affair with Chrystal Allen, a salesgirl in the perfume section of an exclusive department store. Chrystal is a typical gold-digger, tough and mercenary, and will stop at nothing, it seems, to achieve her aims. She attracts men like honey attracts bees and Stephen apparently has succumbed to her charms—or perhaps it was that special brand of perfume Chrystal has been demonstrating that has caused Stephen to fall under her spell.

Disconsolate after Olga's descriptions of Stephen's meeting with Chrystal, Mary visits her mother, Mrs. Morehead, and tells her what she has just heard. Eventually, Mary and Chrystal encounter each other in the fitting room of a dress shop and have a showdown. Chrystal is determined not to give Stephen up and warns Mary not to interfere. She further shocks Mary when the latter suggests that if she is going to please Stephen she should not wear circuslike clothes that he dislikes, to which Crystal replies: "Thanks for the tip, but when anything I wear doesn't please Stephen—I take it off."

Mary soon files suit for divorce and goes to Reno. On the train she meets the Countess De Lave, a middle-aged dowager who has shed many husbands and to whom matrimony is just a lark—not the institution that it was made out to be, and Miriam Aarons, a hardened chorus girl who takes no guff from anybody. The three

230

have booked reservations at a dude ranch, along with Peggy, a sweet type, who has accompanied Mary. Before they know it, Sylvia, who is also divorcing her husband has descended on them with her usual gay tidings, but her gaiety quickly vanishes when a newspaper clipping she finds in Miriam's possession mentioning her husband and Miriam as a twosome prompts her to snatch it from the latter's hand. The two start calling each other some unflattering names, which soon results in a hair-pulling match and a rough-and-tumble fight. Mary tries to stop the brawl but isn't successful. Sylvia and Miriam go at it hammer and tongs until they are exhausted, with Miriam coming out on top.

After her divorce is final Mary and the others return to New York. Mary is grief-stricken because Stephen has married Chrystal and realizes she made a mistake in divorcing him. When she learns that Chrystal has been untrue to Stephen and is now taking up with a popular cowboy radio singer known as Buck Winston on whom the Countess DeLave had prior rights, Mary is resolved to counteract the situation. She puts on a striking new evening dress to wear to a party, plus some red nail polish and surprises her mother by saying: "I've had two years to grow claws, Mother, Jungle Red." With her talons sharpened Mary becomes the predatory female ready to beat Chrystal at her own love game and win back her former husband. She is victorious in her battle.

CRITICS' VERDICT:
"The tonic effect of Metro-Goldwyn-Mayer's film of Clare Boothe's·The Women is so marvelous we believe every studio in Hollywood should make at least one thoroughly nasty picture a year. The saccharine is too much with us: going and coming to syrupy movies we lose our sense of balance. Happily, Miss Boothe hasn't. She has dipped her pen in venom and written a comedy that would turn a litmus paper pink. Metro, without alkalizing it too much, has fed it to a company of actresses who normaly are so sweet that butter (as the man says) wouldn't melt in their mouths. And, instead of gasping and clutching at their throats, the women

The Women: *Dennie Moore and Norma Shearer.*

—bless em'—have downed it without blinking, have gone on a glorious cat-clawing rampage and have turned in one of the merriest pictures of the season.

"Miss Shearer as Mary Stephens, whose divorce and matrimonial comeback keep the cat fight going, is virtually the only member of the all feminine cast who behaves as one of Hollywood's leading ladies is supposed to. And even Miss Shearer's Mary sharpens her talons finally and joins the birds of prey. It is, parenthetically, one of the best performances she has given."
Frank J. Nugent in the *New York Times,* September 22, 1939

"I think probably the movies have made something more solid out of *The Women* than the stage play did. The picture runs two hours and a quarter which is inexcusable in itself, and features Norma Shearer in some of the most incessant weeping and renunciation since Ann Harding—which may not be inexcusable but it's no fun for me. It is a holiday from Hays all right; there is more wicked wit than Hollywood has been allowed since *The Front Page*."
Otis Ferguson in *The New Republic*, September 6, 1939

"The woman is Mary Haines, portrayed with deeply felt finesse by Miss Shearer. She is the wife who, thanks to the whispers and gabble of the contingent led by Sylvia (Miss Russell), finds her marriage headed for the rocks. Of course, there is another woman and she, played with an honesty that is sometimes shocking, is Miss Crawford.

"Fortunately, it has Miss Shearer, and we can cling to decency—albeit desperately—with her."
Edwin Schallert in the *Los Angeles Times,* September 1, 1939

"Good is always at a disadvantage around evil. So is Mary around Chrystal, the Countess, Sylvia and the rest of the women. Miss Shearer, constantly in the

The Women: *Joan Crawford, two players, Norma Shearer, Joan Fontaine, Rosalind Russell, and Phyllis Povah.*

The Women: *Joan Fontaine, Norma Shearer, Rosalind Russell, Mary Boland, and Paulette Goddard.*

foreground throughout the picture, has a battle to hold her own. Her performance, however, is earnestly expressed."
Harry Mines in the *Los Angeles Daily News*, September 11, 1939

"Norma Shearer brings her usual polish and grace to a less showy role as the one really sympathetic character in the piece, Mrs. Stephen Haines."
Picturegoer and *Film Weekly*, March 2, 1940

"*The Women,* like its original is a mordant, mature description of the social decay of one corner of the U.S. middleclass."
Time magazine, September 11, 1939

"Smart, brilliant play becomes sure-fire screen fare finely produced and acted."
Film Daily, August 29, 1939

"Miss Shearer delivers a sparkling performance as the intelligent and loving wife who finds herself unable to cope with both the gossip undercurrent and her husband's indiscretion. Miss Crawford is ruthless and tough-shelled as the wife stealer, while Rosalind Russell contributes a highlight characterization as the sly purveyor of maligning gossip, although her part was a little broadly sketched by direction. Lucile Watson is a sympathetic and male-understanding mother. Virginia Weidler provides several human and dramatic interludes as the child caught in the divorce maelstrom.

"Miss Shearer is on the delivery line of some poignant scenes. Most important are her telephone conversations with her erring husband and explaining to daughter Virginia Weidler the reason for a divorce."
Variety, September 6, 1939

The Women: *Norma Shearer, Joan Fontaine, Rosalind Russell, Mary Boland, and Paulette Goddard.*

The Women: *Phyllis Povah, Paulette Goddard, Joan Crawford, Rosalind Russell, Norma Shearer, Mary Boland, and Florence Nash.*

Escape (Metro-Goldwyn-Mayer — 1940)

CREDITS: Producer: Lawrence Weingarten. Director: Mervyn LeRoy. Based on the novel by Ethel Vance. Screen Play: Arch Obler, Marguerite Roberts. Photography: Robert Planck. Film editor: George Boemier. Art director: Cedric Gibbons. Gowns: Adrian. Recording director: Douglas Shearer. Running time: 104 minutes. Released November 1, 1940.

CAST: Norma Shearer (Countess Von Treck), Robert Taylor (Mark Preysing), Conrad Veidt (General Kurt Von Kolb), Nazimova (Emmy Ritter), Felix Bressart (Fritz Keller), Albert Basserman (Dr. Arthur Henning), Philip Dorn (Dr. Ditten), Bonita Granville (Ursula), Edgar Barrier (commissioner), Elsa Basserman (Mrs. Henning), Blanche Yurka (nurse).

STORY OF THE FILM: Mark Preysing, a young American artist, arrives in a small town in Germany to try and locate the whereabouts of his famous actress-mother, Emmy Ritter, who has mysteriously disappeared. Emmy, a German by birth, had reared Mark and her other child as United States citizens while a resident there, only to return to Germany to sell her house, following her husband's death. In Europe she became a prominent stage star and a continental favorite.

Mark, in making inquiries to find a clue to his mother's disappearance, is shunned at every turn when those he questions learn of his perilous mission. By accident, Mark meets the Countess Von Trek, who is American born and a widow, having once been married to a foreigner. The countess is anything but congenial toward Mark and tries to avoid him. For one thing, she has a lover, who is General Kurt Von Kolb, an important Nazi official whom she is expecting for dinner. That night, the countess asks the General about Emmy Ritter and he tells her that she is in a concentration camp, with a death sentence hanging over her. Her crime is high treason, since she committed a capital

Escape: *Robert Taylor and Norma Shearer.*

Escape: *Nazimova, Robert Taylor, Felix Bressart, and Norma Shearer.*

Escape: *Nazimova and Norma Shearer.*

Escape: *Conrad Veidt and Norma Shearer.*

offense by smuggling money she received for her property out of the country. Under the Hitler regime this is punishable by death.

When the countess sees Mark again she apologizes for having been so cold and indifferent the first day they met and invites him to attend a concert with her. Mark has already learned of his mother's fate and appeals to the countess to use her influence in extricating Emmy. He is soon introduced to Dr. Ditten, a friend of the countess who happens to be treating Mark's mother in the hospital of the concentration camp. The doctor, an anti-Nazi, contrives an ingenious though incredible plan that will free Emmy by administering to her a certain drug that will make it appear as if she had died. The scheme is successfully engineered, despite the presence of the Gestapo, with Dr. Ditten signing the death certificate, while Fritz Keller, Emmy's faithful servant is authorized to bury his mistress. Emmy's body is finally delivered in a coffin to Mark who begins to make the funeral arrangements. Taking Emmy to the countess's home would, of course, mean suicide and

the countess finds a safer place to hide the woman. The funeral, which Mark attends, is held in the village.

From a French girl, who is one of her students, the countess borrows a passport for Emmy and Mark to be used on their flight to Switzerland, with Emmy being made up to look like the girl. Mother and son finally arrive at the airport, shortly before General Von Kolb becomes aware of Emmy's escape. Furious, the general accuses the countess of breaking her alliance with him, and during his excitement he has a stroke, which paralyzes him. The countess receives a telegram from Mark and Emmy, who have arrived safely in Zurich, and is greatly relieved. Although she is resigned to caring for the General until the end of his days, the countess has at least managed to outwit the system she despises and help save a life.

CRITICS' VERDICT:

"The male performances are superb. Robert Taylor gives a fine impression of the distracted young son; Conrad Veidt is properly menacing as the Countess's

237

lover; Felix Bressart is excellent as the frightened but courageous servant and Philip Dorn all but walks away with the picture as the humane camp doctor.

"Norma Shearer, as the Countess, makes up for a static performance by coming to life in the last scene and giving a fine dramatic fillip to the fade-out. Nazimova is splendid throughout, although there is less dramatic stress laid on Emmy's than on Mark's part in the drama. Elsa Basserman, Blanche Yurka and Bonita Granville are fine, too, in the parts they are called upon to play."
Kate Cameron in the *New York Daily News,* November 1, 1940

"One of the most poignantly dramatic films of the year is *Escape*, gripping and spine-tightening melodrama. Both Norma Shearer and Robert Taylor are excellent and the subject matter is very provocative."
Modern Screen, February, 1941

"Outspoken, aggressive little director Mervyn Le Roy lost none of the story in transposing it to the screen. Even the saccharine qualities of Norma Shearer are skillfully tempered to fit the regenerated Countess. Only Robert Taylor, unfairly injected into big league competition, falls behind the pace. But director LeRoy's combination is too strong to be defeated by this single handicap."
Time magazine, November 18, 1940

"Just as the Ethel Vance novel *Escape* had the book-reading public by the ears this time last year, there is every reason to suspect the excellent screen version thereof, which Mervyn Le Roy has prepared for Metro and which opened here yesterday at the Music Hall, will the movie-goers of the land by the nape of the neck as fast as it gets around. For this is far and away the most dramatic and hair-raising picture yet made on the sinister subject of persecution in a totalitarian land, and the suspense which it manages to compress in its moments of greatest intensity would almost seem enough to blow sizable holes in the screen."
Bosley Crowther in the *New York Times*, November 1, 1940

Escape: *Nazimova, Felix Bressart, Robert Taylor, and Norma Shearer.*

238

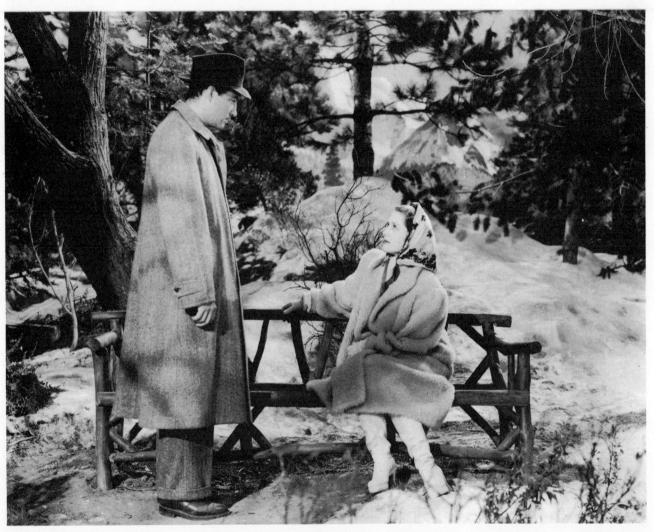

Escape: *Robert Taylor and Norma Shearer.*

Escape: *Conrad Veidt and Norma Shearer.*

Escape: *Robert Taylor, a player, and Norma Shearer.*

We Were Dancing (Metro-Goldwyn-Mayer—1941)

CREDITS: Producers: Robert Z. Leonard, Orville O. Dull. Director: Robert Z. Leonard. Based in part on Noel Coward's *Tonight at 8:30*. Screenplay: George Foreschel. Photography: Robert Planck. Film editor: George Boemier. Musical score: Bronislau Kaper. Art director: Cedric Gibbons. Gowns: Kalloch. Recording director: Douglas Shearer. Running time: 94 minutes. Released March, 1942.

CAST: Norma Shearer (Vicki Wilomirski,) Melvyn Douglas (Nicki Prax), Gail Patrick (Linda Wayne), Lee Bowman (Hubert Tyler), Marjorie Main (Judge Sidney Hawkes), Reginald Owen (Major Tyler Blane), Alan Mowbray (Grand Duke Basil), Florence Bates (Mrs. Vanderlip), Heather Thatcher (Mrs. Tyler Blane), Connie Gilchrist (Olive Ransome), Nella Walker (Mrs. Bentley), Florence Shirley (Mrs. Charteris), Russell Hicks (Mr. Bryce Carew), Norma Varden (Mrs. Bryce Carew).

STORY OF THE FILM: Vicki Wilomirski, an impoverished Polish princess, meets Nicki Prax, a Viennese baron, who is equally as penniless. Despite the fact that she is celebrating her engagment to wealthy Hubert Tyler at the home of Major and Mrs. Tyler Blane, Hubert's parents, in South Carolina, she automatically falls in love with the debonair Nicki as they are dancing to the strains of a waltz. Nicki, a total stranger, has managed, with his usual aplomb, to crash the party. Before the others know what is happening, Vicki and Nicki have eloped, leaving Hubert dumbfounded. Now that they are married, the couple begin to realize that they are professional house guests whose wit and charm have enabled them to live off the rich. Pretending they are single, Vicki and Nicki meet secretly. Linda Wayne, a well-to-do interior decorator,

We Were Dancing: *Melvyn Douglas, Norma Shearer, Heather Thatcher, Lee Bowman, and Reginald Owen.*

We Were Dancing: *Reginald Owen and Norma Shearer.*

We Were Dancing: *Melvyn Douglas and Norma Shearer.*

who had once had an affair with Nicki and who is still in love with him, soon learns of their marriage and exposes them, which reduces the pair in status as extras. Eventually, they are forced to relinquish the more elegant haunts of Newport and Palm Beach and migrate to the midwest, where they ensconce themselves as guests of the diamond-in-the-rough millionaires who have just acquired wealth. Vicki feels that it is time for Nicki to go to work and pleads with him to do so, but he keeps neglecting it. With Linda turning up among the guests once more, she resumes her pursuit of Nicki, which prompts Vicki to start divorce proceedings. Vicki and Hubert are reengaged. Nicki is frantic. One day he visits Linda at her decorating establishment, and discovering how much he knows about decorations she gets him a job decorating Hubert's home, which Hubert is preparing for Vicki. The result of Nicki's work on the house is a thing of beauty. He pays no attention to Vicki

and this inflames her. With her marriage to Hubert approaching, Vicki becomes apprehensive, as does Nicki. Finally, alone together, the two rebuke each other. Nicki asks Vicki not to go through with the wedding, but she tells Nicki that she has an obligation to Hubert and that she cannot walk out on him now.

The scene reverts to the home of Mrs. Tyler Blane, who has since become Mrs. Tyler Fishe. A betrothal party for Vicki and Hubert is taking place. Nicki bids Vicki farewell. The musicians begin playing a familiar tune. It is the waltz which Vicki and Nicki first danced to. They waltz again, then kiss and elope.

CRITICS' VERDICT:

"Miss Shearer acts with dazzling aplomb and wears clothes that will knock your eyes out, and Mr. Douglas turns in another of his devilishly debonair jobs. Lee Bowman and Gail Patrick are present in the customary

second party roles, and Marjorie Main is highly amusing in a brief sequence as a divorce-court judge. But the story sags too often and is dragged out in tiresome length. Its appeal will likely be limited to those patrons who relish a lot of swank. That it has in abundance. You should hear Miss Shearer snap a frigid quiet.''
Bosley Crowther in the *New York Times*, May 1, 1941

"In *We Were Dancing* Norma Shearer and Melvyn Douglas pursue their fervid and often stormy adventure with a maximum of sparkle, touched with a sentiment that is never overdone. Douglas even makes the courtroom scene diverting. Miss Shearer's new hairdress definitely changes her appearance, yet it rather becomes her. The picture will be liked because Miss Shearer has not of late been seen in anything of this

character, although many will remember what she did in the lighter romantic sphere some years ago.''
Carl D. Kinsey in *The Musician Magazine*, May, 1942

"Norma Shearer is grand as Vicki Wilomirski, a penniless Polish princess, and Melvyn Douglas is ditto as Nicki Prax, a bankrupt baron.''
Motion Picture, April 1942

"Too utterly utter and all that sort of rot, my deah.''
Photoplay April 1941

"Tailor-made for Miss Shearer, who has been off the screen for a year. 'Dancing' is a costly, embarrassing picture, whose mood and manners are both dated and false.''
Time Magazine, March 23, 1942

We Were Dancing: *Melvyn Douglas, Norma Shearer, and Alan Mowbray.*

We Were Dancing: *Marjorie Main, Norma Shearer and Melvyn Douglas.*

We Were Dancing: *Nella Walker, Norma Shearer, Gail Patrick, and Melvyn Douglas.*

We Were Dancing: *Melvyn Douglas, Florence Bates, Lee Bowman, and Norma Shearer.*

We Were Dancing: *Norma Shearer and Melvyn Douglas.*

Her Cardboard Lover (Metro-Goldwyn-Mayer—1942)

CREDITS: Producer: J. Walter Ruben. Director: George Cukor. Based on a play by Jacques Deval. Screenplay: Jacques Deval, John Collier, Anthony Veiller, William H. Wright. Photography: Harry Stradling, Robert Planck. Film editor: Robert J. Kern. Musical score: Franz Waxman. Art director: Cedric Gibbons. Gowns: Kalloch. Recording director: Douglas Shearer. Running time: 93 minutes. Released June, 1942.

CAST: Norma Shearer (Consuelo Croydon), Robert Taylor (Terry Trindale), George Sanders (Tony Barling), Frank McHugh (Chappie Champagne), Elizabeth Patterson (Eva), Chill Wills (Judge).

STORY OF THE FILM: Terry Trindale, a young songwriter, loses $3,200 to Consuelo Croydon at baccarat at a fashionable gambling casino at Palm Beach while under the spell of her beauty. He is unable to pay his losses and Consuelo offers to employ him as her bodyguard to keep her from seeing Tony Barling, a suitor with philandering inclinations with whom she is in love. Tony calls at Consuelo's home, but she tells him she is in love with another man, for the sake of making him jealous. Despite all, Consuelo continues to pursue Tony, but Terry, living up to his obligations, forbids it. Terry has just written a new song and manages to borrow plane fare from Eva, Consuelo's servant-confidante, so Chappie Champagne, his song-writing partner can go to New York and sell the composition to their publisher. At the airport, to where Consuelo has accompanied Terry and Chappie, she sees Tony alighting from a plane with some mutual friends. Back at the apartment, Consuelo tells Terry how she feels about Tony—that she needs him. Piqued, Terry departs. A few minutes later Consuelo receives a call and believes it is Tony. She pleads with him to come back to her, but when she opens the front door she finds Terry who confesses to being the caller. At that moment, Tony arrives. Consuelo, equally as furious, discharges Terry, but he insists on remaining with her. Consuelo starts to leave and Terry threatens suicide by jumping out of the window. The sound of a crash is heard, but it is merely a vase Terry has thrown to make it appear as if he had actually made the plunge. However, he comes close, after leaning out and grasping the ledge of the building. Consuelo, fearful that Terry has carried out his threats, faints. Terry climbs back into the room, proud of what he has accomplished, as is Eva, whom Terry had won over in the first place. Later, Terry meets Tony upon returning to his hotel and the two engage in a knock-down-drag-out fight in the basement, which ends in their going to jail. Tony is shortly released, but Terry remains locked up since he lacks the

Her Cardboard Lover: *Norma Shearer and Robert Taylor.*

bail. When Consuelo appears in court, Tony, happy as a lark, begins to embrace her. Terry, who is able to witness this from his cell, finds the scene unbearable. Consuelo is now between the devil and the deep blue sea regarding her two suitors, but she leaves with Tony. While alone with him, she realizes that it is Terry she loves, and Tony, understandingly, bows out. Consuelo goes back to the courthouse to find Terry and Chappie, who has bailed out his friend, leaving. Terry, still fuming, ignores Consuelo and quickly walks past her. When Terry and Chappie arrive at the airport they are suddenly apprehended by the police, with Terry being accused of grand larceny. In court again, Consuelo explains to the judge that she concocted the charges so Terry wouldn't leave because of her love for him. Terry, feeling the same way, forgives Consuelo.

CRITICS' VERDICT:
"If this be Miss Shearer's movie swan song, as has been intimated, she leaves us with a very fine performance to remember her by. True, at times Miss Shearer spreads on the histrionics a bit too thick, but the role is difficult and why shouldn't a love-frustrated woman be a bit hysterical at times? Anyway, we liked her and think you will too."
Photoplay, August, 1942

Her Cardboard Lover: *Robert Taylor and Norma Shearer.*

"It will take the full pulling power of Norma Shearer and Robert Taylor to counteract a dated and generally dull story in this latest transcript of the several times previously made *Her Cardboard Lover*. The Jacques Deval play has been a teaser for male and feminine stars, but seems to have worn out its welcome with audiences as a contrived sex comedy. It seems to be headed for spotty grosses, with dwindling returns as it hits the subsequents. Both stars are alert to winnow all possible comedy from the material and here and there barely triumph over the handicaps, while performing brightly in other sections."
Variety, May 27, 1942

"This undertaking in the zone of sophisticated comedy ranges from boudoir frivolity, such as used to be called continental to knockabout brawling, such as has always been called slapstick. It excels in neither department and serves chiefly as a means of presenting Norma Shearer, Robert Taylor and George Sanders to their fans."
Motion Picture Herald, May 30, 1942

"For the screen play by four weary writers is just a lot of witless talk, and the performances, under George Cukor's direction, are often close to ridiculous. Miss Shearer either overacts deliberately, but without any comic finesse, or she has been looking at the pictures of fancy models in the high-tone fashion magazines. Mr. Taylor, who had finally gotten somewhere as an actor, is back where he began—back as a piece of well-dressed furniture—compelled to make the most inane remarks. And George Sanders, the only other character of any consequence, is just a stock cad.

Metro, the present producers, filmed this story back in 1932 under the title of *The Passionate Plumber*. It should have stood on that production and that title."
Bosley Crowther in *The New York Times*, July 17, 1942

Her Cardboard Lover: *Robert Taylor and Norma Shearer.*

Her Cardboard Lover: *George Sanders and Norma Shearer*.

Her Cardboard Lover: *Robert Taylor, Norma Shearer, and George Sanders*.

Her Cardboard Lover: *Robert Taylor and Norma Shearer*.